W9-BXQ-791

HISPANICS IN THE UNITED STATES

An Anthology of Creative Literature

Volume II

Bilingual Press/Editorial Bilingüe

United States Hispanic Creative Literature

Address
Bilingual Press
Dept. of Foreign Languages
and Bilingual Studies
106 Ford Hall
EASTERN MICHIGAN UNIVERSITY
Ypsilanti, Michigan 48197
(313) 487-0042

HISPANICS IN THE UNITED STATES

An Anthology of Creative Literature

Volume II

Edited by

Francisco Jiménez

and

Gary D. Keller

Bilingual Review/Press

YPSILANTI, MICHIGAN

© 1982 by Bilingual Press/Editorial Bilingüe

All rights reserved. No part of this publication may be reproduced in any
manner without permission in writing, except in the case of brief quotations
embodied in critical articles and reviews.

ISBN: 0-916950-29-8
Library of Congress Catalog Card Number: 80-66273

PRINTED IN THE UNITED STATES OF AMERICA

Cover design by Christopher J. Bidlack

Acknowledgments

The editors gratefully acknowledge the organizations that have
made this collection possible. We express our gratitude to both the
Coordinating Council of Literary Magazines (CCLM), which awarded
this project with a facilitating grant, and the National Endowment
for the Arts (NEA), the parent funding agent, for making this anthology financially possible. We would also like to express our thanks to
the many editors of journals, members of organizations of writers
and other groups, and individuals who helped us get out the word
to the community of Hispanic creative writers that this book was
in the making.

All circumstances in the selections in this anthology are fictional
and none of the characters exist in real life or are based on persons
living or dead. Any resemblance to real situations or to persons
living or dead is purely coincidental.

810.8086873
H673
v. 2
c. 2

Table of Contents

Preface

In the spring of 1980 the Bilingual Review/Press published a special volume of creative literature on Hispanic life in the United States entitled *Hispanics in the United States: An Anthology of Creative Literature*. This volume has received widespread critical attention and acclaim, an example of which is the following review that appeared in *Library Journal*:

> . . . Inside is some of the most vibrant poetry and fiction I've read. Whereas most anthologies focus on segments of the Hispanic community, Keller and Jiménez aim at "providing the reader with sufficient depth and range" into the various Hispanic cultures one finds in the United States. . . . Highly recommended.

As a result of the great success of the 1980 volume as well as our recognition of an ongoing stream of United States Hispanic literature, we decided to publish a second, similar volume. Our intent, once again, has been to provide the reader with a glimpse of the varieties of literature written today that treat the United States Hispanic experience, to encourage literary creativity on this subject, and to offer some insight into the values and lifestyles of Hispanics in the United States, an important sector of American society. It cannot be overemphasized that a deeper understanding of United States Hispanics will bring us closer to an understanding of ourselves and of our country, which is made up of immigrant groups.

United States Hispanic literature, like any other, is a product of the imagination. As such, the themes and perspectives are as varied and multiple as are the experiences of Hispanic groups. However, within this diversity there are common elements, which allowed us once again to organize this anthology into seven broad categories. Naturally, these were largely dictated by the thematic patterns of the manuscripts submitted for possible inclusion in this collection and those that were ultimately accepted for publication.

The categories that we found useful for structuring this second volume are the following: *I. The Immigrant Experience* presents some of the dreams that drive Hispanics to come to the United States and the discrepancy that exists between the ideal they seek and the reality of life they experience in this country. *II. Humor y folklore* deals with that folk wisdom and keen sense of humor so characteristic of Hispanic culture and so often essential for enduring the suffering in a foreign and frequently hostile environment. *III. La familia y la religión* focuses on familial relationships and spiritual values and how these are affected by the majority culture and weakened by the socioeconomic and technological pressures of contemporary society. *IV. Cultural Heritage: Change and Contrast* deals with the efforts of United States Hispanics to save their heritage from the oblivion of assimilation and with those inevitable cultural transformations taking place as a result of the coexistence of the two cultures, Anglo and Hispanic. *V. La Hispana: Portraits and Self-Portraits* evokes the position of women within United States Hispanic culture, revealing both elements of tradition and change affecting this group. The selections in this category present various views on love, sex, identity, women's rights, and relationships. *VI. Obligaciones y compromisos* treats the themes of social justice and human rights and examines the obligations and commitments of United States Hispanics in the political and educational arenas. *VII. War and Death* deals with two universal phenomena deeply rooted in Hispanic history and culture; the two, seemingly complementary and predictable, often yield unexpected results, both good and evil.

The literary pieces included in each of these seven categories, then, reflect United States Hispanic values and lifestyles and are universal in theme. They mirror the variety and diversity of the rich body of literature being created by and about United States Hispanics.

In selecting the works for this second volume, one criterion was followed: that of literary merit, a universal standard that respects no cultural boundaries. From the outset we publicly announced that the literature under consideration could not be previously published and needed to be thematically limited to material dealing with Hispanic life in the United States (including Puerto Rico). However, we noted that the competition for inclusion in the collection was entirely open; contributors did not have to be Hispanic, nor of any specific nationality, surname, or sex. We encouraged both authors who had not previously been published as well as established writers to submit their material on a competitive basis. (To this end we mailed over 6000 printed announcements to universities and individuals throughout the United States and published advertisements in various journals and newsletters.) We emphasized that literary excellence would be the criterion for inclusion in the anthology. As might be expected, we received hundreds of submissions, all of which were read in good faith and painstakingly evaluated. We are extremely pleased with the end result. We hope you will be too.

FRANCISCO JIMENEZ
University of Santa Clara

GARY D. KELLER
Eastern Michigan University

I. The Immigrant Experience

J. W. Rivers

EL CAMPESINO QUIERE IR
AL OTRO LADO

Les hablo franco, sin polillas en la lengua;
vámonos, muchachos, pa'l otro lado
pa' ganarnos unos quintos,
que esta terrezuela ni sirve pa' gusanos.
Dice mi compadre que allá por todas partes
hay trabajo si uno tiene ganas,
y diz que siete ciudades hay de acero
que alcanzan al cielo, y aún más allá.

Subiremos las paredes por escaleras de cuerpos,
seremos hiedra en las chimeneas,
hormiguitas entre tecolotes,
polillas en los roperos.
Lo que es frontera ya ni se ve, pos,
con tantas pisadas de nosotros
se ha borrado, y el otro lado es aquí.

Pat Mora

ILLEGAL ALIEN

Socorro, you free me
to sit in my yellow kitchen
waiting for a poem
while you scrub and iron.

Today you stand before me
holding cleanser and sponge
and say you can't sleep at night.
"My husband's fury is a fire.
His fist can burn.
We don't fight with words
on that side of the Río Grande."

Your eyes fill. I want
to comfort you, but my arms
feel heavy, unaccustomed
to healing grown-up bodies.

I offer foolish questions
when I should hug you hard,
when I should dry your eyes, my sister,
sister because we are both women,
both married, both warmed
by Mexican blood.
It is not cool words you need
but soothing hands.
My plastic bandaid doesn't fit
your hurt.
I am the alien here.

Alfonso Rodríguez

LA OTRA FRONTERA

Para Raúl Leonel Treviño

La lluvia empezaba a arreciar y los transeúntes iban y venían a paso ligero. Por el costado del mercado Zaragoza aparecieron dos hombres, uno apuesto, ya maduro, y el otro, un joven de escasos diez y siete años. Salieron a la calle Real y caminaron apresuradamente hasta llegar al Restaurante Los Arcos. Se detuvieron un instante frente a la puerta, se miraron uno al otro y después entraron.

Afuera, el cielo se estremecía con los truenos. Los automóviles transitaban a vuelta de rueda y las aceras iban poco a poco quedando desiertas, salvo por uno que otro pordiosero o vendedor ambulante que se refugiaban bajo los toldos de los establecimientos comerciales. Era una tarde fría y desabrida.

Adentro, en el restaurante, mientras el mesero atendía a los dos recién llegados, uno de ellos, a quien apodaban el Ingeniero, encendió un cigarro. Con movimientos casi rituales se recargó contra el respaldo de la butaca y echó una bocanada de humo. Era un hombre que rozaba los cuarenta y cinco años, moreno y de frente despejada. Sus gruesas patillas y sus sienes empezaban a poblarse de canas. Portaba un bigote estrecho y bien acicalado. El tono de autoridad que lo investía al hablar revelaba en él la calma de un hombre de mucho mundo. El otro era un muchacho delgado, de facciones indígenas y pelo liso y alborotado. Sus ojos grandes de color azabache dejaban asomar un dejo de ternura mezclada con un aire de lejanía. Le costaba trabajo mantenerse quieto. Cuando no se tronaba los dedos de las manos, le daba vueltas y vueltas al salero que tenía frente a sí. En ratos, masticaba un palillo que tenía entre los dientes mientras tocaba repetidas veces las yemas de los dedos sobre la mesa.

—A ver Ingeniero, si no es mucha molestia, barájemela más despacio por favor. . . .

—Pos mira, la cosa es retesimple. Hay varias maneras de llevar a cabo esta movida. Pero nosotros, esta vez por lo menos, le vamos a hacer así, pon cuidado: Ya tengo a alguien palabreado pa que nos lleve hasta el puente viejo del ferrocarril. De allí, tú y yo caminaremos río abajo unos cuantos kilómetros. Después encontraremos un carrizal espeso donde mero da vuelta el río. Allí nos detendremos pa aguardar la señal. Desde luego, todo esto tiene que ser muy de madrugadita. Pa cuando den las tres de la mañana ya tenemos que estar escondidos detrás de los carrizos. Al chico rato, vamos a oír tres chiflidos largos. Esa es la señal del que nos va a pasar en la lancha de remos. Es un cuate que tiene un taller de refacciones cerca de La Concha. Esto nomás lo hace como pasatiempo, dizque pa no aburrirse, ¿qué te parece?

3

—No, pos cada quien le hace la lucha como puede.

—Acuérdate, tenemos que aflojarle mil pesos tú y mil pesos yo. Consíguelos a como dé lugar, que al cabo esa lana se repone después. Y si por algún motivo no puedes reunirlos, cuenta con un préstamo de mi parte. Viéndolo bien, ese viajecito en lancha no es caro que digamos. Fíjate que por ser a mí, nos va a salir barato. Hay pelados que tienen que aflojar el doble. Es que el cuate me debe algunos favores, sabes. Así es que no se puede mandar muchote. Una vez, por ejemplo, me traje un carro bien paradito del otro lado, era un Doch de esos coludos, recién pintadito y todo. Pos este cuate se enamoró de él. Y se lo vendí casi regalado, por ser a él. Es un chavo servicial.

—Entonces es de confianza, ¿no?

—Claro, hombre, de eso no te quepa la menor duda. Como te decía, entonces una vez que estemos en el otro cachete, nos vamos caminando hasta llegar a la carretera de L'Aguila. Bueno, en realidad no es una carretera, es un camino arenoso que va a una ranchería. Es una caminata de una hora más o menos. Ahora bien, mientras tú y yo estemos en estos trámites, Severiano Flores, el compa que conociste ayer, va a cruzar el río por el puente, en su carro.

—Pero . . . ¿Cómo es posible, Ingeniero?

—Pierde cuidado, hombre, el carro de Severiano es americano, trae placas de Tejas. Además él sabe darse sus aventones en inglés. Y por si eso fuera poco, trae papeles falsos. No te creas, si el compa Severiano es un gallito muy jugado. Ya lleva más de doce años en ese mismo trajín, no hay quien lo haga tonto. Tiene más mañas que un gato bodeguero. Andando con él andas en buenas manos. ¿Ya vas agarrando el hilo?

—Pos más o menos . . .

—Bueno, pues Severiano nos va a esperar en el camino que va pa las rancherías, y de allí todos juntos nos vamos a casa de mi hermana Josefa, que vive en L'Aguila. Ya estando en su casa llamamos a Faustino, un primo hermano mío que vive en un pueblito que se llama River City que queda como a setenta kilómetros de L'Aguila. El entonces se deja venir p'acá en su camionetita y nos da el *sí* o el *no* . . .

—Perdone, Ingeniero, ¿qué cosa es el *sí* o el *no* . . . ?

—Verás. El *sí* quiere decir que no hay peligro y que podemos agarrar carretera, y el *no* es que debemos aguardar en casa de Josefa hasta que pase el peligro.

—Sí, pero . . . ¿qué . . . ?

—Mira, resulta que en ciertos días de la semana se estaciona la Migra en un parquecito que queda a medio camino entre L'Aguila y River City. Como es natural, todo el que pase por allí tiene que presentar papeles. Mi hermano, pues, viene p'acá sólo para avisarnos si está libre el paso o si está plantada la Migra en el parquecito. Si no está, pos ya jodimos, súmele la bota a la carcacha. ¿Cómo la ves de ahí?

—Ahora sí, ya se me va prendiendo el foco. Usted ha de dispensar, con el cuento de que uno es primerizo en estos asuntos le da por hacer preguntas necias. Yo nomás quiero estar seguro de que . . .

—¿De que vamos a poder pasar? ¡Uf! Con los ojos cerrados, hombre. Eso déjamelo a mí. Entonces, ¿qué?, ¿estás en lo dicho?

—Sí, Ingeniero, estoy que no me aguanto. Ya quisiera estar chambiando, a ver si logro juntar unos cuantos dólares. Usted sabe bien que mi jefecita cada vez está peor, y no le va a quedar más remedio que someterse a una operación.

—Así me gusta, que seas decidido. Si uno no se arriesga no logra nunca nada. Mira, te voy a dar un consejo, como vecino y como amigo, porque tú sabes bien que te aprecio. Yo te aseguro que puedes llegar a viejo en la cervecería, cargando camiones, haciendo mandados, matándote todos los días, y no conseguirás reunir ni la quinta parte de lo que necesitas para la operación de tu jefa. Allí los trabajan como burros por una baba de perico. Así pos cuándo vas a dar abasto. Esa no es vida, mano. Ahora suponte que como último recurso, llevaras a tu jefa al Hospital Civil, donde no tienes que dar ningún depósito pa que la operen, allí no te dan ninguna garantía. Es más, puede que te arrepientas para el resto de tus días. Si en algo estimas a la que te dio el ser, no la lleves allí, hombre. Yo sé lo que te digo. Cuando un enfermo de gravedad entra a ese lugar, es muy difícil que salga vivo. Yo conozco a alguien que ha perdido a la mujer y al hijo mayor. Lo que pasa es que hay unos médicos muy bestias, no saben lo que hacen. Por eso te echo el invite a que vayas conmigo al otro cachete, porque yo sé que puedes ahorrar buenos centavos. Y entonces puedes conseguirle a tu jefa un buen especialista. Alguien que la atienda como se merece. Aquí hay muy buenos médicos que le pueden resolver el problema. Claro, hay que aflojar los cueritos de rana.

—Estoy convencido de que eso es lo mejor, por eso quiero irme con usté. Pero me duele tener que dejarla estando como está.

—No dejes que eso te atormente, hombre. Ya sabes que se queda en buenas manos. ¿Quién mejor que Chavela pa cuidarla? Es cierto que ella tiene al marido y a sus chamacos que atender, pero todos los días le puede dar sus vueltecitas hasta que tú regreses, aunque sea nomás pa levantarle el ánimo.

—Dice bien, Ingeniero . . . Pero . . . cambiando de tema . . . ¿usté cree que sea posible salir de casa de su hermano ese mismo día?

—Con el favor de Dios. Mira, quiero que sepas esto, es un secreto de guerra, ¿eh? Por regla general, la Migra no vigila los lunes en la mañana, quién sabe por qué razón. Así que yo calculo que vamos a poder salir ese mismo día. Y mientras llega mi hermano de River City, en casa de mi cuñado podemos echarnos unos huevitos rancheros con café. ¿Qué dices?

—No, pos como usté diga. Y . . . ¿cuándo llegaríamos a Houston?

—En la tarde de ese mismo día. Ya estando allá empiezan a rodar las canicas, ¿me entiendes? Tengo cuates que nos pueden dar una manita. Por chamba no te preocupes, la hay a manos llenas. Si prefieres puedes empezar esa misma noche, tú dirás.

—Pues ya veremos, estando allá . . .

—Estoy seguro que te va a gustar el ambiente. Por lo menos a mí me cuadra. Es mejor que otros lugares donde he chambiado. Una vez pasé un año enterito en Chicago, en el mentado barrio La Garra, y aquello fue de la patada. Lo que es el lugar, pasa, pero lo que es el clima, se lo regalo al que lo quiera. No se aguanta el friazo chingao. A todas horas sopla un viento que corta la cara como navaja de barba. Por eso prefiero Houston, porque aunque se gana un poco menos, y a veces, la chamba es un poco más pesada, no hace tanto frío en invierno. Te aseguro que te irá bien. Eres lo que se dice jalador y tesonero. Además, no tienes vicios de ninguna clase. Vas a lo que vas, y ya.

—Ingeniero . . . ¿y si . . . y si nos agarra la Migra?

—Pos ni modo, mano. Mira, óyeme bien lo que te voy a decir: de mojado uno anda siempre a la buena de Dios. Arrastrado, como quien dice, por la necesidá. El hambre lo obliga a uno a abandonar el terruño, el hogar, los seres queridos. Pero ¿qué le vamos a hacer, mano? Hay que correr riesgos. En la vida hay que correr riesgos. Si no, pos uno no llega a ninguna parte. Tú sabes bien que aquí, uno anda siempre más jodido que las mangas de un chaleco. Así que, mejor jálale pal otro lado, y si algo se logra, es porque Dios es grande, y porque uno mismo no se achicopala. Es cierto que hay que exponerse a toda clase de humillaciones, pero con el tiempo se le hace a uno la concha dura. Una cosa sí te sé decir: si es necesario ir hasta el fin del mundo pa darles de comer a mi mujer y a mis hijos, allá te voy sin vacilar. Me cae de madre que sí. Mira, no me gusta recargár- mela, pero quiero que sepas que a mí la pinche Migra me hace los mandados. Así que, ya sabes, no tengas miedo de que te agarren. Eso es lo de menos, lo de más es aguantar la vara. Créeme, la Migra me viene muy guanga. Nomás hay que tener una gotita de espe- ranza, mano, y un empuje del tamaño de la vida misma. A veces uno se pandea y se re- tuerce, como los churros . . . ¿pero rajarse?—nomás nones. Piensa en que estaremos allá trabajando hasta la Semana Santa, después volveremos pa que se opere tu jefecita. Y si te quedan ganas, nos vamos otra vez. Si te propones, pues hasta podrías venir a poner un negocito. Nada del otro mundo, nomás cualquier mosquero. Se trata de que vivas de- centemente. Si yo tuviera la paciencia que tú tienes eso es lo que haría. Pero yo no nací pa comerciante, me gusta regar la lana y hacer disparates.

—Oiga Ingeniero, ¿y a usté nunca lo ha agarrado la Migra?

—Sí cómo no, tres veces.

—¿Y qué pasa si lo agarran a uno?

—Nada, nomás te avientan pa este lado. Fíjate, la primera vez que me pescaron andaba manejando el carro de mi compadre Salvador. No traía licencia de manejar, y pa acabarla de arruinar tuve un accidente. Choqué con una gabacha que se me atravesó en un semáforo, ya mero me la llevaba de corbata. De buena suerte que ella no sufrió ni un rasguño, si no, allí mismo me linchan los chotas. Nomás le sumí un poquito la pol- vera a un Pontiac nuevecito que ella traía. El Ford de mi compadre era ya el purito cas- carón, pero no se hizo nada. La gabacha se fue echando pestes, y yo quedé detenido. Ese mismo día vine a dar aquí.

—¿Eso fue en Houston?

—No, esa vez andábamos en Dallas. La segunda vez fue en Houston, me acuerdo como si ahorita fuera. Habíamos salido mi compadre Salvador y yo a comprar comida un sábado en la mañana, y cuando regresamos ya estaba la Migra esperándonos. Nunca supimos, a ciencia cierta, cómo se dieron cuenta, pero sospechamos que alguien nos había denunciado.

—¿Y qué les hicieron?

Nomás nos echaron pa acá. Y la mera verdad nos hicieron un favor porque hacía ocho meses que no veíamos a la vieja y a los chilpayates. Lo malo fue que nos dejaron en Matamoros, Tamaulipas. Y de allí tuvimos que viajar en autobús a Monterrey, y des- pués a Saltillo, y de Saltillo hasta aquí. Deja tú, por poco y nos avientan pal sur del estado de Chiapas creyendo que éramos guatemaltecos. Pa allá llevaban un montón de pelados, dizque eran de Guatemala. Y los iban a dejar allá en la frontera de su país. Nosotros tuvimos suerte.

—¡Qué bárbaro! Usté sí que se arroja como los gallos finos.

—Ya te digo es la necesidá que lo empuja a uno. Mira, déjame advertirte algo desde ahorita. De vez en cuando la Migra se da sus vueltecitas por donde uno está chambiando, pero nomás no te acalambres. Cuando los veas llegar escóndete como puedas. Allí te dirán dónde. Los mejicanos del otro lado se enfurecen cuando llega la Migra y les pide papeles. Sabes que han protestado mucho por el tratamiento. Han armando pedorrones de poca madre, y las cosas han ido cambiando un poco. Y ahora a la Migra le ha dado por ir a observar nada más, dizque pa infundir temor. Pa mí son puros, y al amanecer bachichas, los cabrones.

—Oiga Ingeniero, ¿y por qué nunca le ha dado por arreglar papeles pa irse a los Estados Unidos de un jalón?

—La pura desidia. Porque la lana no me ha faltado, ni la palanca tampoco. Además, por ahora, no soy muy amigo de trasplantar a mi familia al otro lado. Si algún día me animo, será cuando mis chamacos ya estén bien crecidos, pa que no pierdan sus raíces. Ya Sergio, el mayor, está estudiando comercio. Tiene mucho empeño en conseguirse una buena chamba en un banco, y no quiero quitarle las intenciones. Por otra parte, mi vieja no tiene el menor deseo de cambiarse pa Gringolandia. Así que, mejor dejo las cosas de ese tamaño.

—¿Y cómo fue la tercera vez que cayó en manos de la Migra?

—La tercera vez cometí una tarugada. Bueno, en aquel entonces pensé que había sido una tarugada, pero ahora la veo como una pequeña aventura. Yo estaba aquí muy a gusto descansando y unos cuates fueron los que me alborotaron. Yo tengo un defecto muy grande, que si me echan el invite no me gusta chiviarme, ¿me entiendes? Me la pusieron de color de rosa, sabes. Me dijeron que era por un mes o mes y medio, a lo más. Y que pagaban bien. Esto fue allá en el norte de Colorado, casi llegando al estado de Guayuma. Resulta que había un viejo que necesitaba cinco manos pa que le hicieran el desahije de betabel, pero no tenía casa. Lo único que prometía era conseguirnos algún lugarcito cerca del rancho. Y como uno, por tal de trabajar, se mete en cualquier gallinero viejo, pos aceptamos. Cuando uno anda de mojado se aviene a todo. Pos allá te vamos, a toda máquina. Yo iba muy esperanzado. Le decía a mi compadre Salvador: "Vamos, nos echamos unos cuantos acres de betabel, y luego regresamos a descansar otra temporadita como Dios manda." Y él me seguía la corriente: "Pos sí, compadre, y sirve de que conocemos el mundo. Dicen que por allá es muy bonito." ¿Qué crees? Cuando llegamos encontramos las cosas todas desconchifladas. Las labores del viejo estaban bien atascadas de yerba. Con razón nadie quería hacerle el trabajo; además, nos dimos cuenta que pagaba una miseria. Pero deja tú, lo peor era que todavía no nos conseguía casa. Llegamos todos mallugados del viaje, y no queríamos muy bien entrarle al desahije esa tarde, pero el viejo insistió en que empezaramos a jalar luego lueguito. Nos aseguró que pa las siete, sin falta, nos tendría listo un lugar donde dormir. Pos le entramos en caliente y chambiamos toda la tarde. Cerca del oscurecer llegó el viejo, y nos dijo: "Síganme." Lo seguimos y nos llevó a una cantina que estaba a la orilla de la carretera muy cerca de una ciudad que se llama Grily. El propietario de la cantina era mejicano, un tal Melesio Pacheco. Allí nos enteramos que la cantina iba a ser nuestra casa. El viejo le iba a dar una comisión a Pacheco pa que nos dejara dormir en la cantina. La cosa no resultó. Llegábamos de la labor todos cateados, casi al oscurecer. Después teníamos que calentar agua pa bañarnos dentro de un cuartito donde guardaban los carros. Y afuera, a los cuatro vientos, teníamos que hacer de comer, en una parrilla. A veces salíamos del desahije tan desmadejados que ni espíritu teníamos pa bañarnos. Dicen que la cáscara guarda el palo. Eso no es nada, teníamos que esperar hasta después de medianoche cuando Pacheco cerraba la cantina. Entonces cada quien juntaba una mesa con otra y hacía su cama. Yo me acordaba mucho de esa canción que dice: "De piedra ha de ser la cama, de piedra la cabecera . . ." No te miento, mano, caíamos muertos de cansancio. Haz de cuenta que dejabas caer un costal de papas sobre las mesas. Ya no nos movíamos hasta por la madrugada cuando teníamos que pegar el brinco pa irnos otra vez al desahije. Pos n'hombre cállate la boca, no aguantamos mucho de ese pelo. Al cabo de diez días le aventamos al viejo con su trabajo y nos fuimos. Pacheco nos consiguió una casita de renta en Grily, y a los pocos días encontramos chamba en una empacadora. Allí fue donde nos pescó la Migra.

"¿Y eso cómo ocurrió, Ingeniero?

—Déjame platicarte. Ah, mira, ya nos traen los taquitos de gallina.

— . . . .

—Entrale . . . sinvergüenzamente . . . Oiga maistro, nos trae dos cafés, por favor.

El joven divisó hacia afuera por la ventana. La lluvia caía a raudales. El único ser humano que se veía en la acera de la esquina era un policía de tránsito que se refugiaba con un paraguas. Permanecía de pie como si se hubiera quedado congelado en el tiempo. No pasaban carros. Lentamente, iba surgiendo la noche y empezaban a brotar las luces de la ciudad. Dentro del restaurante había un ambiente bullicioso, bañado del aroma que salía de la cocina y de la música que despedían el acordeón y la guitarra que pulsaban un anciano ciego y un adolescente. Estos iban tocando canciones de mesa en mesa y recogiendo propinas. El joven siguió comiendo mientras escuchaba al que le apodaban el Ingeniero . . .

—Pos como te iba diciendo, conseguimos chamba en una empacadora. Jalamos por tres semanas a las mil maravillas. Cada semana guardábamos unos centavitos, pero después empeoró el asunto. Era una cuestión que ya venía de tiempo atrás. Resulta que un grupo de obreros—todos ellos mejicanos—estaba protestando los bajos salarios y las condiciones de trabajo. La mera verdá, ya estaban hartos de maltrato, y se organizaron para meter un sindicato. Entonces los mayordomos empezaron a apretar. Llegó el momento en que éstos sospecharon hasta de sus propias madres. Había un mayordomo mejicano, que se llamaba, o se llama, José Sifuentes, pero a él lo tenían allí nomás de adorno. El pobre vivía resentido—y con mucha razón—porque los mayordomos gringos ganaban mucho más que él, y pa acabarla de joder, hacían menos trabajo. Seguramente pensaron que si se la daban a Sifuentes de mayordomo, pagándole poco, de perdido podrían taparle el ojo al macho. Los chavos creyeron que el cuate se iba a vender, ¿mé entiendes? Pero les salió el tiro por la culata, porque Sifuentes acabó uniéndose a la causa de los otros. Entonces se formó la división entre la gente. Por una parte estaban los que no chistaban. A éstos los tenían muy bien amedrentados los gringos, y ni siquiera le dirigían la palabra a los del bando opuesto. Si no, pos ya sabían a qué atenerse los cabroncitos. Y por otra parte, estaban los partidarios de la idea de meter el sindicato, los que eran tenidos por revoltosos. A éstos, los gringos los traían entre ojos. Nomás los andaban vigilando a ver si hacían alguna movida chueca, a ver si daban un paso en falso pa desocuparlos. Una vez, los revoltosos nos invitaron a una junta que tuvieron en casa de Sifuentes. Todos fuimos, a ver qué se oía decir. Pos n'hombre, nos enteramos de un chorro de abusos y barbaridades cometidos en contra de los obreros. En resumidas cuentas, nos pidieron el apoyo, en caso de que hubiera una votación tocante a la cuestión del sindicato. Y les aseguramos que podían contrar con nosotros, aunque les explicamos que como andábamos de mojados no sabíamos lo que pudiera presentarse. Ellos ya estaban enterados de todo eso. Así que, se hicieron compañeros de nosotros, no sólo por el interés del apoyo sino porque los chavos eran de veras gente fina. Buenas reatas, ¿me entiendes? Pos conforme fueron pasando los días, la cosa se fue poniendo cada vez más caliente, hasta que un día se formó el desmadre. Los gringos se pusieron tan histéricos que empezaron a indagar acerca de nosotros y a investigarlo todo. Pos en un dos por tres se dieron cuenta que éramos mojados, y luego lueguito nos denunciaron. La Migra nos echó pa acá y el carro se quedó en casa de Sifuentes. Y hasta la fecha, allí está. No pierdo la esperanza de ir por él un día de éstos.

—¡Híjole! Yo no sé cómo le hace usté, Ingeniero.

—No, mira, todo esto te lo digo pa decirte esto otro: si te vas de mojado, tienes que agarrar parejo. Si te va bien ya jodiste. Si te va mal, ni modo. Nomás acuérdate, las cosas de algún modo se componen.

—Le doy mi palabra, Ingeniero. Estoy dispuesto a todo. Con usté me siento más seguro.

—Así me gusta, que seas decidido. Ya verás cómo va a mejorar tu situación.

Cuando los dos hombres salieron del restaurante ya había escampado. A lo largo de la calle Real las luces bulliciosas se veían reflejadas en los charcos del pavimento. La ciudad había recobrado su pálpito acostumbrado. Rumbido de camiones y automóviles, toque de cláxones, llorido de sirenas, niños vagabundos deambulando, vendedores callejeros negociando sus mercancías a toda voz, canciones de músicos bohemios, pordioseros dándole duro al oficio, borrachos bambaleándose al caminar. Iban y venían los transeúntes.

Los dos hombres llegaron al mercado Zaragoza y doblaron por el costado. Siguieron caminando indiferentes al ritmo citadino. Llegaron a la otra calle confundiéndose entre la muchedumbre. Después doblaron solos por una oscura calleja y se fueron alejando poco a poco hasta perderse en la inmensidad anónima de aquella noche.

José Sánchez Boudy

EL SILENCIO

La miseria lo había sacado de la patria. La miseria y la esperanza. Le habían dicho que en Estados Unidos podía revalidar su carrera de abogado; que le sería fácil porque él tenía una gran habilidad para las lenguas. Y que como no había muchos cubanos en la tierra del Tío Sam sería recibido con los brazos abiertos. Un colombiano que conoció cuando trataba, infructuosamente, de ganarse la vida en su tierra con las pocas habilidades que tenía como letrado, le había dicho: "Con el inglés que tú sabes, en Estados Unidos no tienes problemas. Te haces abogado de una corporación, y ya. Tu problema es que no sabes hablar y en nuestros países el que no es orador está perdido. Pero allá, con los millones que hay, las oportunidades para los letrados son gigantes. Márchate con tu mujer. Además, no hay cubanos por allá. Lo malo es cuando tienes la piel prietecita como yo o ya hay una colonia de tus compatriotas. Entonces te cogen miedo. Pero si no, te dan todo tipo de facilidades."

Como las cosas por su patria no andaban bien políticamente, se decidió a emigrar. Un día vendió, en la casa de empeño de la esquina de su casa, sus muebles y demás andariveles, y con la mujer se marchó al extranjero; con la mujer y el hijo de siete meses que ella llevaba en las entrañas.

Cuando pisó el aeropuerto pequeño de Miami vio los cielos abiertos. Ahora sí que iba a tener una gran oportunidad. "Ahora, mi mujer, vamos a ganar todos los billetes que queramos, y nuestro hijo nacera aquí: será americano."

Pasó fácilmente por emigración porque llevaba visa de turista. La de residente era muy difícil de conseguir. La embajada apenas la otorgaba; ni a los abogados, porque podían ser carga pública.

El Hotel al que llegó en la playa no era de lo mejor. De cuando en cuando una cucaracha se paseaba campante por el medio de la sala, virando la cabeza, y él tenía que hacerla estallar. Pero no era falta de higiene: "es que Miami viejo es un cucarachero. Tanta mata de coco, tanta palma y tanta arena. Además estos hoteles viejos."

Pero a él aquello no le importaba. La esperanza nunca lo abandonaba; la esperanza que llevaba clavada en el pecho como un hongo a la tierra. "Mira, vamos a descansar dos o tres días y después visito los bufetes de abogado y me ofrezco como consultor latinoamericano. ¿Cómo no se me ocurrió eso en Cuba? No hay que ser orador sino saber de papeles. Así que ya todo está resuelto. Vamos a bañarnos en la playa, que aquí todo está tan bueno que ni frío hay."

* * *

El abogado americano lo miraba sonriente. —Cómo no le vamos a dar trabajo hombre. Si necesitamos un especialista latinoamericano. Ganará diez mil pesos.

Se quedó boquiabierto. —Diez mil pesos, ¿dice usted diez mil pesos?

—¿Le parece poco? Si usted puede producir más . . .

—¿Producir más?

—Claro, usted tiene que traer al bufete casos, y de las ganancias el bufete le pagará su salario. Así es como se trabaja aquí.

—Pero para eso trabajo para mí.

—Pero es que su título . . . Además, no se olvide que este es el bufete Smith, Smith, Farley and Francovichky. Oiga como suena: Smith, Smith, Farley and Francovichky.

El abogado americano lo miraba sonriente. Le sonría con cariño.

—Figúrese la situación. Usted no ha metido nada este mes en el bufete. Resulta que es usted el que le debe dinero al bufete. No leyó usted el contrato.

—Leer el contrato.

—No lo leyó. Pueso queda despedido. Smith, Smith, Farley and Francovichky no puede tener un abogado que no ha leído un contrato. Sí, le debe usted mil pesos al bufete. Queda despedido.

—¿Así que tiene un hijo recién nacido?

—Sí, y por eso necesitamos la casa.

La dueña del apartamento lo miraba de arriba abajo. Era gorda, cuadrada como una jicotea, con los pies varilosos por el trabajo de la factoría.

—Pero usted no habla inglés.

—Claro que lo hablo. No me oye.

—¿No lee inglés?

—Pues claro que lo leo.

—No ve lo que ahí dice.

—Miró al letrero: NO CHILDREN. NO PETS.

—Además mi amigo: no nos gustan los extranjeros.

—Pero usted es extranjera. Su acento.

—Yo soy norteamericana. NO CHILDREN. NO PETS.

—No children no pets.

—No children no pets.

—No children no pets.

—No children no pets.

—No children no pets.

Lo volvió a llenar la esperanza. En el bolsillo le quedaban unos pocos centavos, lo suficiente para coger la guagua.

—Es verdad que no nos hemos rozado con esos exiliados para que no nos confundan con ellos, Beatriz. Pero les están dando mucho. Voy a ir al Cuban Refugee Center a hacerme pasar por uno de ellos. Les diré que soy abogado. Seguro me consiguen trabajo fuera de aquí donde sí hay negocios con América Latina. Ya tú verás. O de otra cosa.

La señora del Refugio lo miraba detenidamente. ¿Así que usted quiere un sitio muy tranquilo, lo más tranquilo del mundo?

—Bueno, lo más tranquilo. Donde todo sea paz y tranquilidad. Estoy cansado.

La americana lo miró sonriendo. Lo miró con sonrisa paternal en los ojos:

—Lo tenemos. Formidable. Será para usted lo más tranquilo del mundo. Mire, aquí tiene el pasaje para mañana. Va para Atlanta, Georgia. Allí lo recoge Mr. Dorth el pastor y lo lleva al pueblo donde va a trabajar. El le dará el trabajo.

—¿En Atlanta?

—En un sitio tranquilo. Aquí lo tiene todo. Todo.

—Pero . . .

—¿Acepta o no acepta?

—Bueno.

Recogió el sobre cerrado con los pasajes y la carta para el pastor.

El pastor le sonreía, como la mujer, paternalista. Con una gran simpatía.

—¿Qué le parece la casa? Todo dado por la iglesia. Los muebles un poco viejos pero pintados por voluntarios, como la casa.

¿Y el trabajo?

—Como usted lo quiere: tranquilidad absoluta. Buenísimo. Trabajará poco. Venga que lo llevo.

El auto iba por la carretera polvorienta de las afueras del pueblo. El no había tenido más remedio que irse de Miami. Obedeció al miedo. Por eso ni se atrevía a hacer preguntas. Ni se atrevió. Aunque no fuera de abogado siendo un buen trabajo. El problema era vivir y la angustia de los meses pasados . . .

—El sitio más tranquilo del mundo, mi amigo.

Habían parado frente al cementerio. El pastor le sonreía paternalmente.

—Oiga.

—Muy poco trabajo. Es usted el sepulturero. Aquí se muere poca gente. Un trabajo muy codiciado. Good Luck, Good Luck. GOOD LUCK MY FRIEND. YOU ARE REALLY A LUCKY MAN.

El Huitlacoche

THE MOJADO WHO OFFERED UP HIS TAPEWORMS TO THE PUBLIC WEAL

¡Oyez, oyez! ease your wearies and you shall learn about the case of the State versus the hapless, peripatetic mojao, a surely woeful account in the main—a sucker mojao who slipped across the Bravo stepping stones in a snorkel, flippers, and a toy-store trident—but not without socially redeeming values as well as intimations of brave third worlds, indeed a tale with certain exuberant dimensions of H. Alger-like mobility to which all we citizens of this good nation still (or ought still) respond.

First let me alert you to my editorial intentions. This account as first told to me meandered worse than the Río Grande itself and I mean to edit it. Moreover, I shall want to focus on the moment of conversion, with its sepia qualities of the old print or Far West photo, of the pícaro who once he is scourged and brought to escarmiento (that of course is the moment when our mojao offers up his tapeworms to the public weal) takes to clean living and his place as a far-seeing subject of the State. And it's a totally true story too, I heard it firsthand from a gentleman—digo un gentilhombre—known as one el Rompeculos, in the Trailways station in Earth, Texas. We were casual fellow travelers killing our drudgery as we languished in Earth waiting for the express to come in and take us straight to Ajo, Arizona, and then to San Diego (San Dedo to those who know it well) with blessedly brief pit (piss) stops in Muleshoe, Needmore, Bronco, Humble City, Jal, Wink, Pecos, Boracho, Eagle Flat, Tornillo, Socorro, Chamberino, Bawrtry, Bowie, Cochise, Mescal, Pan Tak, Suwuki Chuapo, Quijotoa, Tracy, and Why. Among the ceaseless hours of waiting and the Chili Dogs, wet and dry burritos, and the juicy jujubes, we took to snorting, piston-like, shots of translucent Pancho Villa tequila (haven't you tried that brand? It's sold exclusively in liquor stores across from bus stations and strictly in $1.99 units), alternating them with swallows of homemade terra-cotta-colored border-town sangrita which one of my companion's amigas had brew-mistressed, tempered with chile pequín, and measured out for Rompe in an ornate onyx flagon.

"Why do they call you Huitlacoche?"

"I choose to call myself that."

"I know it as something to eat. A mushroom or fungus that grows on corn."

"I know him as a boxer I admired some years ago who being a poor Indian became wealthy with his fists and returned wealth to the poor."

"Oh, him. I remember him. Didn't he once fight in the Mexico City bullring?"

"Yes."

"Good."

"Why do they call you Rompeculos?"

"I choose to call myself that. Basically because I'm an arrogant chop buster."

"Good."

This Rompeculos, a muscular brute perhaps about 40 years old with a tattoo of the Aztlanense eagle gorging itself on la serpiente, who as my narration will definitely prove had the gentle, inquisitive sensibility of a schizoid poet, was a sometime hauler of Coors beer along the desert floors and byways. Contrary to what the inside covers of matchbooks so gamely enthuse for ingenues, he really had learned to master the big rigs, and was used to making significant bread—when he worked at this handle—hauling 6000 cases of Coors in a 14 wheel semi and an extra 8 wheeler in tow. He was, of course, a sometime contrabandist, this being the borderland, after all. As for trucking though, as he put it, the "blow job" could get to you. He'd be driving down the Waco run and in the dead night of desert air, all by his lonely, with only a pinup of Sylvia Pinal or María Dolores or Flor Silvestre above his shield to keep him company—Dios es mi copiloto—when suddenly one of those 99 bottles way in back would blow. That's it. They would have been all shook up by their tripping and suddenly he'd hear one blow and a few minutes later another would pop its cap and gush forth and five big ones down the road it would be a third coming to climax. I guessed then that the beer, that was his problem. But I was mistaken. At any rate, here he was, a little down and out in Earth, Texas, precisely where I was.

"What'cha here for, hombre?"

"Well, I needed some chavos to continue my studies at the uni."

He looked at me cross-eyed, like el pícaro that he was. "You a college kid?"

I got very sullen. Being a brutish sight myself, and a higher education gridironist, I felt it an occasional prerogative to be temperamental. "I'm not a kid. I'm back from Nam."

" 'Ta bien. What do you play, middle linebacker? You're huge enough. You here on a bandit run?"

"Something like that. ¡Pero de mala muerte!"

"They fucked you over, ése?"

"Yeah, man. I was supposed to score enough Irapuato green to get me through my junior year. I came down all the way to the central altiplano y pues nada, puro pedo."

"Shit, man. En Irapuato, puras fresas. Ese, that's all they sell there, strawberries. And even be careful with those man, cause the top berries look real good and plump como los besos de una vieja salada but down below they're all huangas and overripe. No, ése, to Irapuato for fresas and to Morelia for morelianas and to Guanajuato, de tan alta alcurnia, for camotes (camo te vienes, camo te vas, camote te meto por detrás—they don't call me Rompeculos for nothing), and to Veracruz for huachinangos, not to mention huapangos, and to Aguascalientes for the best goddamned cockfights you ever saw in your whole life, digo, la feria. But for mota, man, you've got to get way up high, see? Up in the foothills around Toluca, up in the mountains by Amecameca where you can see prince Popo copulating with princess Ixta. Up high, ése, that's where the mota is, Toluca green."

"Oye vato, thanks so much for telling me this shit now that it can do me no good. Aquí pues estoy en mero rasquachi eating pecan chunkies on the bench in Earth, Texas."

"Aw, don't worry about it, ése. Supposing you did score, then you would have had to move your stash across the border. A tenderfoot college vato like you. Who knows what might have happened. You could have ended up like that jerk in the movies, the Midnight Express. It can happen. I'm telling you cause I know." Rompe scratched his head and squinted. "Let me give you some advice, Huitla. Forget about the foliage, it's pure risk man, especially if you're not enchufado into a border brokerage. Next time you come down, run a few parrots. Más vale."

"Parrots? ¿'Tas loco?"

"I'm telling you, man. Pound for pound they'll make more money for you than marihuana. You can buy parrots on the streets of Laredo for maybe 25-30 dollars. You know what they go for in San Antonio? Three hundred big ones! A little further inland, say Kansas City, seven hundred, no más. And with a parrot you've got fluidity. You take your investment to any good pet shop y ahí no más, they exchange it for currency, just like at the bank."

"I don't know, vato loco. I wouldn't buy no parrot but for sure I'd buy a lid of mota."

"That's because you don't know birds, ése. They're the only ones that will accept a human. You can raise a pigeon and it'll do acrobatics but you can't get one to crawl on your finger or hop on your head. The parrot alone will tolerate human companionship. People love them because they become like humans. You teach them to talk, to sing. They've got perfect pitch. I've got one myself. It sings strictly songs of the Mexican Revolution. You know, *Adelita, La Valentina, el 30-30.*"

Finally the Trailways bus arrived. Feeling very tipsy we lurched our way to the Earth men's room to empty our bladders. Then we boarded the bus, picking seats up front where it was less bumpy.

Rompe continued his sermonizing. "All you do is douse their bread with a little tequila and take them over the bridge in a sack under your seat or donde sea. And if you get caught, ¿qué importa? At most a fifty dollar fine, if they even bother. Cause nobody takes parrots seriously, not even the customs agents. With marihuana they can catch up with you 500 miles north of the border. But pericos! ¡Qué ricos! Once they're across you can't prove a damned thing!"

"You're making me sad, Rompe. Real sad. You know how I'm going to spend this summer? Breading shrimp at Arthur Treacher's or grating that foul cheese they use at Taco Bell. Puta madre, and the worst was that my cucaracha conked out in the sierras. It did, it slipped a rod and I had no lana to get it mended."

"So what you do man, you junk it? What's the matter, don't you guys get a football scholarship?"

"Yeah, they throw us a bone, but college is expensive, especially for a Chicano b.m.o.c."

Rompe shrugged his head. "So where's your cucaracha?"

"What could I do, they wouldn't even buy it, a car with U.S. plates in Mexico. Finally some wool brokers in Chihuahua city gave me some lana for it, mostly for the radio although they claimed que tenían modo de arreglar lo de las placas."

Rompe laughed. "I know that Chihuahua wool-gathering crowd, they're enchufadísimo con la aduana. For sure they must've cleared five hundred, maybe a grand on your fotingo. What year was it? What model?"

I just looked at him aggrieved and drank maybe two fingers worth of tequila.

Rompe looked me over as if for the first time, con sospechas y cautela. "You studying to be a doctor?"

"¡Esos! I hate those fuckers."

"¿Pues qué"

"Poet. ¡Pueta! A nomad."

"¿Poeta? What kind of career is that? You're a strange guy, Huitla. And your name is as strange as you. ¿Qué tú haces? You eat magic mushrooms? ¡Hay que vender la mota y no esfumarla!" He had a big poet's belly laugh, a shot of Pancho Villa's best and a good swallow of fiery sangrita, settled back into his pullman seat and told me this tale about a woeful friend of his: un mojao.

Now, this story meandered up and down into every backwater and eddy like the Río Bravo itself. I mean, please don't think that I'm going to bore you with the sort of river flotsam he laid on me—the bit about how this mojao once managed a molino de nixtamal, overseeing the mixing of the corn with water and slaked lime in order to produce the gruel that would then be ground into masa harina while the benditas queued up at 6:00 a.m. for their supplies, or how he landed an RFP from the Yuma, Arizona CETA to offer a crash course to ex-junkies on how to train geese to be industrial watchdogs for the junkyard business (meaner than junkyard dogs! was the program's motto), or how during one period he painted watercolors of cherubs, madonnas and 31 types of chirping birdies on birch barks for los turistas, or how he seduced the wife of el mero chingón jefe de la Falfurrias migra, or the sweatshop he labored in that produced synthetic blue pellets supposed to look like genuine turquoise in order to imitate the jewelry of the Santo Domingo Pueblos, or all those other border conceits. No, none of that, but I must declare, some of this pueta's story—it was like you are panning the Río Bravo for precious substance and all you come up with on your plate is dead catfish after toxic catfish and suddenly there's this clunker, the fabled nugget that made the Golden West— well now, that is something to polish and assay. So, Dios mediante, I would like now to focus on this meandering mojado and that golden moment when he redeemed himself in the eyes of his Anglo overseers through the ordained intercession of the therapeutic tapeworms that thrived in his infected bowels. Let us make a beginning y ahí va de cuento.

Erase un mojado pero muy mojao. According to his cuate el Rompeculos, who knew this wet from the very start and, it could be claimed, dogged him at key intervals like the cartoon angel of good conscience, he was born in the massive wheatfields of Sinaloa, labored in those fields with all told thirteen brethren (and sistern?) reaping the wheat from wither our daily tortillas are patted and fashioned to fill our panzas with cheese and bean burritos. Nothing out of the ordinary, this young, rude, clever, robust, and fearfully ignorant country chamacón, living his days and laboring mightily in the breadbasket of northwestern Mexico, a plains mozalbete who knew no further than Guamuchil to the west and Mocorito to the east. This life was—how can I convey to you the idyll of laborious ignorance?—the bliss of unremitting and unselfconscious routines, an agrarian, Skinnerian utopia (as Keats put it, to think is to be filled with sorrow), until one day, it was about puberty or maybe a bit into it already, he found himself returning the coa to the long white stable of the latifundio and came upon his two older sisters lying on their backs in the straw with their skirts up and their comely legs spread, each with a handsome caballerango on top doing a flopping dance like contrincantes in a cockfight or partners in a horizontal jarabe. Steadfastly he shut the door on the intrusion into su vida. Pero, ¡ay maldito! ya se le entraba el gusanito de las dudas. A dirt road traveling true through the wheatfields was no longer merely a dirt road but a segmented trajectory over time. It was a vector with a retrospect and a prospective future. The signals of nuestra vida natural suddenly took on a new semiotic. What was that arboreal warble that correlated with a young peon's erection? and that long fastidious mutter of oxen that harmonized with a mancebo's inchoate brooding, and finally, passionate resentments? As Rompe judged it, in that establo parpadeo our young mojao had eaten of nuestra manzana del saber and ultimately—as every mojao must feel so deeply in order to be mojao, that is, genuinely driven into border waters—tasted the notion of class.

One day our mojao was musing and chewing his emotional cud by the fire in his adobe home. The firelight made a suppurative dance on the caked wall and ultimately on the breast of his younger sister Consuelo, and for the first time our pre- and protomojado looked upon his sister and himself with foreknowledge. There was young Consuelo, whose breasts rose like certain rivers in times of flood—a natural and irreversible consequence of the springtime or of puberty; poor Consuelo, suddenly and without warning tears streaming down her golden firelit cheeks, her rising, yearning, uncontrollable pechos.

And our mojado knew direction. A triptych the first panel of which put in place the prior conducta of his two older sisters, those very traitors to rural vida who long since had departed flamboyantly on the backs of potros negros, the made mates of mustachioed caballerangos, the kind of varones machos that the Sinaloan wheatfields so proudly boost and supply with field machetes of tempered steel. No longer would his vida contain within it the dulcet periodicity of the three nights a year, el Día de los Muertos, la Nochebuena, el Domingo de Gloria, when these loving archangels would with infinite care fashion festive tamales and fill them with ground walnuts, with coconut, pineapple or strawberries, and feed him, madonna fingers to chamaco mouth. They had been carried away by the implacable, migratory wind and he knew in that moment that he would never see them again.

In the second retable he saw Consuelo, who grew to beauty by days, by discrete moments before the fire that lit adobe walls and the slanted morning sun that illuminated swaying, bread-bearing grasses. Growing to beauty her pechos swelled hopelessly, advertising themselves against her will. She suffered and he suffered with her the bodily rackings of pubertal premonitions, the foreknowledge (and the foreskin) of carnal perdición. He knew this, saw it transmitted from his meaning-laden gaze to the eyes of his dear unsuccored sister, her campesina's eyes, so unused to manifested extremes of feeling, now clouding before revealed truths, a break in the stoic line of her lips. Finally a peasant's sigh issued from inside Consuelo, a sigh patterned on those she had heard from time to time emitted by peasant women who sit in visitation of their loved ones in the camposanto.

And el viejo saw this too, "viejo vivo," chuckled Rompe as he recounted this all on a bus that opened up on the Earth to Ajo trailway like a farting jogger in the clear—"porque más sabe el diablo por viejo que por diablo."

"Yes," said Rompe, who gave high marks—a poet's premium—to those who know even though they cannot act upon what they know. "Los que saben, saben, the viejo just looked up from where he was resting, rose to his haunches on his petate, looked at his son, el mojao sin todavía serlo, with a knowing, señorial air, and then at Consuelo and her heaving, autonomous breasts and said, '¡Ay Consuelo! Parece que tú vas a ser el Consuelo de los hombres.' "

And then, as if this axiological and ontogenetic proposition had been mustered at great physical expense, el viejo crouched back into the adobe shadow, only his eyes visible as brooding points.

And our pobre mojado looked first at his inconsolable sister, for whom the mandates of rural honor and vergüenza would dictate the most vigorous sibling defense of her virginal status, and then at his father, pater noster, nuestro señor de todos los mojados, a man who had conceived and raised a robust and nutrido prole, who had always operated within the narrow orthodoxies of the code of the countryside; now only his eyes were still driven, some message for our mojado in them surely of laissez faire, a blessing of mobility (outward if not upward) from our father of the wetbacks, our viejo who had been a pro-verbial Sinaloan template of a villano en su rincón but for whom no Lope sang paeans of rustic praise, no Fuenteovejuna had risen in defense, no reasoned alcalde had inter-vened against mustachioed machos and their brandished machetes, no Zapata had offered land much less liberty, no Villa, no Orozco, no Obregón had risen a dedo meñique much less offered an arm, not even a Demetrio Macías to offer a fatalistic appreciation of the inertia (punctuated by staccato and unavoidable all-be-them clearly heralded catastrophes) of his wheatfield peonage.

Now to the third retable, himself down low, his member perniciously rising like a volcanic promontory—¡un Paricutín!—from the humdrum llano, an icon erect in the latifundio, feeding itself on the sorrowful solace of autonomous breasts and the acqui-escent despair of worn-out lives, generating libido, as must be the case of any mojao who is truly a mojao, from motives that give impetus to the transgression of taboos. Our mojado knew then in that moment by the shrinking fire of his peon's hearth, in his own swelling, robust sex that was foremost (and foreskin) an act of wet defiance to the social and filial orders, that he would be departed in the morning, onto the dirt road that would become a dusty tar ribbon to Juárez (city in turn founded in the name of a mighty rural leader and iconoclast), there to mingle with a veritable ragtag army of wets recruited from the countless villages, hamlets, and milpas of the sovereign interior of México. This was the Juárez before the maquiladoras and the pleasing rhetoric of the Chamizal, where certain women were paid pesos or dollars to do dirty deeds with donkeys.

As I sorted out this torrent of words which gushed forward from el Rompeculos and doubled back into prefixed rhetorical rivulets, I was at once caught in the web of this hip and coarse narrator, and tugged by a certain anxiety. This man did not fit clearly into the slot or stereotype that I had fashioned for him.

"Did you go to college?"

"Hell no! ¿Y por qué lo preguntas?"

"I don't know. You seem so awfully knowledgeable. Are you claiming that your mojado friend left home because he was aroused by his sister? What am I supposed to think?

That he became errant to maintain the fiction, or perchance more poignantly, the reality of his sister's chaste honor? Or what?"

Rompe chuckled. "Don't exaggerate, poeta. On the other hand a mojado must cross waters to be truly one, isn't that so? And don't ask me again about college. ¡Qué college ni que college! I am a citizen, and a leading one, I might add, of the Third World. Try to understand that. You come down to our world looking for some pin money to carry you through a semester—¿y qué? This is not México. This is not the United States. This is a third land, a band or contraband 2000 miles long and 200 miles wide. It runs from the sand dunes of Matamoros to the seacliffs of La Jolla. It's run by its own logic and psycho-logic; it cooks up its own Tex-Mex food, concocts a language called pocho, musters its own police, la migra. Its felons are sui generis. Where else can a guy get busted for running double yellowheaded parrots, dealing in transnational lobster and shrimp or smuggling flasks of mercury and truckloads of candelilla? Its city-states hang on each side of the frontier, tit for tat, Tecate and Tecate, Calexico and Mexicali, San Luis and San Luis, Gringo Pass and Sonoyta, Sasabe and Sásabe, Nogales and Nogales, Naco and Naco, Columbus and Palomas, Laredo and Nuevo Laredo, Progreso and Nuevo Progreso, like brother and sister—forgive this somewhat Malinchesque although not unjustified analogy—copulating in the night with one eye over their shoulders making sure that faraway parents are not spying.

"While it may pay tribute to remote power centers—Washington, Distrito Federal and other humbug—this borderland, which I will now christen on this pathetic Ajo to Earth express as Mexérica, functions like a satrapy. No borderline here but a wriggling mem-brane that soaks in produce and spits out product. Its city-states own themselves and are committed almost totally to their own introspective, autistic symbiosis—more ap-propriately to the relationship of the shark and the pilot fish, the yucca plant and the yucca moth, or the commensalism of the beneficent tapeworms and their human donor.

"And the currency. That is what is most peculiarly wet. More than the transnational-ism or the transgressions, it's the transactions. As a country we are most like a Wall Street, a brokerage. Power seekers, power brokers, and the impotent; all cross this river, where there is a river. We have dealers in orifices, in euphoria, in human futures and orange juice futures, in man's labor, in the fruit of women's labor, in Christmas tree ornaments, silicon chips and semiconductors, and toothpaste. A friend of mine is the biggest "importer" into Mexico of fiberglass drapes. This is a world that makes a market in sadists and masochists, in siervos and señores, in capitalists and wild-eyed revolution-aries . . ."

"And vatos locos too, right ése? Wild-eyed poets, exuberant truck drivers?"

"Yes, Mr. Huitlacoche, them too, as well as b.m.o.c. Chicanos. Do you know how far we have branched out? Do you know how much certain labor-intensive industries depend on us? I'm not talking about hotels, mister. I mean steel and petrochemicals! Do you know how much San Antonio depends on us; hell, do you know how Chicago de-pends on us? We are branching out mister, we've opened up consulates or dealerships—en esta tierra son la misma cosa—in El Salvador, Nicaragua, Bolivia, Colombia, Perú, you name it, if it's impoverished and still retains some minimal level of aspiration, we've got a presence. Hell, I could show you a store on Laredo's Convent street. A modest, unimposing grocery, where they sell more Tide, Pet Milk and Kool-Aid than anyplace else on this earth. When I read about the developing world, the Third World with its massive infusions of people and currencies, its Aswan dams, its World Banks, I am amused. This is a Third World. Dollars are changed into pesos, pesos to dollars, it is a barterworld and a borderworld, the only frontier on earth where the truly poor commingle with the well-to-do inhabitants of the richest, most spoiled nation on earth. This band, this contraband, my nation Mexérica, Amexica, is a fulsome place of economic growth. It is also a cloaca into which drains the commingled phantasmagoria of the richest and the poorest. And I am one of its citizens and self-adumbrated bards." Our rompeculos of the mojados then chortled, downed another two fingers of Pancho Villa and slumped into his seat.

We had been on the express for over 6 hours and it was a very dark vehicle that sped us to the first reaches of New Mexico. Most of our fellow crew slept fitfully. Here and there one could detect buzzing patches of conversation.

"Tell me then, Rompe, what happened to our young mojao when he reached the wicked city?"

Rompe yawned. "Nothing special. He didn't stay young too long. He learned. He became borderwise and shed his fieldish ways for fiendish ones. From what he told me I figure he was a mite stupider than most. One huckster convinced him to run the river on his own. This poor stupid mojao had saved maybe 60 to 70 bucks as a result of long hours of toil painting little angels and doves on almate bark for the gabacho tourists, and he threw his lana to the coyote who donned him up with a snorkel, flippers, a diving mask, and to add irony to injury, a little trident made of plastic that mocked King Neptune's sovereignty. Then he gave him a copy of one of those 'secret maps' that abound in the Golden West, pointing to everything from treasure to choice bends in the river, and set him off to swim the Río Grande. Except that in that place and at that time of the year the water was so low that he lost his huarache—I mean his flipper—across the stepping stones in the water. Here our mojao was, in the dead of night, dressed up in his sporting-goods store best, slipping over the dead bullheads beached on the riverbed stones. And all the time the officers of la migra are waiting in their cop car, trying so hard to muffle their laughter that they're shitting. You see, it was all a set-up. A cruel practical joke. When wettie gets over to the other side they flash a beam on him and fall down in mirth. One by one the officers go to relieve themselves by the river. Then they apprehend their delincuente, fleece him of his garb and throw him back across the border. When el mojao gets back to the cantina all his acquaintances are clued in."

"Hey hombres, here comes el indito!"

"The one who dressed up like the Creature from the Black Lagoon!"

"He just got back from el coloso del norte!"

"What's the matter, Macario? You look all wet!"

"Oye, indio triste, lend me some money from what you made pizcando melones!"

The "Mojado According to Rompe" follows a different story line from there, and then it turns again and takes a third direction. What seems to be clear though is that this ése of rural honor, perhaps partially because of the warped joke, turned to re-enacting the role of mojado, emerging baptismally from the Río Bravo time and time again. For one, although he was as clever and adroit as any, he refused to learn much of the English language. Moreover, basing himself on the Mexican side of the river he sought out opportunities that required continual round-tripping. That's apparently how Rompe met our mojado: they were working double yellowheaded parrots plus an occasional scarlet macaw. This became a big bull market around the time that the Baretta television show peaked. Buyers competed to bid up parrot futures to unprecedented river highs.

Rompe and the wet would go down into the interior and dicker with the Indians who trapped parrots in the coastal jungles. "Make them young," they told their Indians. "For every young parrot you get a premium because those are easier to train. The maldito older ones are so wild, all they want to do is bite off an index finger." From the jungles of the interior the parrots traveled by fotingo to the Río Bravo. Rompe and the mojado would feed them a little bread soaked with pulque so that they would get drowsy and then they put them in a long flat cage that went atop a raft of inner tubes. Y pues, así no más. Facilito as Tzintzuntzan. They ran the river and picked up their van on the other side. From there to the parrot jobber who had orders on account from all over. There were birds for Houston oilers, Dallas bankers, Wichita ranchabouts, Norman, Oklahoma, academics, and Chicago fashion plates.

In his prime our mojado was a grand sight. Dressed in a cordobés hat, finest Mexican leather hand-tooled boots, a Spanish bolero vest, with a superb pawn bolo tie fashioned from an old serpentine Tarahumara arrowhead studded with forty pieces of turquoise, he would find himself from time to time in Rosa's Cantina, lunching on short ribs soaked in red chile and catching up on the latest news from the Third World commodity market. When the city's Visitor and Convention Bureau decided to shoot a promo film he landed a bit part as the incarnation of Old Mexico. He looked like a Casasola sepia photograph of a 1910 Mexican revolutionary.

After sauntering to the post office or the telégrafos to wire some money to Sinaloa, he might, when business called for it, pack some clientes from out of town into his Winnebago and drive down to the zona de tolerancia where each bar had its own prostitutes licensed and medically supervised by the municipal authorities. Lots of college kids would be there mixed in with truckers, oil hands, ranchers, salesmen, other whatnot, and especially políticos. Our mojado didn't like to go there much. He didn't like the way the gabachos used the place as their pigpen. It seemed that a gabacho could be a faithful one-woman husband and church-going Elk or Moose in the coloso but once he crossed the border he figured he could paw, puke and otherwise make a fool out of himself with impunity. They were right. One night a well-heeled, distinguished looking black dude was trying to get laid. The hooker turned him down flat and suggested he try a lesser club down the street. It seemed that the management didn't cotton to the girls taking on black customers cause a class joint like theirs could start losing their gabacho clientele. El magnate was stunned. Jesus Christ, it was the last place in the world where he was expecting discrimination. He had to convince the puta that he was really a Puerto Rican grown up on the continent who had never learned Spanish. That made it o.k. and flushed with pride he paid his money and together they went on back.

Just one problemita. Anonymity was the virtuous precondition of transriver entrepreneurship in Mexérica. Or to paraphrase Heraclitus, a bandit oughtn't step into the same river twice. Our mojado began to earn himself a pretty big handle. While he had always stayed away from the aguas mayores, flesh and leaves in their various formats—these, under any account, being controlled by conglomerates of certain orders—even

21

his long position in aguas menores was eventually compromised, and even undermined, by his air of haughty and driven defiance. A rural, Calderonian curandero of his propia honra, this mojado arrogated and amalgamated notions of robber bandit and Robin Hood even though he was riverwise enough to "know better." So then, while at the beginning his transgressions, when uncovered by the border patrol, were punished by the customary petty fines and slaps on the wrist—who really gets fired up about smuggling parrots or the prime ingredient in chewing gum?—his wet attitude of villano pero honrado quickly began to impress an indelible mark on the crowded, bored and hurried courtrooms where novelties could quickly be seized upon to alleviate the crushing monotonies imposed by the blur of contraband cohorts that filed past the judges' gavels. Similar was the attitude of the law enforcement community, some members of which apparently began to call him epithets like el superwet, el mojado en ajo, et alia. Our mojado noticed that his capture rate, which had an initial background level approximating a random walk, had risen off the charts to the point where at the close of his career it was more like an águila/sol tossup. He was worried, business was badly down, and his familia, now living in better quarters in Culiacán, began to voice remonstrations over larga distancia. But in misfortune too our mojado soberbio reveled in his own way, coming out of the bends in the river with parrots under his arms and an air of feverish anticipation (la migra ¿sí o no?), reliving in each crossing the river renaissance, this our San Juan Bautista, guardián de todos los mojados.

What is clearly apocryphal, claims el Rompeculos, yet certainly symptomatic in its being attributed to our bedeviled and vainglorious mojado en ajo, was the so-called "wet warranty," which made its presence known for a few years around the time that Chrysler, G.M., and the others promoted it in a different economic sector. The way it worked was that for a certain insurance premium the exporter of a commodity could in effect guarantee delivery of goods (or their dollar value) across the border irrespective of confiscations, water damage, dust storms, or acts of God. Indeed it was the "wet warranty" that destroyed el mojado's brokerage, which, given his high capture rate, could not afford to reimburse suppliers at any reasonable premium. Ni pedo, some insensitive souls blamed the new market circumstances on the arrogant mojado who indeed, while not a conceiver of the warranty, had, in a paradox that operates elsewhere in México (vid. Partido Revolucionario Institucional), attempted in a certain sense to institutionalize what had always been conceived as a peripatetic roll of the bones. Contrabandists began to mutter darkly (this, by the way, was during the period when Joe Columbo organized the Italian-American Civil Rights League and paid so dearly for his gesture) about the new affront to the truer days of caveat emptor, of river skullduggery, even as they had to comply with the economic writ of the period.

"Maldición. There are too many coyotes desgraciados who are making an effrontery of the perils of the river!"

"Precisamente. These pendejos are giving too high a profile to our dealerships."

Our mojado, like so many other Mexican revolutionaries and freethinkers over the decades, took a cue from caution. One moonless night, making sure he wasn't being tailed, he packed his personal belongings and drove to a place way upriver—a hardship spot with steep banks and a dearth of landing places, but one that also claimed the advantages of few sensors and virtually no patrol. He ran the river for one last time, never to return again.

Our mojado quickly descended from his comfortable bourgeois life into the vast anonimato of the undocumented worker. In a sense he wanted it and needed it that way. He shaved his Zapata mustache, cut his hair a different way, and took a humble job sorting remnants at a blue jeans manufacturer with an infamous reputation for its abuse of illegal aliens. He felt safe there; he blended in. He cut off relations with everyone, even his family. It would only be a few months, he felt. His only connection was with his compadre, el Rompeculos.

Clearly la vida was softening up our pícaro for a spectacular conversion. Those forces of fate that redress Tex-Mex hubris were conspiring against our San Juan Bautista on two juxtaposed fronts. One was that the border entered into one of those sporadic periods when potentates in Washington become "deeply concerned." El mundo tightened up. There were delays on the International Amistad bridge for three and four hours. The United States Army Corps of Engineers busily installed a "tortilla curtain" to keep out illegal aliens, a reinforced steel mesh wall supposedly incapable of being cut but which was riddled with holes by sunup. The Border Patrol issued a list of persons it wanted to nab for high questioning, or rather, to pin some delitos to; payment was offered leading to the apprehension thereof, and our mojado made the list. His person became of some value and soon a co-worker in the remnant division developed a certain inkling. The other factor, according to Rompe, must have been the "Huevos Whateveros."

"Huevos Whateveros," I asked him. "What the hell are those?"

"Third World food," said Rompe. "They're delicious. Let me share my own recipe. Take the remains of the last few nights of Mexican meals—chilaquiles, pico de gallo, frijoles refritos, ruptured enchiladas, a foresaken chile relleno and so on—and lard them into a deep frying pan. Add sufficient stewed tomatoes to obtain a brew and on top of this bubbling riverbed crack open as many eggs as called for, yolks intact. Over a low heat grate some braided Chihuahua cheese and sprinkle with as much cilantro, green onion, and epazote as coraje would prescribe. ¡Qué rico!"

"My God!"

"Well it probably was the huevos whateveros that gave him the tapeworms. After all, you can't use ingredients that are too stale or you run certain risks. At any rate, one day I received an emergency call from the mojado. Come at once! Can you believe it, the bridge was so tight with migra, aduana, fiscales, and the rest of that riffraff with their sniff hounds going through the gabachos' dirty underwear that I had to borrow my neighbor's water wings from his pool and cross the river that way. When I got to the mojado's I was confronted with a grotesque scene. A bullnecked, rednecked Texan with a name like Bubba was directing his skeptical, Spanish-surnamed migra underlings who were gingerly stepping over the wet's vomit as they pulled on each of his arms. El mojado was pleading to be taken to the hospital. He was in the throes of calambres and slumgullion upchuck. The mojado's pet parrot (and if truth be known, only true companion over the years) was hysterical, ranging at full blast from the famous aria from *Figaro* to *La Cucaracha* to multiple pocho groserías.

"Hi there occifer! Where are you taking my compadre?"

"Haul off, scudsball! I'm taking this border bandito off to the slammer! He's on everybody's hit list, the Border Patrol, the Texas Rangers, the T-men, Batman and Robin, you name it. He must be a mastermind behind some Bolivian cocaine ring. Do you know how

23

many times this shitheel has been up the river? Thirty-six count'em convictions, thirty-six!"

"Aw, come now occifer, don't hyberbolize. You know he's small potatoes. Why get so excited over a few lousy parrots that bring so much delight to lonely suburban housewives or a bargain basement lobster dinner for eight? Besides, I'm not asking you to let him go or nothin. Put a ball'n chain on him for chrissakes but get him over to the hospital. If he's D.O.A. at patrol headquarters our trade association is going to hold you strictly to account." Rompe looked severely at the two Hispanos. "I see you two Judas-lackeys have gotten wetback barf on your Gucci loafers."

The scene at the hospital was no less poignant. The migra overlord stood fidgeting in the wings and growling into his walkie-talkie. The internist was chattering excitedly with the hospital administrator while Rompe sat with the mojado who, one hand on his underbelly, was in a state of stoic dejection.

"¿Por qué están tan excitados?" the mojado asked.

"No sé. El médico anda discutiendo con el jefe del hospital. No sé de que se trataría. Quizá de la migra."

"No, eso no es. Ha de ser que voy a morir al momento." The mojado was quickly becoming convinced that he was an accelerated terminal. A fitting denouement for the life that he had lived.

The internist came over to the Mexicans. "Mr., uh . . . Mojado. It's not serious at all what you have. All they are are tapeworms. Taenia saginata to be exact. They're fairly common in some parts of the underdeveloped world, but not at all common around here. Actually, they're pretty valuable. . . ." The internist looked disarmingly at the wetback. "I mean, not really valuable, but useful, experimentally useful."

The mojado looked at the doctor with incomprehension.

The internist turned to his compadre. "Go on, Mr., what's your name, Mr. Rompeculos."

"Diz que tienes gusanos. Diz que no te hacen daño y a lo mejor valen más que todo el oro de la mina de El Dorado."

The mojado brightened up measurably. He thought the worms in his body must be along the lines of Ponce de León's fabled elixir if they were worth their weight in golden nuggets.

The internist smiled ingratiatingly at the mojado. He made a little wriggling motion with his index finger as if it were a cutsie worm. "Sí, Mr. Mojado. That's right, el gusano."

The mojado smiled back and reciprocated with the same wriggling finger. "Oh, yes, meester doctor . . . the worm."

The internist turned to Rompe and explained the conditions of the barter. It seems that the hospital could put fresh specimens of taenia saginata to excellent use for their medical students. Fresh, living specimens—these would be so much better than mere mounted fantoches. Their medical students could be so much better prepared in the field of contagious diseases. Mr. Mojado would be doing a genuine service to society, a true charitable donation to the public weal. And incidentally, the doctor and the hospital administrator noticed that Mr. Mojado was having a bit of a problem with the Immigration Service? They were prepared to vouchsafe for Mr. Mojado, offer him a job on the spot as a matter of fact, nothing too strenuous of course, they couldn't . . . put any strain on their valuable flesh and blood test tube. All Mr. Mojado had to do was agree in writing to let them have . . . access to his tapeworms. They would do the rest.

By now the redneck had gotten very un-red. Images of a nice bonus and a commendation that had been dancing in his mind's eye were going under like a bloated, toxic catfish sinking into the Bravo for a third time. "Say here, doc, what do you mean about this felon being a worm factory or some kind of one-man maquiladora? This here border bandito's a known major criminal with 36 convictions and he's gotta be taken to justice. No way is he gonna be gainfully employed except maybe at the rock quarry."

"Not true, not true," shouted Rompe. "Worst he ever did was cross the river with a soused-up parrot. He's a fine citizen, sends all his income over to Culiacán where he's got a sick old father and twelve brothers and sisters."

"Well now, Mr. Bubba," said the hospital administrator. "I'm sure we can accommodate every one in this regard. We certainly think that your apprehension of this rascal should go recognized, and we'll help you see to that. But now that we've got him, let's give him some meaningful social role. Think, Mr. Bubba, this gentleman here, Mr. Mojado, can perform a vital function in the service of the public weal. As a matter of fact, and I'm sure you're not aware of this, your own chief of the Immigration Service is a patient of our head internist here, Dr. Buggy, whose helping him along with the duodenal ulcer that this frustrating wetback situation has brought on to him. Don't you see, it's with the experimental data that fellows like Mr. Mojado can provide that we may gain a real breakthrough and help you patrolmen out with medical solutions!"

The mojado had suffered another stomach spasm. Having no food left in him he had expectorated a small portion of phlegm mixed with blood. The hospital administrator snapped a finger and a silent indocumentado came out with a pail and mop (all the orderlies were wets, they were the only ones who could "afford" the pay). The doubled up mojado moved to face the internist. He pointed to his underbelly. "Is pain!"

"Oh, we'll take care of that, Mr. Mojado. Soon as you sign up with us we're going to give you a superb medicine that will control your tapeworms so that the pain will be just about eliminated. We need to control your supply of tapeworms, don't we sir? That's the essence of experimentation, isn't it, observation and control!"

"¿Qué dice?"

"Dice que si firmas te quedas aquí con una medicinita y si no te dejan morir de gusanitos hideputas o te llevan a la pinta o las ambas cosas a la vez."

"Dile que firmaré. Pero que me ayude. ¡Que me ayude!"

"He says he'll sign. But help, auxilio, socorro, amparo!"

"Mr. Mojado, I'm so glad that you are cooperating. I knew you would. I could tell you wanted to be of service to the community. Now, whenever you defecate, Mr. Mojado, you know, move your bowels (the internist made an indicative gesture with his hips), do so in a special vessel we'll be giving you. You see, the tapeworms are nested in your fecal matter."

"¿Qué dice?"

"Que tienes que cagar en una olla."

"¿En una olla?"

"Sí, es muy importante."

"Está bien. Lo hago. Con estos dolores cagaría en los cojones del Buda si fuese necesario." The spasm was easing and the mojado felt a little better. He had heard the word "fecal." It sounded like a place in the Yucatán where some time ago he had bartered for parrots. "¿Qué es, 'fecal'? El médico dijo, fecal."

"Es la caca."

"¿La caca?"

"Es la caca, es la mierda. Quieren que tú cagues en una olla para pizcar los gusanos que van a estar horadando en tu materia excremental."

The mojado was stunned. "¡Ay, fuchi!" He turned to the internist and pointed to his butt. "¿Fecal?"

"Sí, señor," the doctor replied and shyly patted the wet's ass. "Very valuable!"

"¡Mierda!"

"What's that, Mr. Mojado? No comprendo."

"¡Caca!"

The doctor looked quizzically at the mojado, then at Rompe and back at the mojado. The mojado screamed at the top of his voice, "Eshit!"

The internist blushed. "My, señor Mojado! You do speak pretty good English after all. I think you're English is much better than my Spanish!"

Burn out. The last six hours on the bus together we spent in a restless hush. A half-hour in front of Ajo, Arizona, the sun had risen over the desert. There is no finer color to the desert, no finer air than that of a desert dawn. We were by the Organ Pipe Cactus National Monument and here and there the sun shone through the giant flowering saguaro cacti and through the ironwood trees that seemed like dwarfs in comparison.

"You'll be off this bus in minutes, Rompe, and into a cup of fresh coffee. That'll be nice."

"Yeah, Huitla. Appreciate passing spirits and gas with you. There is one last thing I ought to tell you though."

"What? That you are the mojao?"

He looked startled. "How'd you know that?"

"I guess it was your impassioned grasp of details. Also, a no-name mojao. Más sabe por viejo que por diablo, right?"

"God damn!" He punched my arm affectionately. "That's right, you clever college vato."

"You still into tapeworms?"

"Hell no! Those nasty little critters! I got out of that indentured servitude some years ago. Learned English real good—I'm even a resident of the Coloso now. I mean, I'd never become a U.S. citizen, but I'm strictly legit. I've seen the re-Hispanization of the deep Southwest over these two decades or so, the demographic effects of migration, the palpable result of raza versus Anglo birth rates, the Hispanic changeover of officials ranging from mayors to county clerks and police officers. I used to think that it all meant the re-conquest of the Southwest by the Republic of México, gradually and in evolutionary increments. Now I realize it's another thing, a new patrimony that is more than the mere sum of its parts, the Third World." He laughed. "Maybe we ought to join with you college intelligentsia vatos and call it Aztlán."

"That would be fine with me, Rompe."

"Yeah, but it would be quite an undertaking, wouldn't it? Students and river runners, hand in hand? We'll do it quiet, in desert stealth, right? No use building up big recognition. A rep could be bad for this border. Although, I don't think anything except maybe a totally East German goose-stepping mentality could put a real lid on the Bravo."

"What about the family back home?"

"Good, ése. Consuelo's 32 now and she's still not married or anything. Isn't that grand? She's thinking of taking her dowry and entering el convento. Never in our maddest dreams did anyone in our family figure that one of us could have the lana to enter the Church. Or maybe she'll marry after all, maybe to some gente de bien, alguien de villarica. It's her choice."

The bus was pulling into the parking lot of the Ajo Cantina and Grille. Rompe whispered in my ear, "You know what I'm really here for? I'm into running cactus. It's strictly part-time, but it's real good bread, a seller's market. I've got a bandit run going for two 60 foot saguaros. Got a big rig loaded and waiting. I understand some outfit like Bank of America or American Express wants them for the front office grounds. Hay que cumplir, ¿verdad? Hell, cactus—pound for pound there's more money in them than coca leaves. And nobody, and I mean nobody's gonna bother you about a cactus. What's the worst it's gonna do you? A few stray thorns in your paw?"

"Wear heavy gloves, ése."

"Now you're talking, vato habilidoso. ¡Cógelo suave! Ai te huacho."

He walked out of the Trailways bus with his cocky air of rustic indio vergüenza and coraje.

I thought as I sat back in my seat, immediately missing his camaraderie, that they had taken much from the Rompemojado. They had taken his loved ones, his puberty, his sense of honor and of shame, his indio way of life, his mother tongue, and the very fruit of his bowels. But they had given him uniquely new family ties, a sense of coraje and varonía, a novel-fashioned lengua, a Third World identity and a river baptism in fire. Add up each column, then, and call it a waterworks wash.

And then, finally, there was the matter of the fecal matter—the aguas mayores. It's not every hombre who can claim his turd as a deduction to the common weal.

II. Humor y folklore

Pat Mora

CURANDERA

They think she lives alone
on the edge of town in a two-room house
where she moved when her husband died
at thirty-five of a gunshot wound
in the bed of another woman. The *curandera*
and house have aged together to the rhythm
of the desert.

She wakes early, lights candles before
her sacred statues, brews tea of *yerbabuena*.
She moves down her porch steps, rubs
cool morning sand into her hands, into her arms.
Like a large black bird, she feeds on
the desert, gathering herbs for her basket.

Her days are slow, days of grinding
dried snake into powder, of crushing
wild bees to mix with white wine.
And the townspeople come, hoping
to be touched by her ointments,
her hands, her prayers, her eyes.
She listens to their stories, and she listens
to the desert, always, to the desert.

By sunset she is tired. The wind
strokes the strands of long, gray hair,
the smell of drying plants drifts
into her blood, the sun seeps
into her bones. She dozes
on her back porch. Rocking, rocking.

At night she cooks chopped cactus
and brews more tea. She brushes a layer
of sand from her bed, sand which covers
the table, stove, floor. She blows
the statues clean, the candles out.
Before sleeping, she listens to the message
of the owl and the coyote. She closes her eyes
and breathes with the mice and snakes
and wind.

Alberto Ríos

THE FEELING OF BIRTH

Cuts reveal us
who must make evidence of our hearts
to no purpose greater,
who fill often October skies
in ourselves with nothing
more than what is there.
As cuts, these open only skin.
Appeared bruises and rings and masks
on October faces in me,
faces been to Lima
to the Indian heights of Peru
to El Paso in the daytime.
Cure me Curandero!
Cure me Doctor!
Together they mimic:
aspirin is the bark of the willow,
cinchona the quinine that cools fevers.
The differences in them
walk in different directions
than the words that reach me.
They agree: *a man who cannot hear*
cannot be cured.
Wrong with me,
nothing and nothing right,
the words that do reach me
are my only consolation:
The future will be no names,
but the colors will lose only their names
and the bruises of birth will not go,
will color, then, Novembers.

ALBERTO RIOS

THE DEATH OF ROSA

In 1851, a man was carved
from stone. Joaquín Murrieta's wife was raped
and thrown away by men who beat Joaquín,
but he escaped. They posted a reward
for all men named Joaquín: it was a name
not used by white men whom he killed now, paid
a little back; he knew a price the spit
of which not even rock could disregard.

In '53, his Rosa saw them shoot
a ghost. The man, Joaquín Murrieta, rides
the galloping Sierra Madres through
the Californias, where he never died
and where he meets with la Llorona, who
screams screams that comb his hair,
                        that soothe his nights.

31

Arnoldo C. Vento

DESDE EL OJO DE ALLEN

(relato picaresco del valle)

Pos aquí estoy en casa ajena esperando a este gringo pachorro que nunca llega. Dicen que se llama un tal Allen. Hasta parece que viene en carreta. Y las tiendas que no dan abasto con tanta gente alocada. . . . ¡Esto ya se volvió puro pedo!

Que para cuando llegue al valle central, que va a llegar a sólo 80 millas por hora. ¡Tanto guato pa' nada! ¡Ni siquiera se le arrima a aquella mujer que le llamaron Beulah! ¡Eso sí era llover!

¡Nomás unas 26 pulgaditas!

¿Qué tal mi Chencha? Hasta le hicieron una bola de corridos en disco.

¿A poco le van a dedicar unos corridos a este gringo pachorro?

¡No pueden los gavachos!

Todos sentaditos en aire acondicionado en butacas del Astrodome tomando su cervecita y atacándose de hot dogs mientras que la raza está tirada aquí a manadas en el valle en pisos de las escuelas, gimnasios, y otros edificios públicos con tanto niñerío, con tanta colcha vieja y con comida hecha a la carrera.

Fíjate que le preguntó un locutor a una chicanita con un bebé de un año si le gustaba al niño lo que estaba pasando.

¡Qué ocurrencias!

La pobre no pudo más que contestar que "no es más que un bebito".

Ya toda la raza (y algunos negritos para darle sabor) están amontonados en Brownsville. Dicen que ya se pasa de 15,000 almas en los *shelters*. Y hasta la gente de México que ha tenido que salir de sus jacales ha pedido auxilio en este lado. Y se les ha dado permiso. ¡Qué picada estará la migra!

¿Y si dan luz a niños por acá? Pos, como dice la canción: "Y sigue la yunta andando. . . ."

Pos yo creo que este bolillo cabrón es miedoso, chismoso y puro pedo. Primero, salieron con que andaba a 24 millas de la boca del Río Bravo. Luego que estaba a 35 millas. Y ahora, a 40 millas. Pos, ¿qué pasó? A mí se me hace que es puro pedo. ¿No te parece así?

Pos, sí. Fíjate que la comadre que es pachorra con las tortillas de harina, ya se hubiera aventado bastantes para pavimentar la 83 del Valle.

N'ombre, ¡qué barbaridad!

Este aigrecito apenas para rasurarme los pelitos de la barba. ¡Qué se me hace que el gallo de la tía Hortensia se va a echar sus toques al amanecer!

Que, ¿Qué pasó con los perros?
Busgos, cabrones, y flacos, nomás de pata suelta en los barrios . . .
Pos, ¡cada quien a su santo! Ni modo. Yo tengo bastante jale con tanto huerquerío . . .
¡N'ombre, ese perro prieto del tío Ruperto es más vivo que un político chicano!
Fíjate que acaba de llegar la familia Zúñiga desde Illinois. Llegaron todos en una pick-up con camper y toda la cosa. Pero ni tuvieron tiempo de lucirla porque llegaron sólo a tiempo para saludar al chubasco gavacho.
¡N'ombre, no te creas de esos chavos!
No es la primera vez que nos visita un huracán. Mi agüelita me contaba que nuestros antepasados se preparaban desde muy antes del chubasco. Sí señor. Veían las señas de la tierra y del cielo. Veían como andaban los pájaros, las nubes, las hormigas y los venados. Sabían qué iba a pasar. No andaban con tanto pedo de televisión, de entrevistas con el sheriff, el mayor de McAllen, o el senador de Washington que avisa sobre reglamientos burócratas y que luego dice que su hija acaba de gastar 100 dólares de comida en preparación del huracán!
¡Te huachaste al superintendente de "Halinche" con esa cachucha colorada de agricultor pendejo bolillo?
¡Qué puntadas!
No, ¿sabes qué?
A la otra, cuando téngamos un huracán, que sea un huracán con huevos, que no ande con pendejadas; luego le llamaremos "El cañon de la viuda Tencha" y entonces vamos a barrer con toda esta pudrición, todo este pinche zumbido que siempre nos tiene amarrados.
Pos, sí, tienes razón. Se va a matar mucha de nuestra gente. Pero ni pa' que se las saque, ¡muchos de ellos son puros vendidos y cabrones!
¡Ya verás!
Bueno, al fin, sólo la arena clarita, suavecita y lisita de la playa quedará. . . .
Como si fuera una nueva renovación, una nueva limpieza para empezar otra vez. . . .
¿Entonces qué?
Pos, ¡entonces le damos gas! comadrita . . .

Alvaro Cardona-Hine

THE MEXICAN DONKEY

Strange, but in describing this woman I feel as if I am describing the Museum. If I say—as she had to be—that she was a sixty-year-old virgin, I am doing no more than presenting a historical survey of an institution which survives to this very day untainted by reality.

Similes are weaker than metaphors so let's be clear about it. I am not saying that she and the Museum were like each other; I am saying that they were one and the same albeit totally separate and distinct entities.

This is not a puzzle. Many institutions come to resemble those who attempt to run them. Museums often imbue their curators, docents and directors with not a few of their characteristics. In our case, common sense can be pushed to its furthest limits; the Midwest is, after all, home of the only genuine American tall tale, the doings of Paul Bunyan and Blue Ox. The resemblance between Miss Trinity and the Museum was what we find in mirrors each morning when we try to make heads and tails of our reflections. Even more: two mirrors face to face, waking up in 1975 or in 1925, either way with the blank look of yesterday in mind.

Miss Trinity was ecumenically ugly: she would have been found ugly by a 19th century Abyssinian with failing eyesight, an l8th century French cavalry officer blinded by sunstroke or by Ben Turpin coming around a corner.

Her ugliness differed from that of her unemployed sister in that it was of the benign, saccharine variety. This does not mean that it was harmless; on the contrary, it had the power to disarm by its dulcet innocuousness. It worked on your pity and softened you for the kill. Her "We'd like to have you and your wife over for tea soon" came at you with the suddenness and ruthlessness of a locomotive on tiptoe. It gave you no time to conjure up a family death or an out-of-town trip on the spot.

Her face, once you managed to take in all of its incongruous detail, produced the effect of belonging, double chin and all, to an intelligent gargoyle or a dumb French king. But the dominant note was sounded by the rouge, powder, eyeshadow and other material by which it was transformed into a mask underwritten by wrinkles, managed by a litany of moues.

Her sister was not as charming. This creature would steal in around four o'clock in the afternoon and hover about until closing time. Everything around us would acquire the furtive ictus of a muted but persistent appetite, faint echo of this woman's limitless hunger. She was on the verge of chronic anemia; it took her tremendous physical stamina to muster a tepid smile because her facial muscles, disillusioned after decades of unspecified longings, had forgotten the trick and much footwork was needed just below skin level to get the tortured look off the face and replace it with a semblance of the most fleeting and evanescent happiness. The effort, repeated over the years, had cost her the right to walk upright. True, she still used only her legs, but you sensed that crouching over a bone or a ginger cookie was the natural stance. She seemed to tremble as if before some invisible morsel of misfortune held by a perverse angel just in front of her at chest level: the angel of envy, as orthodox as the saliva of a saint.

It would have been impossible to have imagined her in the morning. She began to take corporeal form towards three in the afternoon, awakening from a stupor as dense as the night of *maya*. And this awakening, this activity in which some minor god must surely have taken pride, would center around a stale piece of white bread and a cup of coffee so dismal that it chose to reflect her features as she sipped it, out of revenge for having to course through her digestive tract.

Surviving beautifully on an intake of protein that would have harmed the starving children of India, this sister would then put on her hat, a hat that was once confused for a rainbow of inanities by a septuagenarian butterfly. But that had been its heyday; all its component colors had faded into a listless purple like the purple of bigots. With that hat on she would arrive at the Museum to fetch her sister. And her sister, who from habit walked around with her hands held idly in front, as if they were wet and she needed a towel to dry them with, this sister would expand psychically until you felt that in putting on her rubbers and her scarf and her overcoat and gloves and her hat she was putting on the various offices in the executive suite, because she said goodbye to each of us in different stages of her preparation for departure, and in so doing sucked off all architectural space, all air and all ideas.

All the while, her sister would sit down to devour, with a thoroughness that would have done a third world dog justice, the other's leftovers from lunch, liberating onion, garlic, pickle and mustard odors which permeated the air-conditioning system and circulated until we had lost all sensitivity to them and had to learn from shocked visitors that, indeed, we worked in an atmosphere as rank as that of a delicatessen refrigerator.

My staff, given to youth and rebellion (the last recruits of a federal plan meant to inculcate the new generation with love and respect for the work ethic), loathed the pair. They forced me to assume a conciliatory attitude so that our unit (a rather amorphous and much maligned Education Department) should not appear outrightly seditious. But there was nothing I could do when they chose to decorate the walls in the office suite with Mexican posters for Day of the Dead celebrations. In this they were technically correct, for Education was operating at the time on directives to emphasize the beautiful ethnicity of our neighbor to the south, a tortuous political move on the part of the city's establishment to show the restless Chicano population that their culture was taken into account.

Since Miss Trinity was personally horrified of death in any way, shape or form, and went into paroxysms at any verbal or visual allusion to it, this bit of decorating on the part of my indecorous staff was a slap in the face of her adamant mortality; it kept her in a state of nerves for which I had to pay because she would visit my office two and three times a day to complain that her delicate emotional balance was in jeopardy.

We had some profound exchanges on the subject—not on her emotional balance, which I suspected to be stronger than mine, but on death itself. I found myself having to defend, on more than one occasion, the need to die, as if death were an institution about to default for need of partisans. Making desperate efforts to appear charming and lofty, with her face held up to numinous presences revealing themselves only to her, she would deny the existence of death. I would counter that if that was the case there was no need to be so upset over a few childlike posters. Ah, but they were in bad taste, she would come back, as if everything else in the Museum was in better taste . . .

If death was hard to discuss, taste was ten times more difficult. Miss Trinity was an elitist. With Wagnerian intensity she would confide in me that she thought great art to be immortal. As far as our misguided attempt to do justice to Mexico through its folk art she was critical on two counts: Folk art was only a craft wedded to the needs of the moment, to daily life, and thus lacking in the sublime. Secondly, it dealt with death much too much. A museum should be dedicated to life, she would say, her cheeks vibrating with the energy of her vision. That I could have found convincing—male chauvinist pig that I am—if she had been devastatingly beautiful or even passably good-looking. As it was, with flecks of rouge and face powder falling all around her like a pertinent little shower of dandruff from a Fourth of July fireworks display, I could only appear weak and imply that I could not dictate to my employees how they should decorate their immediate surroundings any more than I could present Mexico with less than a measure of its tragic vertigo.

Ironically, I was the one who had exposed Miss Trinity's secret dread of death, that immense lagoon whose waters had never known the keel of an inquisitive search party. One innocent afternoon I had playfully shaken Nicanor at her as I was on my way out to lecture a fourth-grade class at some school on the wonders of Mexican life. It was a foolish prank, I admit, done only because I was in love with Nicanor, a life-size papier-mâché skeleton, the only skeleton I have ever seen go to the trouble of keeping his moustache in the face of death. Well, Miss Trinity nearly lost her wig and swallowed her dentures. Even though I was late for my lecture she came out of her office (I had waved loose-jointed Nicanor in front of her door, keeping myself out of view) and tearfully explained that her father had died just 14 months before and that it was . . . it was horribly painful (hand on heart) to be reminded of such . . . of such things.

The next day was the next day for everyone but Miss Trinity. We noticed that she still trembled, that she talked to sundry persons about her father for most of the morning. It was he who had made her what she was, who had introduced her to the fine things, to poetry, to painting, to music, so that at 28 she had not only won third prize in a state-wide watercolor show but been elected Poet Laureate of the state (a position she still held by default, no other poets having been able to snatch the title from the indomitable lady). To hear her talk you would have thought her dad had died three weeks before.

It wasn't long after that that the Day of the Dead posters had proliferated on the walls of the large hall and reception area where my people had had to be put for lack of space, their desks bathing like hippopotami in public waters. Within days, nothing but Mexican death, cheap, garish, munificent, surrounded us on all sides. One poster in particular showed a rather ominous death peeking out from behind a smiling cookie skull. It should have pleased a child. Miss Trinity's sister got the hiccups when she first laid eyes on that one and these hiccups didn't leave her until two afternoons later when a terrible man exposed himself to her outside the Museum doors.

Miss Trinity took silly little mincing steps from her office to mine (she always walked as if she were falling) in order to tell me how mortified she was over the emphasis on such morbid things but I stopped her in her tracks that time. I asked her if she knew the root meaning of the word *mortified*. She looked at me with her squirrelly eyes narrowed in thought and I said M.O.R.T., Miss Trinity, and right then and there I knew her heart had become a bitter almond of hate ten inches above her drooping left tit, the only tit that had studied French and understood how to be properly mortified without the use ever of a man's rough fingers.

Tuesdays and Thursdays were especially mortifying because it was then that we mounted our pageant: Death in a Mexican Village. A classroom of children would arrive bright and early, the same ones whom I had visited a few days before with Nicanor. Miss Trinity, never happy to see loose hordes of children in the sacrosanct temple of art to begin with, just could not believe that the National Endowment for the Arts had poured two hundred thousand dollars into a project that, for three hours at a time, allowed the little ones to scream and wet their pantaloons over a carefully choreographed scenario of blood and carnage. Not without pride did I take credit for discovering a primordial subject of fascination for children: Death, the most tabooed subject of conversation since Sex was taken over by the advertising media in the Twenties and Thirties. American children are starved for news, gossip, anything having to do with Death. And Mexico is Deathland. There, children wallow in its syrups; they themselves perish in droves, clutching wooden effigies of their Redemptor, to be buried with as much splendor as their happy parents can afford, because, after all, the little angels do not have to suffer any more, they have gone to Happy Bunting Land where they can intercede with the Virgin or some patron saint for a better job for Papa.

Of course, if you can enjoy the death of others and stay alive, so much the better; then it's a festival. And a festival it was we created for our noisy fourth graders who, with wild-eyed joy, cut out and colored their own death masks, made their own bullfighting outfits and step by step learned the roles they had to play. The bullfighters, for instance, had to choose the one from among their number who would be gored by the bull. Bleeding tomato juice from all sides, the victim was taken over by *curanderas*, healers with rattles and raw eggs, who would try to save the bullfighter's life with their grey magic. The raw egg sinking into a glass of water indicated that there was no hope for the wounded hero. His raucous dying opened the way for an honest-to-God Mexican wake.

Here we demanded the utmost. The primal scream, the tantrum scream and the Tarzan howl. His companions would carry this bullfighter, who had died in his glory owing fifty pesos to his barber and who had left a trail of pretty girls with broken hearts in every town, and parade him together with Nicanor through the halls and galleries of the Museum; that is, past the endless works of regional painters who had daubed in oils all their lives as if neither Matisse nor de Kooning had ever existed.

But then the children's grief would turn to joy. The climax of the festival was a piñata filled with candy. When the piñata broke and those children leaped in and fought for their share of the loot, the Museum was given over to bedlam, the chandeliers swayed, the paintings hung awry and Belinda Pontchartrain, in whose hands rested the entire financial structure of the Museum, working in the furthest confines of the office suite next to the Director's office, adding her singular columns of numbers, would understandably transfer one or two zeros from right to left or from left to right, to the discreet benefit of certain parties.

Meanwhile, Miss Trinity would be swallowing five or six aspirins to try and head off the onset of another massive migraine headache, aspirins which, for all practical purposes, only made her lower lip hang loose so that the contents of her thoughts—such as they were—oozed out, as if her whole being had been left leaning at an angle in the pantry of conventional small talk.

The curator of Western Art had already, long before, taken to drink, so that her behavior could not be blamed on Education, but Segismund Pencil, the Museum Director, did begin at this time to exhibit some physical irregularities; oh, nothing serious, just minor motor lapses that lent his military bearing a touch of comic relief. Of these the facial tick was perhaps the most arresting: one eye would turn up while the other would plunge floorward, as if the personality behind his implacable detachment were beseeching not only heaven but hell as well for a way out of the holocaust. His dilemma was understandable, alas. The only grants coming to museums in those days were education grants tied to actual programming. In turn, these life-giving agencies required a significant head count before they would give again. The institution—which had been supremely and provincially elitist—had to prove that hundreds and thousands of the downtrodden passed through its marble halls. This explains the efflorescence of Arts Awareness programs throughout the country, programs to attract the young, the ignorant, the contemptuous, the ailing, the handicapped, the elderly, and the loony.

We had many such programs at the Museum but, somehow, Death in a Mexican Village went against the grain. It was too successful, too full of life; it had dangerous overtones. Instead of being inane it was as raucous, unbridled and acrid as an unsolicited visit from Pancho Villa.

Still, I believe that, given the inertia of most institutions once something has gotten underway, Death in a Mexican Village would have survived had it not been for the behavior of one of the small wooden toys on exhibit, a wooden donkey.

The guards, who at the high point of our little bi-weekly festivals would take refuge with the janitor in the latter's broom closet in favor of some Jack Daniels, discovered one day something beyond their comprehension beneath one of the brightly painted animals inside a glass display case in our special Chicano exhibit area. Naturally, they activated the alarm system, emptied the Museum of visitors and came looking for Segismund. I asked one of them what was happening.

"Something serious; we need Mr. Pencil."

"He's in Patagonia," I told him, "investing his money in a land scheme." The news dismayed the guard. He called two others to his aid. After a minute of consultations, they were at a loss.

"Are you aware of what's happening in case 34?" the first guard asked me.

"Why, that's in the Chicano environment . . . What's wrong?"

"One of the animals is acting strange."

"Acting strange?" Shades of the Nutcracker Suite.

I followed the guards to the gallery. Sure enough, a little donkey had done his business. I tried to make a joke of it but they would have nothing to do with levity. I wondered what all the excitement was about, all I could see was an inch-high cone of wood dust beneath the donkey.

"I noticed it yesterday," the brightest guard volunteered, "but Bill here wouldn't believe me. He thought I was joking."

Bill didn't like the responsibility being placed on his shoulders. "Stan is always joking around, Sir. It just sounded like a joke . . ."

Stan was out for a promotion. "I just told him like I saw it. Today it was twice as high."

"When will Mr. Pencil get back?" asked Bill.

"Why do you need Mr. Pencil?"

"Any change in the galleries must be reported immediately . . ."

"Look, this is not a damaged Degas. Do you realize how little that poor donkey cost? No more than a buck-fifty."

They looked at me aghast as I opened the case and pulled out the offending donkey. I showed them the donkey's underside. Sure enough, there was a small round hole from which all that wood dust had come.

"See that? That's where the crap is coming from." I showed the animal all around.

Bill closed his eyes in order to think better. Stan covered his ears in disbelief and the other guard his mouth in amazement.

"Haven't you guys ever heard of termites?"

"Termites?"

"Tropical and semi-tropical insects that love to eat wood. There is one in this fellow's belly."

Visions of paintings and tapestries perforated by boll weevil extravaganzas from the malarial jungles of southern Mexico crossed all three men's faces.

"He won't come out while he's having dinner so let's treat him to a surprise."

"What kind of surprise?"

"A taste of winter."

"Of winter?"

"We'll stick him in the office refrigerator. That is, if Trinity has left any room. Unless he's wearing an overcoat it'll be the last we see of this termite."

"When will Mr. Pencil be back?"

"He's not due back till next month. I read somewhere where the Argentine government has outlawed time."

"You'll have to take responsibility for this, Sir . . ."

"I will. Termites I understand, leave it to me."

I went and placed the donkey next to Miss Trinity's spaghetti medley of three day's running.

"Too bad the termite didn't go for one of the wooden death masks!" one of my assistants quipped later, "that way the spaghetti would have made a terminal meal for you-know-who . . ."

"Let's not push things too far," I replied drily.

In half an hour the Museum was back to business, minus a cold donkey in an impossibly crowded refrigerator. Of course, news of the termite-infested donkey spread fast. One salutory effect of its presence in the refrigerator was the fact that Miss Trinity went on a drastic diet; within days she was using safety pins to keep her plaid slacks up. Her sister, on the other hand, not one to look a gift donkey in the mouth but to place it there, put the finishing touches on the spaghetti that same evening, her largest windfall in our recollection. A week later, the donkey was out on display again, as if his belly were full of himself and not air and a dead mite.

I thought the matter closed and even did a little jig in the style of Adolf Hitler when he got to Paris a conquering hero, all for the benefit of my staff. But, as with the illustrious German, it was premature. You might say the jig was up. None of us had expected our Patagonian investor to return unexpectedly. Miss Trinity's wire reached him during a crucial moment in negotiations when a quarter of a million dollars hung in the balance. The wire read: "Termites in Oaxacan donkey frozen by Ed Dept stop gallery possibly overrun stop please advise."

When Segismund stormed into the Museum and began screaming indiscriminately at everyone, each of us, without exception, felt that we too would have carried on in a similar fashion had we lost a three million dollar deal because of a single bug. On the other hand, Segismund did not stop to reflect that no termite had interfered in his five previous unsuccessful deals: The Saharan Aquacentennial Oilcapades, the condominiumizing of the Tower of London, the Florida Home for Deposed Latin American Strong Men, the research into yak butter, and the transfer of the Taj Mahal to the outskirts of Tulsa, Oklahoma. But he was a born autocrat and born autocrats have their quirks. What was inspiring was his unstated but implied assumption that had he been there when the cone of wood dust first appeared it would not have been caused by termites. Thus, no major crisis would have existed.

For a major crisis existed. Museum authorities fear termites the way a saint might fear the odor of sulphur. To hear the talk of curators on the long distance line one would have thought the creature possessed such wondrous reproductive powers that within months every single piece of lumber in the United States of America would be a thing of the past.

Insurance companies got into the act. They recommended we consult the Smithsonian. Within the week, a team of experts from that revered institution arrived with their white smocks and their microscopes, their tinctures and scalpel knives. They proceeded to dissect every Mexican toy in the exhibit, a sort of mass autopsy that saw the end of fourteen donkeys, three burros, five peasants, six saints, and ten doves and yielded the lone termite in the belly of our initial donkey frozen along its dinner route, the ersatz intestine of its host. When the massacre was over they looked in the direction of the art collection. This was art so no massacre was called for but each and every painting, collage, watercolor, print, woodcut, tapestry and sculpture was frisked for extraneous substances, hidden life and host receptivity. The building itself had to be inspected. Beyond that, an area of five city blocks was quarantined and the lovely old Roxanne Building, which the city had been planning to refurbish, was torn down since it was made almost entirely of wood.

Miss Trinity's sister came temporarily under suspicion at the time. It could not be proven conclusively that a small number of termites might not have abandoned their carrier and contaminated the spaghetti during the first hour after I had placed the donkey in the refrigerator. This theory was based on a Smithsonian study made to test the survival strength of termites in refrigerators set at different temperatures. A mean survival ratio was established and we were given to understand that our termite/termites could have survived the cold of our refrigerator for fifty-nine long minutes. During that time, of course, venturesome termites could have wandered out of the donkey and into the spaghetti. Had Miss Trinity's sister eaten the spaghetti on the spot or had she taken it into the offices and perhaps left it unattended for crucial minutes? She was a notoriously slow eater so some termites could have escaped being eaten alive.

I had raised doubts about the existence of more than one termite, pointing out that there had been only one cone of wood dust and one long tunnel leading to the afore-mentioned frozen termite, but the Smithsonian scientists had smiled condescendingly. What about termite eggs? they had countered.

From all this it can be inferred that my position at the Museum was precarious, to say the least. I conducted myself with dignity and reserve but Miss Trinity's glee was so evident on her face that it began a new series of wrinkle patterns crisscrossing the former ones and before long giving her face the look of a minutely designed, endless checker-board.

Checkerboard or not, Miss Trinity was named head of all Museum programming. In addition, she retained her duties as Director of Membership, a position she loved because it meant hobnobbing with bishops, duck hunters, and retired Italian restauranteurs. These vast new powers meant that my young rebellious staff had to go. Out they went. Out went Death in a Mexican Village and in came an all-plastic Mexican folk art exhibit guaranteed to house no termites if only because it was manufactured in Billings, Montana. It was so perfect in all its detail that I could not complain. The new theme of our programs was Songs and Dances of Old Mexico. The emphasis was on the much ballyhooed respect for elders in Mexican society. This program was an even greater success with the school district—if not with the children. The schools' representative, a gal who could have amount-ed to something human if she hadn't been at the mercy of a severe case of self-inflicted menopause (old-fashioned teacher syndrome), had originally adored my scheme. You can lose your job within hours in ethnic matters so she had played it safe. The new pro-gram, with its Mexican hat dance and its Shriner convention mentality, fitted to a T her Manifest Destiny chromosome memories of how things South of the Border should be.

I didn't mind shaving my beard and impersonating a Mexican señorita and strumming a guitar but I put my foot down when there was no one else to warm Miss Trinity's lunch at twelve-thirty nor its leftovers at four-thirty for her sister. The temptation to put a little strychnine in the food was just too great.

On my last day, Belinda Pontchartrain asked me to sign pro forma expense accounts for the period when I had directed the program. I took one look and understood why the program was so vital to the Museum. A liberal estimate of what I had actually spent on the folk art collection would have come to no more than four thousand dollars. The forms specified $28,000. Installation and running costs were similarly magnified until one would have thought one was looking at an Arab sheik's expense account while visiting Las Vegas.

When I pushed the pen away, Miss Trinity was called in to sign in my stead.

She giggled. "Won't this mean that I was in charge all the while?"

"Of course," Belinda chimed in, "you've been in charge all along. Aren't you the one who is always saying how death is only an illusion?"

41

THE MEXICAN DONKEY

"Bullseye!" I exclaimed, unable to hold back my admiration. The remark had gone clear through me, pinning me to the chair. It wasn't easy to get up and walk out. It took pull, the kind of pull only a donkey can muster at the end of a long, hard road.

Jim Sagel

EASY

"Ooh—another *family* scene," thought Isadoro "Easy" Trujillo as he surveyed the garage where the party was barely toddling out of infancy. "Not even a PG."

And he counted off all the "married chicks" sitting placidly on the wooden benches and steel folding chairs lining the two by four-studded walls like junior high cherubs quarantined on the south side of a sock-hop gym. Only two he knew of who weren't taken— well, *one* he was sure of. The other he'd never seen before, or at least not straight enough to remember, but anyway, she wasn't all that hot (though she *was* blond). Most of Easy's carnales had been married for years now. C.A. (Chris Atencio, or "Crusty Ass," as Easy liked to refer to him when C.A.'d get wound up and start spouting off his cultural-religious horseshit like he was sure to do at the party tonight, since he always did when more than two people gathered together in his midst—or was it "mist," Easy chuckled silently)—well, C.A. even had a son already at McCurdy High School.

But they could have it, Easy reiterated in his mind. All the headaches—bills, kids, house, new car, clothes, bitching, brow-beating and ball-bruising. He had all the female company he wanted in his weekend rendezvous with la Chata (Charlene Ortega, his off-and-on-again ten-year steady) when they'd cruise down the back roads of Chima, talking about nothing in particular, parking in the sandy-cliffed dead-end of the third arroyo to make a standard but sufficiently passionate love in the back seat of "El Mentado," Easy's baby-blue 57 Chevy. Which was cramped but cool enough except for an occasional high school invasion. Once, when an ogling entourage of wet-eared kids had come at the most inopportune point possible, Easy had just had time to scramble into his shorts and leap over the seat, jamming "El Mentado" into reverse and up to the axle in the ultra-fine sand in the middle of the arroyo, forcing him to squirm on his levis between "chingados" and "jodidos" while the Coors-charged, sex-famished beggars pulled up directly opposite his window asking him "si necesitaba ayuda" and sneering unblinkingly at Chata cringing beneath a wrinkled green dress in the back seat. And Easy would've pulled his "cuete" out of the glove compartment to enforce a little respect, but he was far too occupied struggling to engage his fly, while the rear wheels kept chewing voraciously into the sand.

It was then that Easy had decided to find some other place—any location where there wouldn't be these slimy suckers messin' up his movidas. His jefa's house, where he still lived alone with his mama at thirty-two ripe years of age, was definitely out. She *never* slept. Oh, she lay down in bed for a couple of hours just for show, but she never lost consciousness. Just stretched out there and ran through a couple dozen novenas and then jumped up and cleaned the hardwood floor in the hall.

43

No good at Chata's house either. Her old man *lived* in front of the color T.V., knew exactly how to spell R-O-L-A-I-D-S, and laughed even before Ed McMahon at Johnny Carson's driveling inanities. Plus Chata's jefe couldn't *stand* Easy and still, after a full decade, would remark, in a routine but disparaging tone, that his daughter had better not be going out with that "damned overgrown pachuco" again, just as she was about to slip past the recliner and out the den door.

But at last Easy had hit upon one of the "great truths" he humbly blundered into with such uncanny frequency in his life. People, he'd discovered, tended to ignore the obvious. And what could be more obvious, he pep-talked a reluctant Chata as they pulled up behind the apple shed right off the highway and a few hundred feet from several *unquestionably* Christian households. But as it turned out, Easy was right—no one bothered them behind the warehouse of delicious reds, no matter how compromising their position.

Ah, but not tonight, reflected Easy—esta noche no me va a valer. Chata was pissed at him, the full rag. Had been for a *week* now, and just because he'd forgotten her birthday. He'd seen her at the Credit Union where she worked and he'd withdrawn fifty bucks and she just naturally figured it was for a dozen long-stemmed roses, a heavy box of gooey candy and dinner at Ranchos, and she was righteously indignant when, two days and not even so much as a phone call later, she found out the bread had gone for some "good Lumbo" Easy now wanted her to share when he knew *good* and well she got paranoid when she toked. And when she reminded him that she had had to see in her third decade all by her lonesome, Easy had quipped in one of his patented, fatally mistimed jokes that "¿qué importaba anyway?—it's just another birthday, nomás otro año más vieja y un poco más acabada." Needless to say, Easy's little chiste wasn't exactly warmly received—in fact, Chata'd refused to speak to him ever since, leaving Easy to wonder whether his nickname shouldn't be lengthened to "Easy *Trouble*," judging from the facility he had for getting into it.

The original source for his sobrenombre, by the way, had been the tongue-tied, gringified grade-school teachers who, finding Isadoro an impossible mouthful, had rechristened the little greñudo "Izzy." Then, as he had developed into a sly, smooth-stepping man-on-the-make in late adolescence, it had seemed a simple and logical jump from "Izzy" to "Easy." Plus, most of his bros already pronounced "Izzy" like "Easy" anyway, ése.

And tonight, well he'd be "easy"—light and loose, a cool cat on the prowl. No damn bitch would wrinkle his style, although it might not be all *that* easy, with all these *casadas* around, but, well, he couldn't let that bother him either. No, life was like the Schlitz commercial, he reflected, gazing pensively at his own can in his hand—"you only go around once" and you'd better make it easy. That's what he said anyway and even though it sounded like a fuckin' cliché, well, no one'd ever shown him nothing better.

Though that pinche C.A. had *tried* enough, Dios sabe, telling him to change his lifestyle, get out of politics, get married, settle down, carve bultos out of cottonwood roots and live the general "good life" of a genuine latter-day santero—and he could get welfare too. In other words, live just like C.A. himself. And the bad thing was that Easy'd fallen for it for awhile and had hermitized himself and got fitted for a free government hair shirt, but it hadn't worked out. Mostly, he figured in the end, because he had gotten bored, and if there was *one* thing Easy couldn't abide it was sitting around all aburrido.

And, as irony would have it, as Easy meandered through these thoughts and tripped over viciously situated scraps of lumber and random apple tree roots—parked outside the garage for eventual chainsawing—on his way out back for his first piss of the evening, who should he stumble upon but old peasant-shirted C.A. himself, in full session with a smattering of disciples nearby.

"Quihubo, bro—" and Easy let his stream glide into the star-pocked darkness while C.A. plunged back into his oration.

"You know those mutilators have gotten quiet now—¿dites cuenta? You know why? Pos—it's because they know who it is. They know it's esa plebe de Los Alamos out buscando por uranium—tú sabes. Pos, sí, mira—it makes sense, hombre. That's why they cut out the ojete—pos that uranium shit's got to pass through the asshole too, man. That's how they know if there's uranium out here. ¿Dites cuenta?—that's why you don't see none of them mutilators in the East—nomás out here and over by Grants. It makes sense, hombre. And who else'd have all that maquinaria anyhow? They're probably the same vatos who are the flying saucers too, man."

But by now the conversation had spaced into far too cosmic oceans for Easy and he excused himself and hauled ass back to the action.

What there *was* of it anyway.

It looked like it might be a pretty tough jalecito tonight—and if he was going to have to work, well, he might as well do it on a full stomach, so he headed into the house and copped himself a plate of food. Yes, Linda and Mike sure knew how to throw a party— the *food* end of it anyhow, Easy thought as he heaped up enchiladas, posole, frijoles, chile colorado, salad, bizcochitos, and arroz con leche on his precarious paper plate and steered into the garage "a comer."

As per custom and time-worn tradition, most of the vatos were grouped together by the door and the women sat in a cluster or two, with the daring exception of a few more recently married couples. Kids ran *everywhere*—darting past, playing their unconscious roles in the ancient ritual of pursuit and spiriting beer from the icy tubs. Easy shifted his sagging plate from hand to hand, alternately clasping Chicano shakes and slapping compadre-abrazos on backs. Santiago Mata was there, grey-eyed and gay writer, as well as José Dolores Martínez, electronics instructor at the T.V.I., bearded, tanned and relaxed as a Bermuda tourist now that the summer had come. Balding gringo construction worker Joe Single was holding up the door frame listening to Mano Pete tell another "chiste de verdad" about his experiences in Sacred Heart School and the United States Army, equally insensitive institutions that rumbled along on remarkably similar gears of repression. Local postmaster and painter Antonio Luján was repeating the familiar and tragic legend of George Padilla, the Hernández artist who had busted up in Hollywood working for Walt Disney and who had thrown away his career, marriage, family, and home and returned to Española, cracked up and solito, to wander the streets bien borracho before he froze to death in his early forties, a waste of one of the "best talents we ever produced up here," Antonio was saying. "And you know, the poor old vato would come into the post office every few days trying to talk me out of a few centavitos just to go out and buy another damn pint of Saint Lucy. And I'd usually give it to him too—prestarle la feria, I'd say—because he was still a proud old vato even all smashed, and he'd do me a drawing— have to leave me a picture before he'd take off, even if it'd been a while and he'd be shakin' so hard he couldn't hardly hold onto his pencil. And I kept all those drawings—some of them mountains and animals, and some just of the gente there inside the estafeta, you know, like portraits. And I bet they're worth some money now. I mean, that's how they *always* do, isn't it?—your work ain't worth shit till you're dead? ¿Cómo has estado, Easy?" Antonio asked, trying to corral him with his magnetic, whiskered grin, but Easy broke away with a "bien bro—ahí te watcho después," as he sauntered over to the table to eat. Of course, he could have sat down on the end of the bench beside Antonio's primo Gilberto, also an artist, but a dark, brooding, Mr. Hyde-opposite to the eternally cheerful Antonio. Gilberto was a cloud-browed apprentice to the "master-santero" C.A., carving a series of carretas de muerte, penitente death carts with disturbingly intricate and accurately workable aspen bones, ribs and joints and horrific realistic details like the real silver-grey hair hanging around doña Sebastiana's hollow eyes and actual human teeth in her razor-sharp death grin. Gilberto worked for the phone company during the day, but Easy could only guess what strange metamorphosis engulfed him by night when he would gouge a llorona's howl out of a dormant chunk of cedar. Gilberto nearly scared Easy, a vato who made it his business, like every self-respecting Chimayoso, to *never* be afraid of nothing.

Still, he decided to venture over to the folding table where Antonio's wife, Debra, sat across from Priscilla, Gilberto's overweight but effusive mate. At the far end of the table, C.A.'s long-suffering wife Dolores was engaged in a tight knot of gossip with her cuñada Juanita and the halter-topped and dark-eyed Rita, Single's spouse. Easy, as was his wont, checked out the entire scene instantly and calculated his best bet would be Debra, since it looked like couples night anyway and she was the youngest and blondest of the group. "Hello ladies," he saluted as he walked up with his Schlitz and dripping plate and, in a gallant but misfortunate gesture with the wrong hand, remarked to Debra about how pretty she looked tonight and drizzled bean juice all down his pants.

"How's the kids?" Easy began unimaginatively, his customary wit and flare suffering for his soggy crotch.

"Fine. And you, how've you been? Where's Chata?"

"Don't ask," he winced between mouthloads of enchiladas and posole, "don't *ev*-en ask."

"Okay," Debra laughed coquettishly and shook her yellowish curls while Easy fantasized how he wished *he'd* had first shot at this one, cute, a good cook and mother—and güera too. That pock-faced postmaster wouldn't have had a chance up against *his* charm!

If only—someday—he could find someone to match up to his ideals. Just a simple girl, beautiful and loyal, who could keep the house clean and not hassle him but give him all the good loving he needed—a good "bod" and, yes, a decent cocinera too, because if there was one vice Easy had, it was a weakness for fine cooking. That's what he needed—a woman who would always love him, never question or challenge him—in short, his mother in Bo Derek's body. Why, there was nothin' in the world he'd rather do than take that perfect creature and settle down and build her a house and have a line of sons and quit this damned movida he was too old for anyhow. Yeah, he needed someone like his old lady—una mujer de antes—but she'd have to be a fox too. And this Debra, well, she might have come close. She *was* blond, but too bitchy for Easy's blood—too bossy. He liked a docile woman. But not too docile.

"So how's the Raza Unida doing?" Debra asked.

46

"En lo mismo—tú sabes. Still fighting that cabrón de Ferminio," Easy replied, referring to the heavy-handed political patrón who had controlled every detail of life for the last quarter of a century in sprawling, mountainous Río Arriba County from the schools to the jails to the county maintenance crew to the New Mexico State Senate. Easy had joined forces with a Christ-eyed young radical named "Teddy" who had founded el partido de la Raza Unida in the north to prick the soft belly of Ferminio's political patronage with criticism in the press, demonstrations, rallies, and an exhaustive run of lawsuits, a number of which "primo Ferminio" had lost in spite of his control of the local judicial system to the tune of tens of thousands of dollars and nagging morning ulcers over coffee and glazed donuts in his private restaurant, where business was routinely done under the table, extricating folks from various hassles that ranged from murder raps to overdue hospital bills in exchange for a lifetime of correct poll-booth lever pulling. Of course, la Raza Unida was no more than a thorn in the machine's side and nothing was really changed after seven years of skirmishes; Ferminio *still* claimed there wasn't a family in the entire county that didn't owe him a favor and continued guaranteeing the truth of the statement. And, though he had been found guilty of perjury and had even had to resign his beloved post of State Senator as a convicted felon, truth, justice and the political payoff had triumphed in the end and he had been exonerated in the Court of Appeals, thereby regaining his leather chair in the Roundhouse.

"¿Pero sabes qué?" Easy said, leaning conspiratorially and conveniently closer to Debra. "They've got my phone tapped. ¡A lo serio!" he added, when she hadn't recoiled in horror.

"Really. They're after me, you know—Ferminio's goons. That's why I don't go nowhere without my *cuete*, tú sabes. And then that bastard's in with the FBI too. Did I tell you what happened to me the other day at Mr. G's . . . I was in the back checking out the boots when all of a sudden I look up and there's this gabacho staring at me. Real *weird* dude—crew-cut, business suit, the whole bit. I mean, what would a guy like *that* be doing in Mr. G's? And as soon as I look at him, he just turns and leaves—walks right out of the store, as fast as he can without lookin' too suspicious. 'Stá cabrón, sabes—it's rough, man. You never know when those guys are just gonna find you out in the middle of nowhere and arrange it so you're permanently lost. I mean, who'd ever know the difference, man?"

"You know what you need?" Debra said in an authoritative tone. "You need to get *married*. You need to settle down and quit fooling around with all this cops-and-robbers BS. I mean, look at you—how old are you anyway?"

"Twenty-seven."

"*Look* at you—twenty-seven years old and still cruising through town like a teenager. You ought to settle down—there's plenty of girls around who'd be ready and willing."

"Yeah, I know—I know you're right, but it's hard. I just can't find the right girl, you know. 'Stá *duro*, mano—it really is." And then, before he could begin enumerating the ideal characteristics of his elusive perfect girl, Linda cranked up the music on the stereo to an ear-rattling decibel level that would have easily read off the scale, and Debra's post office box husband stepped up and took her out to dance. Antonio, of course, never hung around his esposa at social gatherings—no self-respecting macho would! But he *was* consummately jealous and possessive of his prize of a wife—"un gallo muy celoso," as Al Hurricane Jr. sang in one of Antonio's all-time favorite canciones.

Oh well, Easy thought to himself—too damned smart anyway. He didn't like his women too smart. But, then again, not too dumb either. So he leaned against the wall in his chair, drained his Schlitz, and kicked back in his head, just taking everything in nice and easy. He thought about lightin' up a toke, but reconsidered. Too much family scene here— somebody'd get bent out of shape. Of course, he could get up and do it outside, but C.A. was probably still out back homilying his star-struck attendants and, anyway, he was pretty mellow already. But who knew how much longer he would be with that damn disco blaring in the tweeters right behind him.

Linda and Mike were the perfect hosts all right—kept *everybody* happy. Had both Coors *and* Schlitz in abundance. And they continued alternating music. Yes, it was definite- ly a segregated bunch here tonight, with several cultural contingents represented in the scattered nuclei in the garage. And so Linda played the Bee Gees, who seemed to be "staying alive" interminably so the Albuquerque clique could get down and boogie. Then Tiny Morrie sang "Por el amor a mi madre, voy a dejar la parranda," and the España gang left their cervecitas to polka and two-step twirl around the room. And, apparently for her cowboy brother-in-law and the secret Tex-Mex freaks in the crowd, she unleashed Country Roland García, who vacillated twangingly between cultures in one selection after the other, moseying from "The Red River Valley" to "El Rancho Grande," from "Truck Drivin' Man" to a honky-tonk version of "Gabino Barrera" that made that classically famoso heart-break- er and child-disseminator sound like a shiny-levied redneck out of Waco.

Bueno, you've got to keep the plebe contenta, Easy thought. And he could relate to that—he did it all the time too. Easy liked to communicate with *all* types—vatos locos, gringos, viejitos, women—of course, all kinds of women. And he prided himself on his associations with varying folks—why, one of his best amigos was the fuckin' vice-president of the county Republican party! But he wasn't too sure about this "younger generation," as the Village People started stomping out a repetitious, atonal jam about young boys at the Y.M.C.A. What mind-deadening *shit*, Easy thought, and wondered whether he shouldn't go out and smoke that weed after all. It *was* good dope—home-grown too. First cosecha of the year, harvested from between his blue corn stalks. Though Easy annually nurtured a few dozen dope plants to supplement his commercial "happiness," he never allowed the leafy contraband to grow any higher than the maíz because Ferminio's goons were watching him and just waitin' for a chance to bust him. That's why he never used the phone much either. It was tapped—hell, they were just lookin' for an excuse to put him away. And if they didn't find one, they'd plant some shit on him like they did with Noel or they'd arrange a little "accident."

But Easy did have a nice huerta this year, he thought, as the sweaty bodies gyrated in front of him. He and his mama planted a huge garden every year—chile principally, and that was retetrabajoso. But they hoed, irrigated and weaved it into ristras that Easy'd sell for twenty-five bucks each at the Farmer's Market in the Big Rock Shopping Center. And both of them wove too—for borderline slave-labor wages turning out identical, bright- ly colored pieces for sale in DeAguero's Weaving Shop, but it *was* steady money that bought the groceries and paid the gas.

Easy's mother had taught him to weave and it had been in the family for generations, as the now-tattered and faded rag rugs his great-grandmother had woven and which covered the worn "ule" on the kitchen floor attested. And though Easy's mother was content to crank out the DeAguero's monotonous patterns—with an occasional road-runner thrown in for excitement—Easy got into the art of weaving on a more creative level, executing wall hangings for their pure aesthetic value.

And most of his weavings had a religious motif because, for all his blustering and hustling, his "big-barrio" paranoia and the "cuete" in his "glove department," Easy was a religious man. A member of the penitente hermandad, he took his religion seriously and personally, explaining it was probably the most important thing in his life (often as not, shortly before cruising off in "El Mentado" to throw a little party). But he never missed a holy day of obligation, and still sang alabados at velorios in Truchas and Río Chiquito and wove a lot of crosses in his jergas. His masterpiece to date had been a seven-foot pictorial tapestry of a crucified Cristo he had taken from a postcard picture of the main altar in the Santuario de Chimayo.

Yeah, he should go out and smoke that toke, but now Linda'd finally put on some *good* music, an Antonio Aguilar album, and old Tony was wailing with sentimiento about another in the long string of "mujeres ingratas" who seemed to make his life so melodically miserable, and Easy figured the time was right to dance. Anyhow, the mosquitos were bad outside unless you stood right in the smoke of the smoldering estiercol Mike had strategically placed around the yard to ward off the bothersome bloodsuckers.

He could ask one of the married mamasotas—that would be all right. It'd be heavy, but he could dig a shot at something that might *lead* somewhere at least. But shit, this place was filled with more couples than "Bingo Night" at the Knights of Columbus, yet there was that chick over there with the Burque locos—the one he'd spotted when he first walked in the door. She didn't look *too* bad now, after a few birrias, and she seemed to be alone—and she was, of course, blond.

Bueno, pues, Easy hitched up his chile-stained jeans and chuco-stepped up to the babe, all nonchalant and natural-like.

"Hi." Pause. Give her a chance to check him out. "Hey, you wanna dance?"

The güera flashed a toothpaste smile and replied, "Okay." But as she got up, so did a six-foot-seven Nordic giant of a dude in unison with her.

"Listen, guy," he growled, squinting down through the stratosphere at Easy. "She's my wife and I got *first* priority. She dances with *me* first!"

"Bueno, bueno bro. No hay pedo—it's cool, man. No hay pedo." And Easy retreated to his original seat, watching the couple spat all the way out to the dance floor and then finally tramp back to their seats, obviously engaged in some kind of domestic war, and Easy wondered where the hell that "Viking" had come from. He'd seen him over there but figured the dude was standing when, in reality, he'd been sitting down!

Oh well, so much for Antonio Aguilar and "Sin Sangre en las Venas." Another blond bites the dust. Así es la vida, mano.

Shit—maybe he oughta pintarse. Go on home. It was already gettin' a little late any-way. And he should give Chata a call. See what she was doin' tomorrow. Maybe she'd decided to forgive and forget. And he could sweet-talk her a little—throw in some choice madera about how much he missed her and everything. Of course, he couldn't apologize. After all, he hadn't *done* anything wrong.

But that's exactly what she'll want, he thought—that's what she always wants when-ever she gets mad. But this time he wouldn't do it. This time he wouldn't give her the satisfaction. Of course, he could turn it around and smooth it out so it sounded like he was apologizing when he really wasn't. That might work.

Shit, she probably missed him so much by now that she'd take him back right away, no questions asked. After all, he was a pretty good catch—maybe she didn't even deserve him. She oughta consider herself lucky.

That's what he'd do. Grab another Schlitz and split and call her up. Hang up if the old man answered first, though. But what if she wasn't home? Well, where else would she be?

She'd *better* be home.

Yeah, he'd go call. If for nothin' else, to check up. One thing you could never trust was a single woman—especially if she wasn't a virgin. He should know.

And, as he stood up, who should walk by but Debra. Did he want to dance, she asked.

"Sure. ¿Cómo no?" he replied, making a quick check of the garage and noting that Antonio was absent, with a good percentage of the other carnales—probably out echando toques themselves.

Bueno—why not? They'd be gone for awhile. And Debra was pretty good. A little too smart, but pretty good anyway.

And she *was* blond.

III. La familia y la religión

Leo Romero

MEMORIES OF
YOUR FATHER

A short
stout man
who worked
at a steelmill
Played the horses
And once came home
and gave you
a hundred dollar bill
after he had hit it big
But he would always
clench his fists
and say
Which one, which one

The fist
which held the money
would be held tightest
and if you missed
you got nothing
But you knew which
hand held the money
from the way
it trembled
from the strain
of holding
so tight

Rafael Jesús González

A ROSARIO, MI ABUELA

Tres años he tenido el lápiz
suspendido sobre la página de tu alabanza—
    no quería que el dolor
    manchara su blancura,
    dañara con su lija el cutis
    de tus nardos y tus espuelas.
Es confuso el inventario de tu memoria
como la historia de un país
         de una época
         de un santo.
El sueño, el mito, el hecho se confunden.
    ¿Es cierto que a los quince en Durango
    les robabas las lenguas hasta a las campanas
    al pasear en domingo luciendo
    tu sombrero de plumas blancas de avestruz?
    Dicen que los caballos del coche familiar
    pisaban con más garbo al reconocer tu peso.
No hay documentos—
    en un momento en que te sabía amarga la sal
    quemaste las cartas de mi abuelo.
(Te pudo después—te hubiera gustado que yo las leyera—
hubieras querido un testigo de tu sangre
       para tu belleza, para tu amor.)
¡Y qué amor debe haber sido!
    Altiva, encinta con mi madre te lanzabas
    en mula contra las tormentas de las sierras.
    ¿En San Andrés soñabas con los bailes del gobernador?
    ¿Te soñabas esmeraldas, diamantes y rubís?

II

¿Y cuando tuviste que dejar los viajes a las minas, el montepío,
el piano, el zaguán con sus golondrinas y su buganvilla,
los criados, la tumba de tu primera hija
para una tierra extraña cuya lengua era de lija?
Nunca te oí lamentar el robo de tus joyas.
    Te recuerdo en excursiones por el bosque:
    como cabra escalabas las lomas
    buscando musgo, helechos y violetas blancas
    aquellos raros tesoros de la primavera.
    Y luego al regreso, silenciabas el miedo
    al aguacero lanzando contra la carcajada
    del arroyo ruidoso el gorjeo de la tuya.
        (Y ha sido tu risa
        la medida del goce—
        en donde esté la busco—
            el concierto
            el baile
            el aula
            la esquina de las luces rojas—
                París, Barcelona, Atenas, Edinburgo.)
Tu casa siempre estaba llena:
    Contabas tus nueve hijos, tus nietos y bisnietos
    como las cuentas de tu nombre
    y eras eterna.

III

Siempre me gustó hacerte regalos—
    inútiles,
            extravagantes—
más para darme gusto a mí
que a ti en lucirlos:
            crucifijos de plata
            camafeos,
                del Japón, cajas de marfil
                mantillas de España
                de Francia cajitas de Limoges
                prendedores de Italia—
            y flores, más que nada flores—
            aquellos claveles color de rosa hinchados
            como el dulce, nubes de azúcar,
            que venden en los circos;

aquellos claveles casi sin olor,
pobres rivales a tus mejillas
 amasadas de crema, rosas, y duraznos
 acentuadas por tus aretes de acerinas
  lustrosos como los ojos de aves nocturnas—
  talismanes de regiones obscuras.
Bien conocí tus ángeles
(hasta casi creer que eras toda ángeles)
y nunca tus demonios
 que han de haber vivido encerrados
 como vírgenes vestidas como nardos prietos.

¡Pobres demonios de mi abuela—
eran tantos sus ángeles de perla!

CANCION DE BAILE

para Rosa

¿Si recogiéramos un ramo de danzas,
si combináramos sus formas y colores
 y lo lleváramos a Dios Itlatzonantzin
   la Señora del Tepeyac,
 se retrataría el mundo en nuestro manto?
Y ¡qué templo se elevaría!
 Entonces sería Nuestra Señora de la Danza,
 parte guerrero, parte ángel, parte payaso.
Así se pisa la tierra—
así se ríe y se llora—
así se hace la hermandad.
 (Piedad a los que no saben celebrar,
  los que por celos y temores
  aprietan el corazón de la tierra.)
  Ay, macehualtin, benemérito—
   no penitente sino danzante,
   no sacerdote mas bailarín.
Entonces en el estruendo del zapateado,
en el jarabe, en el huapango, en el chotis,
en los silencios entre los pasos y la canción,
en lo eterno que justifica a cada cosa,
nos llenaría de dichas y de pavores
la celeste zozobra de la rosa.

Guadalupe Ochoa Thompson

MECIENDO COBARDE

Meciendo . . . meciendo
entre la carne seca
la cebolla y el ajo

Meciendo con la lengua
de fuera y los ojos saltantes
Te ves en la mente
de nieta meciendo
meciendo bajo tus pies
su madre niña llorando sufriendo

Meciendo cobarde
entre la carne seca
la cebolla y el ajo
Meciendo con la lengua
de fuera y los ojos saltantes

Judith Ortiz Cofer

MY FATHER IN THE NAVY:
A CHILDHOOD MEMORY

Stiff and immaculate
in the white cloth of his uniform
and a round cap on his head like a halo,
he was an apparition on leave from a shadow-world
and only flesh and blood when he rose from below
the waterline where he kept watch over the engines
and dials making sure the ship parted the waters
on a straight course.
Mother, brother and I kept vigil
on the nights and dawns of his arrivals,
watching the corner beyond the neon sign of a quasar
for the flash of white our father like an angel
heralding a new day.
His homecomings were the verses
we composed over the years making up
the siren's song that kept him coming back
from the bellies of iron whales
and into our nights
like the evening prayer.

EN MIS OJOS NO HAY DIAS

*from Borges' poem
"The Keeper of the Books"*

Back before the fire burned in his eyes,
in the blast furnace which finally consumed him,
Father told us about the reign of little terrors
of his childhood beginning

at birth with a father who cursed him
for being the twelfth and the fairest
too blond and pretty to be from his loins,
so he named him the priest's pauper son.
He said the old man kept:
a mule for labor
a horse for sport
wine in his cellar
a mistress in town
and a wife to bear him daughters,
to send to church
to pray for his soul.
And sons,
to send to the fields
to cut the cane
and raise the money
to buy his rum.
He was only ten when he saw his father
split a man in two with his machete
and walk away proud to have rescued his honor
like a true "hombre."
Father always wrapped these tales
in the tissue paper of his humor
and we'd listen at his knees rapt,
warm and safe,
by the blanket of his caring,
but he himself could not be saved,
"What on earth drove him mad?"
his friends still ask,
remembering Prince Hamlet, I reply,
"Nothing on earth,"
but no one listens to ghost stories anymore.

Alberto Ríos

DINNER

As Tacaná erupted in the south
Mexican jungles, my father was born
and this is the sound he makes
when he eats.
I am afraid of volcanoes,
or I think I am, like anthills
and he spits the small seeds out.

Elías Miguel Muñoz

LOS NIÑOS DE
NEWPORT BEACH

Hay sol y mar
en sus arrugas blancas
granos de sal
y juguetes de fuego
Sólo pueden hablar
de sus hazañas
de sus velas
Allí los ves
en sus gafas de espejo
Casi parecen hombres
Llevan sus shorts
de felpa
y en cada mano
una cerveza amarga
(Dicen que surge de la tierra
 que esa cerveza brota de
 las piedras)

Da gracia verlos
divertirse
Salir del mar
como los camarones
Desde el azul marino
de sus patios
escribirán sus nombres
Y les será difícil
porque apenas empiezan
(Del pasado heredaron
 nada más
 una biblia de cifras)

Y los niños bronceados
dan lecciones al mundo
Desde su pequeñez
amos de sus casitas
y de sus barcos
de papel

Nadie puede tocarlos
Ellos no saben escuchar
Juegan sin conocernos
y sin vernos
Porque no hay sol ni espuma
en nuestra esquina
Pero tú y yo
Los dos
ya lo advertimos
Ellos sólo podrán ser niños
Siempre

ESTOS HIJOS DEL SOL

Si das la vuelta
ellos darán la vuelta
Si te fijas en la cima del árbol
ellos también se fijarán
Si les hablas
de esa necesidad
de crear héroes
de esa obsesión que ya
no disimulan bien
de ese querer cubrir
con papel de aluminio
la no-historia del hombre americano
no seguirán tus pasos
ni mirarán la copa
Te mirarán a ti
en silencio
Si les dices
que es mejor
no creer en el sol
callarán

Si les hablas del pobre
callarán
Si les hablas del rico
no sabrán qué decir
Si te tiras al pozo
(Porque no compras el Sueño
 de estos hijos del sol)
te irás tú solo bocabajo
y ellos te observarán
desde sus copas
mudos

Enrique R. Lamadrid

GALLOS Y GALLINEROS

para Jaime y Teresa y mi suegro

Andy drove the last u-shaped nails into the fencepost with a rain of victorious blows. "Ahora sí está bien clavado," he thought, amazed that even his innermost musings had been emerging in Spanish for some time now. The two layers of mesh wire were well nailed, buried at the bottom, and tightly strung around a scrap wood shack which looked like the best gallinero he had ever seen. The six dozen Araucanian chickens living there were already taking on careless cosmopolitan airs as they strutted brainlessly around the compound, relentlessly attacking certain pebbles.

An old blue pick-up that had been bouncing along the acequia road suddenly turned and skidded to a halt in a cloud of dust. A spry old man leaned out the window, shaking his head:

"¡Tanto trabajo por nada! You're wasting your time. I can't tell if it's a fort or a hotel, but it's not going to do you a bit of good."

"Mira, no más, Felipe," Andy told him, slightly irritated, "look at that wire. It cost me plenty. No dog can get through that, I don't care what you say."

"Bueno, so what if ese cabrón perro del vecino got a chicken last week, ¿qué le hace? At least the other ones could get away. Better to leave them loose," he laughed, and spun the truck back through the trees as the younger man shook his head.

Andy, or Andrés as people were beginning to call him, sauntered over to a huge fallen limb underneath an ancient cottonwood. He pulled an iced jug of yerba buena tea out of a hollow place, drank deeply and sat down. Two weeks before, the limb had come crashing down during a rain storm, narrowly missing the gallinero and pulverizing a row of drying adobe bricks. Andrés was furious about it still, but was secretly relieved at the minimal damage that it did. He had worried about it for seven years, the length of time that he and Rosina had been living in the nearby adobe house they built with their own hands. Her father had begrudgingly given them the little piece of land when she appealed to him for her herencia. She was appropriately humble, but the request took him by surprise. Andrés recalled the words of the grizzled patriarch.

"Hija, first you quit school, then you bring your greñudo boyfriend home with you, and now you ask me what your sisters haven't yet dared to. ¿No tienes vergüenza?"

His daughter was as stubborn and proud as he was, the qualities which most fascinated and frustrated Andrés about the people he was learning to call his own.

The tree had been a source of conflict between him and his suegro for a long time.

62

As soon as Andy saw the gnarled limbs twisting out at incredible angles from the main trunk, he felt a compelling urge to crank up his chainsaw to make his world a little safer, according to the way he looked at it. He was used to the symmetrical mountain cottonwoods of the lush valleys of his native Colorado. When they first staked out the foundations of the house he told his father-in-law:

"Felipe, just look at the way those limbs hang down. That dead one could break off in a breeze and kill a man. I'm going to cut it."

"No seas miedoso," his suegro laughed, "just calm down your nerves. That limb was in the same shape fifty years ago when I played under it as a kid."

The next fall after working all morning in the woodpile, Andy approached the tree with saw in hand. Out of a cloud of dust appeared Felipe's pickup as if from nowhere.

"What the hell are you doing, cabrón, you trying to get yourself killed?" he said with an angry smile. "Just leave well enough alone. Besides, I want you to come to town with me." Not another word was spoken about the tree for years.

With the passing of each season, Andrés came to love the valley as much as he loved Rosina. Through her family he steeped himself in local culture and learned northern New Mexican Spanish well enough to hold his own in the endless pláticas with viejitos and vatos locos in the little bar out on the Chama highway. People were beginning to accept him as "uno de nosotros, casi," a rare honor for an Anglo. Of course, if anyone became jealous, drunk or abusive, he would occasionally get called down for being what he was, but it never shook him anymore.

"Culture is learned, something that is cultivated and treasured, not just a gift that happens to come with your blood," he convinced himself. He often fought back sarcastically too, saying "There are plenty of Chicanos in this valley who are so agringados that all they want to do is sit in their trailors all day soaking up TV soap operas and second-hand football."

What was most important to Andrés, however, was gaining the respect of his suegro. He didn't realize it, but the harmless crash of the huge álamo limb was the start of a new era. His seven-year apprenticeship of paciencia, respeto and vergüenza had ended. Andrés stretched out along the wide limb and took another drink of the yerba buena. He sensed something had changed, but still felt unsettled. As he gazed up into the branches of the tree, he saw a grace and strength he never noticed before:

"The people in this valley are like these trees," he thought. "There may not be much rain, but the roots are deep enough to get them by for hundreds of years. Besides, the acequia is just right over there . . ."

Rosina's call roused him. He closed the gate of the gallinero and went into the house for supper. Andrés felt strange, but content. They made love that night and slept so soundly that the only thing that woke them up the next morning were the rifle shots.

Felipe's pickup was in the driveway and he was putting his rifle back in the rack. In silence they buried all the chickens along with the dog that had killed them. Andrés felt the anger and frustration burning in his throat when he felt Felipe's hand on his shoulder.

"No te preocupes, hijo, no es nada."

Andrés felt a surge of relief as they went back inside the house for coffee.

Diana Rivera

THAT CHURCH SPECIFICALLY

Perhaps I decided to be an artist when I went to mass. Unconsciously, you see. For all I know about my childhood I went to church regularly for as long as I remember. And, really, the church made me dream, that church I went to, specifically. I mean everything about it, its hugeness, the incredible dome, the gigantic porcelain statues, the crowds. Well, for a child, this can be an incredible experience and, since you're not supposed to talk, you're bound to fantasize. And you can imagine what fantasies can lead to . . . well, in my case they made me pass out, I mean literally pass out, swear to God, because, you see, they were not always pleasant ones.

I suppose I was a susceptible child. I think I was, anyway. In any case, doing something for a prolonged period of time can cause you to become that thing. I became a dreamer. Dreaming became a habit, I guess, something unavoidable. I mean, really, I was there, in that church specifically, every Sunday. Not only was I there every Sunday since I was seven but I was there every first Friday of the month also. See, my mother believed that if you went to mass every first Friday for nine consecutive Fridays you would go to heaven. This was supposed to be a sacrifice to the Sacred Heart of Jesus. Not to the Virgin Mary, remember, but to Jesus. If you did that, then you were promised heaven. But you had to do it consecutively. If you missed one Friday, for example, you'd have to start over again, like some sort of game. I mean, not you, but me, of course.

Well, anyhow, I had to start over again several times until I got to high school. In high school we went to mass every first Friday. We wore white pleated skirts and vests instead of the ordinary navy blue uniform 'cause it was a special day. Anyhow, since I was never absent from school, I thought I was definitely going to heaven. Oh, I forgot, you also had to have communion. Of course, you had to go to confession, which we did every first Thursday, and be sinless. Well, I felt sad for all the people in elementary school who went to church on other days 'cause it was the privilege of older high school students to go on first Fridays and be saved. The poor little things . . . Anyhow, when I was as young as them, I thought I'd be a saint, or an artist. Special, anyhow.

I had lots of great experiences in church. I thought I was some sort of mystic. Everything about that church fascinated me, even its color. Bright blue, like heaven. But the floors, big checkers in black and white, had a strange peculiarity to them. I looked and looked at them, my hands clasped and folded in prayer, looking down, wondering why. There was something very mysterious in their stark repetitive patterns and in the way different shoes and all those people stepped on them back and forth or simply stood and waited during those long ceremonies as if for something. Then, one Sunday, the thought came to me, suddenly and impetuously and unexpectedly, like all thoughts come to me. I knew it was a revelation. I knew something that nobody else knew. My God, I thought, at my age! But in reality I did not think it odd then. In fact, I thought it was most natural and I cherished the secret that God had given me. I looked at the people. The woman with the pink frock and the emeralds and her hair tucked up with barrettes, she stood with both feet on a black checker—I knew she was going to hell; and then there was the big fat man with the crooked nose and curly hair, he was definitely in between, one foot on the white tile, one foot on the black; he was both good and bad and still had not decided which way to go, exactly what to become; I supposed he was going to purgatory. And then there was that little pale boy with shiny black hair and deep, black eyes; he stood there so still and quiet but one whole foot was on the black checker and his other foot was half on white and half on black, so really, three-quarters, as I had learned in school, were on the black. Too bad he was going to hell. And the lady seated on the side bench waiting to be confessed, the one with the eyeglasses that hung from her neck from a golden chain, she was going to heaven!

Well, I guess I spent most of my time passing judgment on people, or, really, playing games in my mind because I was too bored, or, simply, I had to be quiet so I had to invent something to do when I got tired of praying. And if I giggled with my sisters my father would punish us afterwards. Anyhow, I was always cautious to stand with both of my feet on the big white checkers. Somehow though, as I grew older, I would sometimes forget the game which had become a form of truth to me and find myself standing on the black tile; alarmed, I'd move quickly onto the white one! The nicest thing, though, was that no one else knew this simple truth and it was *my secret*.

What? Well, I didn't mean to say that I began to paint right away because of it. What I meant was that going to church became an outlet for fantasy to me and that the increasing fantasies perhaps contributed to my becoming an artist. I mean, I'm sure I weaved lots of fantasies elsewhere and at other times but since I found myself in church so much . . . Do you see? It was there, really, where I began to know myself, many things about myself that, perhaps, elsewhere were different. Imagine! I even thought I was a visionary! You won't believe that several times I had visions! Well, at least I thought I had them and, at that age, you really don't know . . .

You won't believe it if I tell you that one day I saw halos around the heads of the statues of the Virgin and Jesus. I mean, actual bright yellow light around their heads. Well, I could not believe it, but, you see, I thought it was one of those incredible secrets God gave me, powers that no one else had and, a little anxious and frightened, I looked around at other people's expressions to find them casual and ordinary. Then I looked at the statues again and the halos had disappeared. But then, suddenly, something unbelievable happened. A floating purple haze spread out from the statue of Jesus. It was a beautiful yet haunting shadow that grew out of it slowly, farther and farther out, as if trying to separate itself from the statue. Then I looked at the porcelain virgin with the blue veil over her head and the same thing happened. I looked around again but no one seemed to notice it. It was a miracle, I thought, wondering what God had in store for me, wondering if perhaps He wanted me to become a nun.

I felt a sublime, tender feeling. I knew God loved me and I had never felt his love more intensely. But I was a little scared. The real soul of Jesus and Mary was there, quivering inside those plaster casts trying to get out. What if they did separate completely and they suddenly appeared? My God! They would be here, in this church, and I happened to be here too! But would they talk? What would they say? Then I began to sweat a bit. Maybe, I thought, maybe the end of the world will come today. On the other hand, I felt like shouting: By God, by God, it's a miracle! It's a miracle! But then I looked around and everyone remained calm. I looked at the purple shadows and they had not yet separated. I felt a sense of relief and then, suddenly, they vanished. Then I saw the halos again. Then the shadows. God had given me a special power. I must be one of those chosen ones, I thought, and all I had to do was *look* in a different way. All I had to do was to focus my eyes on the brightness behind the statues, obliterating the people, the priest, the altar, focusing only on the brightly lit space behind the statues, and golden halos and purple shadows would appear. It was wonderful, I thought. I took to doing it every week and had lots of fun. One time I even saw a halo around Father Lozada's head. I felt elated to have a saint for a priest and realized, as the nuns had taught, that priests were truly the messengers of Christ—that they *were* Christ. Yes, that's right. After a while my eyes began to grow tired and it was no longer fun. I grew a little suspicious that those great apparitions did not come as easily, yet for a long, long time I thought I was a visionary.

No, not that young. Ten, eleven perhaps, but this type of thing continued to happen until I was fourteen or so. But it happens today too, you see, when the body makes strange things happen to you and you cannot control it. I mean, I don't know if it happens to you, but it happens to me. But now it's different, it's frightening—there's absolutely no innocence. Sometimes it's horrible, when your fantasies are morbid and grotesque, a bizarre feeling indeed. It didn't take a long time for me to get to that point. Somehow, around the time of puberty, my fantasies grew darker. With sex and all that. Do you understand? I know, I know. I'm getting to that. I mean, that's what I came here for. Right? Right. Well, needless to say, that's when I began to get sick. Mentally and physically, I imagine you know. Maybe. And I could not control this feeling. Where before I took delight in looking at people walk down the aisle, genuflect, walk in and out, now it made me sick, utterly sick to my stomach. I mean, really, when I was a kid and saw cartoons where little mice shook their knees when the big cat got near, I did not suspect anything like that could really happen to people—and to me! More than butterflies!

. . . And people fainting, that's another trip—people fainting in movies when someone died or when they got scared, I could not believe that happened either. But now I know, don't worry, I know for sure! I began to faint in church myself. Of course I know why! I was darned scared! Scared of damnation! Scared of the hell I thought I had been saved from! What else could be more frightening to a young girl? I mean, except for parents. You see, when I began to play with myself, I mean, after it had happened naturally, I felt deliriously guilty and panicked. But I did not feel guilty when I found out about it for the first time.

I'm sure you know, yes, sure, it was wonderful. And the way it happened to me, specifically, was more wonderful altogether. I mean, not that I know how it happened to you, but it happened in a very natural manner to me. I remember clearly. I was at the swimming pool at the country club near home, swimming of course. Why, yes, about eleven. By now I'm probably blushing I suppose but, anyhow, I got hold of a line of buoys, those that separate lanes for swimming races, held it tight, and as I swam from one side of the pool to another holding the line of buoys tightly underneath, they began to cause friction against me. Between the speed and the friction, it happened. Of course, I did not know *what* had happened. But, perplexed, I knew I liked it. I swam back in the same manner but nothing happened the second time. Anyhow, I felt great delight in having another secret, which unlike the others, I supposed, did not happen to a selected few, but, I was certain, only to me. It was wonderful and mine only and I took delight in keeping it a secret and, of course, I tried to see whether it would happen again in my bedroom and it certainly did.

Well, Dr. Freidus—I know my giggle is nervous—I'm sure glad I had my own bedroom; I'm sure that contributed to my stored secrets. Part of the pleasure of it was that it was a secret and I did not want anybody to know not really because I thought there was anything abnormal about it, but because it was my own secret, my own. If I had been discovered it might not have been as pleasurable afterwards. But somehow I found out that it was wrong. I don't know how. Maybe because nobody talked about it. Maybe because one time, bathing with my little cousin—I was very little— I touched his tiny penis and his mother, impulsively, took him away from the tub. I don't know. Maybe because when I was in the hospital after appendicitis my mother helped me shower and, as I cleansed myself—there—she jumped and said, "Oh, use the soap!" "Oh God," I said, "C'mon"— wait, that was later . . . well, I really don't know how I found out it was bad, that *I* was bad, but I found out. So I *had* to confess it. If not, I could not have communion first Friday and I would have to start all over again.

Not only that, but on Sundays, if I didn't have communion, which I began to do as I grew older, my father, after the mass was over and we had gathered in the car, would ask, "Why didn't you have communion? Why?" and his small eyes would become smaller, piercing into mine trying to discover the devil. I would be frightened, speechless, feeling guilty because I felt too guilty to have communion. Sometimes I ventured to say that one really had to have a feel for it—if not, it became a mechanical act—but most times, though, I had communion because I did not want to go through the interrogation. Yes? Oh yes, indeed. I did go to confession quite frequently but . . . but I really despised it. In fact, I usually lied when I confessed, made up sins, you see, or covered up others, especially masturbation, and, in the long run, I would feel that I had more sins after confession than prior to it, because I had lied.

Imagine! Lying to the priest! Somehow, the only great sin was *that one* and *that one* was precisely the one I didn't confess. The others—I disrespected my parents, when I meant I really didn't like them; I fought with my brothers and sisters (I didn't have any brothers)—I had gathered and memorized in a list which I changed, shortened, and lengthened depending on the priest. If the old, white-haired, half-bald priest was in the confessional, I would shorten the list because I knew he was old-fashioned; if it was the younger, attractive black-haired priest, I would confess as many sins as I could. Sometimes, with him, I would confess: "I committed impure acts." And he was really cool and told me to pray four Hail Marys, one more than he usually gave for penance. Anyhow, when I didn't confess it, my last sin confessed would be "I lied," hoping that God would be as merciful as they said He was, and included the present tense sins as well as the past ones. And I thought lying was not as bad. But somehow I would come out feeling more ashamed. The priests were God and I had lied directly to them, to God. But instead I figured that God knew it all anyway and He would try to understand.

One time, though, all the high school students were going to confession one Thursday when the burden of guilt was truly choking me and I decided I must be courageous and confess my sin. I was really unlucky. There were so many kids in church the priests had to use those extra confessionals, the mobile ones that are simply a piece of board with a screen. Everybody could see you when you confessed. But I was determined not to lie. I told the priest I had committed an impure act. Well, he happened to be the old, white-haired man and he wanted to know what the act was. I gulped and became nervous. I tried to think fast. No, I couldn't tell him, no, not my secret, I tried to think fast. Hansey, an older boy I liked, came to my mind. Hansey did not even know I existed but . . . I really loved him. "Tell me, my child," the priest asked, "what was the nature of your act?" "Well . . . ," I said, "it has to do with a boy." A boy? I asked myself. What about a boy? I didn't even have a boyfriend. I hadn't even been kissed. "Yes?" the priest asked again, by now more interested, "What about him?"

I asked myself the same question and thought of Hansey. That day in the country club, when I swung on the swings, I could hear him laughing, telling the other boys something about my panties. What a terrible thing for him to say! I felt like crying. Oh God, I kept thinking, I hope he didn't see, I hope he didn't . . . And then afterwards I checked myself and noticed there was no blood, relieved. But how horrible of him, an invasion of privacy, of intimacy . . . How I hated him then, fiercely. "Well," I told the priest, "every morning, as I walk to school, I look at his house, to see him . . . I, I think I like him." "Yes, and . . . ?" he sort of asked.

"Well, Father, I like a boy." "Oh," he said, "my child, there's nothing wrong in liking a boy." "There isn't?" I asked. "No, my child, it is a most natural feeling." I made a sound of relief. I had lied once again. Again, I had a double reason for feeling guilty, guilt increased guilt and there was no way I could stop. So I stopped confessing the sin altogether. I hated to have to be direct, specific; I loved my impure voyage more and more and every day it grew better and better. And, then, I was also forced to have communion, Dr. Freidus, because of my father, you see, to please him—sometimes, when I didn't have communion, I knew he condemned me, even if he didn't speak to me (which we didn't do much of anyhow), with his eyes. . . . So I had communion after having sinned and my guilt was tripled and quadrupled, and that's when it began to happen.

Why, those collapses! It was as if I had to die before going for communion. It was as if my father were God and I feared his punishment, his suspicion. And so one day, before the time of communion, I fainted over the pew. Another time, on a rainy day when all the church windows were shut and I wore my blue velvet jumper with long crepe sleeves, as I walked the aisle towards the altar, I fainted again. This time my parents were vacationing in St. Thomas and my poor grandmother, who happened to be behind me, held me as I fell. When I regained consciousness I lay on a pew. I opened my eyes to see lots of heads looking down on me, hands fanning me with pieces of paper. And then—this is the epitome of guilt—I noticed that my slip was showing and I pulled it down. Ha! My slip was showing! In church! In that church in particular!

Isn't that odd? Isn't it funny and strange—the guilt, the confessions? Well, sure, I realize that's exactly what I'm doing now. But it's different, you see . . . oh, I just remembered something awkward that happened with my father. He . . . What? Did you say the session is over? God, an hour passes by so fast! What? The last two bills were not paid? Are you sure? You are. Well, I'll definitely send you a check tomorrow morning. I'll have to talk to my husband about it. He pays the bills. I'll have to talk to him this time.

Alma Villanueva

GOLDEN GLASS

It was his fourteenth summer. He was thinning out, becoming angular and clumsy, but the cautiousness, the old-man seriousness he'd had as a baby, kept him contained, ageless and safe. His humor, always dry and to the bone since a small child, let you know he was watching everything.

He seemed always to be at the center of his own universe, so it was no surprise to his mother to hear Ted say: "I'm building a fort and sleeping out in it all summer, and I won't come in for anything, not even food. Okay?"

This had been their silent communion, the steady presence of love that flowed regularly, daily—food. The presence of his mother preparing it, his great appetite and obvious enjoyment of it—his nose smelling everything, seeing his mother more vividly than with his eyes.

He watched her now for signs of offense, alarm, and only saw interest. "Where will you put the fort?" Vida asked.

She trusted him to build well and not ruin things, but of course she had to know where. She looked at his dark, contained face and her eyes turned in and saw him when he was small, with curly golden hair, when he wrapped his arms around her neck. Their quiet times—undemanding—he could be let down, and a small toy could delight him for hours. She thought of the year he began kissing her elbow in passing, the way he preferred. Vida would touch his hair, his forehead, his shoulders—the body breathing out at the touch, his stillness. Then the explosion out the door told her he needed her touch, still.

"I'll build it by the redwoods, in the cypress trees. Okay?"

"Make sure you keep your nails together and don't dig into the trees. I'll be checking. If the trees get damaged, it'll have to come down."

"Jason already said he'd bring my food and stuff."

"Where do you plan to shower and go to the bathroom?" Vida wondered.

"With the hose when it's hot and I'll dig holes behind the barn," Ted said so quietly as to seem unspoken. He knew how to slither under her, smoothly, like silk.

"Sounds interesting, but it better stay clean—this place isn't that big. Also, on your dinner night, you can cook outdoors."

His eyes flashed, but he said, "Okay."

He began to gather wood from various stacks, drying it patiently from the long rains. He kept one of the hammers and a supply of nails that he bought in his room. It was early June and the seasonal creek was still running. It was pretty dark out there and he wondered if he'd meant what he'd said.

Ted hadn't seen his father in nearly four years, and he didn't miss him like you should a regular father, he thought. His father's image blurred with the memory of a football hitting him too hard, pointed (a bullet), right in the stomach, and the punishment for the penny candies—a test his father had set up for him to fail. His stomach hardened at the thought of his father, and he found he didn't miss him at all.

He began to look at the shapes of the trees, where the limbs were solid, where a space was provided (he knew his mother really would make him tear down the fort if he hurt the trees). The cypress was right next to the redwoods, making it seem very remote. Redwoods do that—they suck up sound and time and smell like another place. So he counted the footsteps, when no one was looking, from the fort to the house. He couldn't believe it was so close, it seemed so separate, alone—especially in the dark, when the only safe way of travel seemed flight (invisible at best).

Ted had seen his mother walk out to the bridge at night with a glass of wine, looking into the water, listening to it. He knew she loved to see the moon's reflection in the water. She'd pointed it out to him once by a river where they camped, her face full of longing—too naked somehow, he thought. Then, she swam out into the water, at night, as though trying to touch the moon. He wouldn't look at her. He sat and glared at the fire and roasted another marshmallow the way he liked it: bubbly, soft and brown (maybe six if he could get away with it). Then she'd be back, chilled and bright, and he was glad she went. Maybe I like the moon too, he thought, involuntarily, as though the thought weren't his own—but it was.

He built the ground floor directly on the earth, with a cover of old plywood, then scattered remnant rugs that he'd asked Vida to get for him. He concocted a latch and a door, with his hand ax over it, just in case. He brought his sleeping bag, some pillows, a transistor radio, some clothes, and moved in for the summer. The first week he slept with his buck knife open in his hand and his pellet gun loaded on the same side, his right. The second week Ted sheathed the knife and put it under his head, but kept the pellet gun loaded at all times. He missed no one in the house but the dog, so he brought him in the cramped little space, enduring dog breath and farts because he missed *someone*.

Ted thought of when his father left, when they lived in the city, with forty kids on one side of the block and forty on the other. He remembered that one little kid with the funny sores on his body who chose an apple over candy every time. He worried they would starve or something worse. That time he woke up screaming in his room (he forgot why), and his sister began crying at the same time, "Someone's in here," as though they were having the same terrible dream. Vida ran in with a chair in one hand and a kitchen knife in the other, which frightened them even more. But when their mother realized it was only their hysteria she became angry and left. Later they all laughed about this till they cried, including Vida, and things felt safer.

He began to build the top floor now but he had to prune some limbs out of the way. Well, that was okay as long as he was careful. So he stacked them to one side for kindling and began to brace things in place. It felt weird going up into the tree, not as safe as his small, contained place on the ground. He began to build it, thinking of light. He could bring his comic books, new ones, sit up straight, and eat snacks in the daytime. He would put in a side window facing the house to watch them, if he wanted, and a tunnel from the bottom floor to the top. Also, a ladder he'd found and repaired—he could pull it up and place it on hooks, out of reach. A hatch at the top of the ceiling for leaving or entering, tied down inside with a rope. He began to sleep up here, without the dog, with the tunnel closed off.

Vida noticed Ted had become cheerful and would stand next to her, to her left side, talking sometimes. But she realized she musn't face him or he'd become silent and wander away. So she stood listening, in the same even breath and heartbeat she kept when she spotted the wild pheasants with their long, lush tails trailing the grape arbor, picking delicately and greedily at the unpicked grapes in the early autumn light. So sharp, so perfect, so rare to see a wild thing at peace.

She knew he ate well—his brother brought out a half gallon of milk that never came back, waiting to be asked to join him, but never daring to ask. His sister made him an extra piece of ham for his four eggs; most always he ate cold cereal and fruit or got a hot chocolate on the way to summer school. They treated Ted somewhat like a stranger, because he was.

Ted was taking a make-up course and one in stained glass. There, he talked and acted relaxed, like a boy; no one expected any more or less. The colors of the stained glass were deep and beautiful, and special—you couldn't waste this glass. The sides were sharp, the cuts were slow and meticulous with a steady pressure. The design's plan had to be absolutely followed or the beautiful glass would go to waste, and he'd curse himself.

It was late August and Ted hadn't gone inside the house once. He liked waking up, hearing nothing but birds—not his mother's voice or his sister's or his brother's. He could tell the various bird calls and liked the soft brown quail call the best. He imagined their taste and wondered if their flesh was as soft as their song. Quail would've been okay to kill, as long as he ate it, his mother said. Instead, he killed jays because they irritated him so much with their shrill cries. Besides, a neighbor paid Ted per bird because he didn't want them in his garden. But that was last summer and he didn't do that anymore, and the quail were proud and plump and swift, and Ted was glad.

The stained glass was finished and he decided to place it in his fort facing the back fields. In fact, it looked like the back fields—trees and the sun in a dark sky. During the day the glass sun shimmered a beautiful yellow, the blue a much better color than the sky outside: deeper, like night.

He was so used to sleeping outside now he didn't wake up during the night, just like in the house. One night, toward the end when he'd have to move back with everyone (school was starting, frost was coming and the rains), Ted woke up to see the stained glass full of light. The little sun was a golden moon and the inside glass sky and the outside sky matched.

In a few days he'd be inside, and he wouldn't mind at all.

IV. Cultural Heritage: Change and Contrast

Alberto Ríos

DECIDING ON
A FACE

1.

White Mexican
skin poured
from a wax
carton, fingers
pulled from
a picket
fence, you
look into a
mirror and
see angels
not at all
what you
expected but
the angel
smiles, I
brush my
teeth on my
shirtsleeve
but the teeth
stay, wrinkled
white suits
at a formal
concert with
a red stage.
I think of
white breasts.

2.

I watch the black
hole of the oven

early in the morning
and I think of
the small brown faces
in black veils
on the way to church:
each face
a little blacker
with each year
until face and veil
become indistinguishable.
But the process
continues: a black veil
begins to show, becomes
suddenly obvious in a
brown face, in the space
of an open mouth,
in the nostrils viewed
by a child, in
the holes of the ears
when the hair
is tied back, in
the centers of the eyes.
The intricacies of
the lace veil become
imprinted on their
faces, on my grandmother's
face, everything
is black lace, patterned,
an expensive skin.
I watch the black
hole of the oven
as she bends
to take out
breads, praying
they are not burned,
the bend as prayer.

3.

We sit to dinner
three for manicotti,
checked cloth, white
wine, garlic bread.
We order and

no one is offended.
The waitress lights
our candle.
My father said once
during the war
he saw the sign no
dogs or mexicans
allowed but this
must not be
that place.
We eat our large
dinner, and I
wonder about that
other place, the
beautiful young girls
who ate on a patio
a dinner like
ours, who tasted
the garlic bread
in my hands.

4.

The face by which I had
known her is a lie.
The pointed blades of
her back reach out,
letting go or holding
her to the large bed,
giving the illusion
of weight.
From the bed she
extends stiffly her
arms, thin praying
extensions of a mantis
and a loud noise
makes her breathe in,
she jerks her arms back,
shivers like an animal
stupidly caught between
a door and its jamb.
In that moment she
frightens her history
out onto her body
as if the past were

a shield or the small,
creased and glove-worn
cover of a Catholic Bible,
the kind with yellow
pages like old teeth
and illuminated letters
that look like doilies,
intricate but useless,
painstakingly produced.
Last month she said
she would not have pets
when she got home
because they die
in their various ways
and she had not the
strength to bury another.
Today she has said
nothing until we are
ready to leave, she
has opened her eyes,
someone has placed her
glasses properly but has
forgotten to remove
them—they will fall when
she sleeps—she asks,
looking at me,
what is your name?

5.

Not all nuns creep
not those arthritics
with steel implanted
voluminous hips
always lopsided
making those nuns
secretly beneath
their large skirts
bicycle riders
out too far
without water
but coming downhill
unfunny, without
subtlety, or comfort.

6.

Pinned on his oversized lapel
an illiterate arrow pointed north.
Was this north? he asked me.
His parents had died
who were too poor to have left
anything behind except him.
Neighbors sent him now
northward to relatives
who had big rooms, they said.
A car would pick him up
if he stood next to the road
and he could explain
or perhaps the bus driver
would take pity on his size.
Neighbors had reassured him.
Regardless, I faced him now.
Yes, this is north, I said
and I watched him walk.
I would have invited him home.
He might have stayed.

Elías Miguel Muñoz

HERMANITA NACIDA
EN ESTAS TIERRAS

Para Vicky

Al escurrirte
lenta y cariñosa
entre mis dedos
sin poder sujetarte
y explicarte mil cosas
Cada vez que sonríes
o me muestras
tus zapatos de broche
o me cuentas
una historia de vuelos espaciales
(Como quisieras ser princesa
 de esas guerras absurdas
 y sangrientas)
Cada vez que me intrigas
con tus *riddles*
con tus palabras
que serán siempre extrañas
a la experiencia nuestra

No es un reproche
hermana
hermanita nacida en estas tierras
Es que nunca sabrás
de gallinas echadas
(¿Habrá en tu infancia
 emoción parecida?)
ni de huecos de ratas
en la tierra mojada
Hubo una vez un niño
sobre lajas muy blancas
y paseos a pie

y juguetes de lata
Hubo también
misterio en las cañadas
Hubo piratas malos
y corsarios bravíos
Hubo lecciones
para sacar al hombre
de las piedras
Hubo crema de leche
y boniatillo

No es un reproche
hermana
hermanita nacida en estas tierras
Es que tú sólo tienes
la alegría minada
de los héroes de Disney
Animales que arrastran
con vergüenza
la estupidez del hombre
que los crea
sus valores gastados
y sus vicios
Porque sonreirás
sin darte cuenta
cuando el señor genial
de los muñecos
haga de ti
de cada niño
un payasito plástico
y ridículo

Al escurrirte
lenta y cariñosa
sin poder inventarte
otra niñez
regalarte la mía
que aunque también
se alimentó de héroes
tuvo sabor a palma
y mamoncillo
Y no sufrió la burla
de los juguetes caros

que te regala
el fantasma engañoso
de diciembre

Al escurrirte
lenta y cariñosa
sin que podamos juntos
enterrar en el patio
(Aquella tierra tibia
 y siempre abierta)
esos modelos sucios
que se irán imponiendo
que te acechan
desde su cartulina
y sus letras de molde
en un vaso de leche
o Coca-Cola

No es un reproche
hermana
hermanita nacida en estas tierras

Rafael Catalá

SUNRISE NEUYORKINO

Trasplantados en una maceta declaramos nuestra hispanidad
desde un subway neuyorkino
Los camastros me llaman sonriendo porque el correr
de las mañanas no me deja pensar
                    Es dormir corriendo
Las calles sofocadas levantan la mirada
y en el Greenwich Village a shopping bag lady es coronada
                    reina del Arco de Washington

Nacen los 60 y yo llego con ellos
al palpitar de guerra, el santoral sexual de las miradas,
el vértigo universitario obsesiona lactantes
                            La turbulencia
como principio físico encarna
                    estalla mis cabezas
El compromiso con mis huesos se va formando
                    poco a poco
                            y en quánticos detalles
salto a la noche de las calles, las aceras no hablan
La noche finaliza a una mañana helada

Y en el trasplante se quedaron costumbres
   y fue un morir de tíos
   y fue un nacer de un hombre
que nació a los sesenta, que dejó los sesenta,
que se siguió a sí mismo
y nace a las mañanas mojado de rocío

Noel Rico

THE PLAZA IN PONCE, 1979

The old men who sit within the shadows of the trees
Complain that Ponce is not what it used to be;
Back in the old days
The young men on Sundays
Would walk
On one side of the plaza
And the young ladies
On the other side:
Everyone was neatly dressed;
Even the poorest man conducted himself
Like an aristocrat. Every now
And then
A few of the local rich boys, drunk,
Would drive their big fancy cars
On the sidewalks;
Some of them would bathe
In the fountain
That sits in the middle
Of the plaza.
Some would even mount
The stone lions that sit at its edge,
Shouting obscenities
At the starched shirts
Walking past them.

Jim Sagel

BACA GRANDE

*Una vaca se topó con un ratón
y le dice: "Tú—¿tan chiquito
y con bigote?" Y le responde
el ratón: "Y tú tan grandota—
¿y sin brassiere?"*

It was nearly a miracle
James Baca remembered anyone at all
from the old hometown gang
having been two years at Yale
    no less
and halfway through law school
at the University of California at Irvine

They hardly recognized him either
in his three-piece grey business suit
and surfer-swirl haircut
with just the menacing hint
of a tightly trimmed Zapata moustache
    for cultural balance
and relevance

He had come to deliver the keynote address
to the graduating class of 80
at his old alma mater
and show off his well-trained lips
which laboriously parted
    each Kennedyish "R"
and drilled the first person pronoun
through the microphone
like an oil bit
with the slick, elegantly honed phrases
that slid so smoothly
off his meticulously bleached
    tongue

He talked Big Bucks
with astronautish fervor and if he
    the former bootstrapless James A. Baca
could dazzle the ass
off the universe
then even you
    yes you

Joey Martínez toying with your yellow
    tassle
and staring dumbly into space
could emulate Mr. Baca someday
    possibly
well
there was of course
such a thing
as being an outrageously successful
gas station attendant too
    let us never forget
it doesn't really matter what you do
so long as you excel
    James said
never believing a word
of it
for he had already risen
    as high as they go

Wasn't nobody else
from this deprived environment
who'd ever jumped
    straight out of college
into the Governor's office
and maybe one day
he'd sit in that big chair
    himself
and when he did
he'd forget this damned town
and all the petty little people
in it
once and for all

That much he promised himself

JIM SAGEL

EL VECINO VA PA' HAWAII

el vecino vendió más madera este año
que ningún otro vendedor
top salesman third year in a row
at Española Mercantile
and he had already turned down
two expense-paid trips
to Las Vegas
and the Bahamas
in favor of the cash
pero este año su vieja
se aferró
        Hawaii
why that was her lifetime dream
(wasn't it everybody's?)
y al cabo que la casa
ya no necesitaba más trabajo
hadn't he already tacked on
enough additions and appendages
to transform the multihued monstrosity
into a sprawling pentagon
pegado al arroyo?
y aunque el vecino
tenía un shope nuevo en la mente
pues al fin se dio
pulled his "Rockybilt" cap
down over his bushy black eyebrows
and boarded Trans-World Airlines
flight number 267 for Honolulu
though not without
severe reservations
for he'd never liked riding
in nothing
he wasn't driving himself
y todo el viaje
mirando por la ventana al mar
pacífico
he thought about what
his papá would think of him now
el hombre que lo mandó
a cuidar las borregas
desde ocho años de edad
the man who had driven

hard work
into his soul
asistiendo los animales
ordeñando en la madrugada
barbechando con el caballo
batiendo zoquete para hacer adobes
cortando zacate con la hoz
encerrándolo con la horquilla
viajando pa' Colora'o a piscar
papas, pepinos y cebolla
cortando madera y clavando
cortando
        y clavando
¿qué pensaría su papá
 si lo viera ahora?
and as you might have expected
el vecino tuvo mal tiempo en Hawaii
not terrible of course
for his wife was radiant
having never travelled beyond
Colorado Springs in her life
pero el vecino pasó todo el tiempo
nomás pensando en la madera que
él hubiera comprado con este dineral
que andaban tirando
you can see it in every snapshot
la vecina nos pasa
allí está él
parado en la orilla del mar
in his baggy bermuda shorts
salvaged from a trunk last opened
in 1945
and his bleached fish legs
and the smile is properly frozen
but the eyes are distant
and thirsty
        for his saw and his shovel
and his parched red earth
donde el maíz germina
solamente
con su sudor

Carlos Morton

THE MEETING

Scene 1. Introduction

(At rise two narrators enter from opposite sides of the stage to address the audience.)

SECRETARY: Ladies and gentlemen.
AIDE: Damas y caballeros.
SECRETARY: This is the story.
AIDE: El cuento.
SECRETARY: Of a meeting.
AIDE: De un encuentro.
SECRETARY: Between two of the greatest leaders the world has ever known.
AIDE: De dos de los más grandes líderes que el mundo ha conocido.
SECRETARY: Denied by all historians, the people in the streets know it to be true.
AIDE: Aunque negado por los académicos, la gente del pueblo cree saberlo ser verdad.
SECRETARY: A meeting between two presidents—the United States and Mexico.
AIDE: El encuentro entre dos presidentes—los Estados Unidos y México.
SECRETARY: In the early 1860s.
AIDE: En la primera parte de la década de 1860.
SECRETARY: Some say in Washington, others believe El Paso, Texas.
AIDE: Algunos creen que fue en Washington, otros dicen en El Paso, Texas.
SECRETARY: But one thing is for certain, they were bad times, full of danger for democracy everywhere.
AIDE: Pero algo sí sabemos, fueron tiempos malos, llenos de peligro para la democracia en cualquier lugar.
SECRETARY: The United States was fighting a bloody Civil War.
AIDE: Los Estados Unidos estaba luchando en una sangriente guerra civil.
SECRETARY: In which the Confederate forces, exponents of slavery, were winning.
AIDE: En donde las fuerzas de la Confederación, exponentes de la esclavitud, estaban ganando.
SECRETARY: In Mexico the French army had installed the imperial reign of Maximilian.
AIDE: En México el ejército francés había impuesto el reinado imperial de Maximiliano.
SECRETARY: To oppress the Mexican people.
AIDE: Para oprimir al pueblo mexicano.
SECRETARY: Two men stood in the way of tyranny.

AIDE: Dos hombres se enfrentaban contra la tiranía.
SECRETARY: Abraham Lincoln.
AIDE: Benito Juárez.

Scene 2. Lincoln Waits

(Blackout. Exit aide, enter Lincoln, agitated.)

LINCOLN: Is Juárez here yet?
SECRETARY: No, Mr. President, no word as yet. He may have had some trouble getting through the Rebel lines.
LINCOLN: We're running out of time, I should be down at the telegraph office.
SECRETARY: Our runner will keep us informed, sir. The last message received said that General Lee had driven our Union troops out of Hagerstown, Maryland, and then crossed into York, Pennsylvania. The mayor turned over the city.
LINCOLN: He did what?
SECRETARY: He gave up the city and paid a tribute of $28,000 in U.S. Treasury notes, 40,000 pounds of fresh beef, 30,000 bushels of corn, and 1,000 pairs of shoes.
LINCOLN: He should be tried for collaboration. But I guess if I were in his shoes, I would have done the same thing. Was he a Democrat?
SECRETARY: Yes, I believe he was, Mr. President.
LINCOLN: That's the trouble with fighting a war where the enemy speaks the same language—it drags on forever. That is my biggest fear, Miss Kennedy, that this war will destroy us all.
SECRETARY: The latest dispatch had Lee, with 100,000 men, 250 cannon, at Greencastle . . . no, Gettysburg.
LINCOLN: Gettysburg! I wager they are having a field day, those Johnny Rebs. Strutting and striding, off on a great adventure! Why, some of those butternuts are probably wearing shoes for the first time in their lives!
SECRETARY: *(Dashing off stage.)* More reports are coming in now, Mr. President!
LINCOLN: Quickly, Miss Kennedy, quickly!
SECRETARY: Lee attacked Meade's left wing the first day and the right wing the second day. But Meade sends word that the enemy is being repulsed on all points.
LINCOLN: Good, they're holding. But I wish we hadn't rotated those 58 regiments of northern veterans and filled the ranks with raw recruits.
SECRETARY: We promised that the men would only serve six months, sir.
LINCOLN: This war may take six years!
SECRETARY: Yes, Mr. President, but the draft is an unpopular thing, if you don't mind my saying so, sir.
LINCOLN: Especially among the Irish in New York, eh, Miss Kennedy.
SECRETARY: It's not fair when a rich man can buy his way out for $300 so a poor man can take his place, Mr. President.
LINCOLN: Very logical . . . that's why I hired you as my secretary. Hmmmm. But logic tells me we are not winning.

SECRETARY: It's only a matter of time, sir. We have the numerical superiority, the industry, the treasury . . .

LINCOLN: Tell me, why is it that within seven months and two contests they have routed, sent reeling, and threatened to crush the Army of the Potomac? All Lee has to do is repeat his victories at Fredericksburg and Chancellorsville. He then moves on to the state capital and barracks, replenishes his needs, and marches through Philadelphia, Baltimore, and Washington. He lays hold of the money, supplies, munitions, wins European recognition, *and* wins the war.

SECRETARY: Oh please, sir, that will never happen!

LINCOLN: What would we do then?

SECRETARY: Here is the latest dispatch! Pickett smashed into Meade's center with 15,000 men. The Rebels marched seven-eighths of a mile in broad daylight under fire. Only half reached the Union lines at Cemetery Ridge. The line held! We beat them back!!

LINCOLN: Thank God in Heaven!

SECRETARY: At night a heavy rain started to fall. Lee has ordered a retreat towards the Potomac.

LINCOLN: We've got them now, the river will be too flooded for them to ford!

SECRETARY: Estimated casualties. 23,000 wounded, missing, and killed for the Union and 28,000 for the Confederacy.

LINCOLN: 51,000 . . . in two days!!!

SECRETARY: I think that's Juárez now . . . I see a carriage rolling up. (*Exit Secretary, leaving Lincoln alone with his thoughts.*)

Scene 3. First Encounter

VOICE: (*In Lincoln's mind. All voices can be prerecorded.*) Durn it, Abe, you know I don't cotton to that booklearning a yurn. It's a waste 'a time. I need you out in the fields.

VOICE: But Papa . . .

VOICE: See that little boy over there, that's Abe Lincoln, the smartest pupil in class.

VOICE: Poor little feller, looks just like the ugly duckling. Look at his baggy breeches, they lack by several inches meeting the top of his shoes.

VOICE: Go on, ask him, go on.

VOICE: Young man, tell us, what do you want to be when you grow up?

VOICE: I, sir, am going to be President of the United States. (*Laughter, laughter.*)

SECRETARY: Juárez is here now, sir, he's on his way up.

LINCOLN: Who called this meeting? What am I doing waiting for the President of the Republic of Mexico when we are fighting what could be the deciding battle of the Civil War?

SECRETARY: Mr. President. President Juárez came all the way from Mexico City at great risk to his person.

LINCOLN: Show him in, Miss Kennedy.

SECRETARY: President Juárez of the Republic of Mexico!

LINCOLN: President Juárez, I am glad to make your acquaintance.

JUAREZ: El placer es mío, Presidente Lincoln.

LINCOLN: I wish that we could have met under more pleasant circumstances. Miss Kennedy, will you get us some coffee. *(As Secretary exits.)* Please sit down, we haven't much time. Now then . . .

JUAREZ: Presidente Lincoln, en este momento tan histórico quiero decirle . . . *(They stare at each other, embarrassed and ill at ease.)*

LINCOLN: President Juárez, I'm afraid I don't speak Spanish! Shall I call for an interpreter?

JUAREZ: No, no es necesario, I understand English. I spent some time in New Orleans, in exile.

LINCOLN: Good, my knowledge of other languages has always been limited.

JUAREZ: Yes, Napoleon III and his puppet Maximiliano would have us learn francés.

LINCOLN: We haven't much time, due to our own misfortunes, to formulate a more vigorous reply to the French intervention. But the Monroe Doctrine remains the cornerstone of our policy.

JUAREZ: Precisely the question I want to deal with; you see, both our countries are under attack by reactionary forces . . .

SECRETARY: *(Rushing in.)* President Lincoln, excuse me, sir, I have General Meade's latest communiqué.

LINCOLN: Please excuse us, President Juárez.

JUAREZ: I understand, go right ahead.

LINCOLN: Read it to me, Miss Kennedy.

SECRETARY: *(Reading.)* "The enemy has withdrawn from the contest."

LINCOLN: My God! Is that all?

SECRETARY: He goes on to say that Lee's army is in full retreat, back into Maryland!

LINCOLN: Meade let them cross the Potomac! He let them get away! We had them in our grasp. Why can't I find a general who can *fight*! Excuse me, Señor Juárez, I must leave at once.

JUAREZ: I wish that you did not have to go.

LINCOLN: I'm sorry, but this is the worst possible news. Excuse me.
    (Exit Lincoln.)

Scene 4. Juárez Alone

JUAREZ: *(Obviously disappointed.)* Will you please send in my aide, Señor González?

SECRETARY: Yes, of course. *(Exit secretary.)*

AIDE: *(Rushing in past the secretary.)* ¿Qué pasó, no te quiso ver?

JUAREZ: No pudo, estaba muy preocupado.

AIDE: ¡Esto es un insulto! ¡¡Por qué siempre están tan apurados estos malditos gringos!! *(Noticing the secretary staring at him.)*

JUAREZ: González, this is Miss Kennedy, President Lincoln's private secretary. My aide-de-camp, Señor González.

SECRETARY: Pleased to make your acquaintance.

AIDE: Señorita, the pleasure is definitely mine!

JUAREZ: González was asking me why you Americans are always in such a hurry. I was going to reply, perhaps because time runs here, el tiempo corre, in our country time walks.

SECRETARY: Excuse me, I'm going to see what President Lincoln is doing.

AIDE: *(Helping himself to Lincoln's coffee.)* Ugh! What terrible coffee. And the food is horrendous, all they eat is salted pork, white bread, and whiskey . . . Humph! So this is Washington, where the streets are lined with gold!

JUAREZ: Yes, and you can never go home again.

AIDE: In spite of their technological advances, their science, industry, I still prefer our so-called "primitive" country to theirs.

JUAREZ: But do you realize how far they have gone to eradicate poverty and to educate the minds of their citizens? I never even knew my own parents. I was raised by an uncle to be a shepherd and would have remained so all my life were it not for the chance straying of a sheep. I *let* the sheep slip away; then I too escaped.

AIDE: I never realized . . . Señor Presidente.

Scene 5. Juárez Flashback

JUAREZ: I was twelve years old, couldn't even speak Spanish! I walked forty miles to the big city of Oaxaca to search out my sister, who was working as a cook in the home of a wealthy man. It was hot and dusty, I was hungry, my feet swollen.

MARIA: *(Enter María.)* ¡Benito! ¡Qué haces aquí tan lejos de tu pueblo!

JUAREZ: ¡María Josefa! I explained to her that I wanted to obtain an education.

MARIA: Voy a preguntarle al patrón, a ver si te podemos encontrar un trabajo.

JUAREZ: She was going to ask the patrón if I could work for him. Oh, I had dreams even then—I could see myself, a man of letters, a scholar, a teacher.

MARIA: *(Handing him a broom.)* Andale, vete a la granja.

JUAREZ: They put me in charge of the stable! I was so confused, it was another world. But little by little I began to open my eyes.

MARIA: Tenemos que encontrarte un patrocinador.

JUAREZ: ¿Patrocinador?

MARIA: Tú trabajas por él y él te dará una educación, ves.

JUAREZ: In those days a poor Indian lad like myself could only hope to educate himself through the good graces of a patrocinador, a patrón. I soon realized that the majority of the boys and girls who served in the wealthy homes of Oaxaca came from my own village.

AIDE: Like indentured servants!

JUAREZ: I will never forget the last words my sister told me before she died.

MARIA: Benito, mi hermano, escucha, aunque te vas a educar y ser un hombre culto . . .

JUAREZ: . . . although you will get an education and become a learned man . . .

MARIA: Nunca olvides a tu gente, nunca olvides tu raza.

JUAREZ: Never forget your people, never forget your origins.

MARIA: No hagas lo que me han hecho a mí, ni hagas que te avergüences de ser zapoteca, de ser indio.

JUAREZ: Don't let them do what they have done to me, don't let them make you ashamed of being a Zapotec, of being Indian.

Scene 6. Lincoln Returns

AIDE: That's why Lincoln didn't see you . . .

JUAREZ: No, no, no González . . .

AIDE: He thinks he's superior to you!

JUAREZ: You are presuming something. Don't let this embitter you. Conquer those feelings. Seventeen years later I married the daughter of that wealthy white man my sister cooked for!

AIDE: Doña Margarita!

JUAREZ: The only wife I have ever had!

AIDE: Don Benito, would that I could have as much knowledge of worldly things as you.

JUAREZ: Well, stop wrestling with the world, González, you're asking for a fall. What is the news from Mexico?

AIDE: The French are still firmly in control of the capital, the puppet Maximiliano is installed at Chapultepec, and we have yet to win another victory like the one at Puebla.

LINCOLN: *(Poking his head in momentarily.)* Juárez . . . Oh, you're still here!

JUAREZ: Perhaps we should be gone!

LINCOLN: I am sorry, I did not mean that. There are a million things running through my mind. I can't concentrate. General Grant has just won at Vicksburg, but the war is far from over yet. I regret your having come all this way . . .

JUAREZ: President Lincoln, don't you realize that we are fighting for the same cause . . .

LINCOLN: I promise that someday I will make it up to you.

JUAREZ: *Someday* may be too late.

LINCOLN: Presidente Juárez, I have the Confederate Army to contend with.

JUAREZ: And I have the French army with a dagger at my throat.

LINCOLN: I can't help you now!

JUAREZ: Perhaps *I* can help you . . .

LINCOLN: Juárez, excuse me. *(Leaving.)* I can only deal at this time with the United States of America.

JUAREZ: *(Going after Lincoln.)* Don't you see, if the French Empire conquers Mexico they will ally themselves with the South! *(Lincoln returns.)* And together they will make slaves out of all of us! *(Lincoln pauses, looks at Juárez, fade to black, except for a spot on Lincoln's face.)*

Scene 7. A Second Meeting

VOICE: Daddy, why's that man so black?

VOICE: 'Cause he's got the mark 'a Cain on 'im.

VOICE: What's the mark 'a Cain?

VOICE: Mean's he kilt Abel, his brother, so God made him a nigger. *(During this interchange, the set has been changed somewhat. Juárez' aide and Lincoln's secretary are rearranging a setting similar to the first. The year is now 1865, El Paso, Texas.)*

SECRETARY: Is it always this hot in El Paso del Norte?

AIDE: Only in the summer time. You should take a siesta.

SECRETARY: Mr. González, I haven't got time to be sleeping.

AIDE: Miss Kennedy, a siesta in this part of the country is not a sign of laziness, it is a necessity. "Only mad dogs and Englishmen walk around in the midday heat."

SECRETARY: Is that why they call this the land of "mañana?"

AIDE: How is everything in Washington, Señorita?

SECRETARY: Oh, much better, that's why Mr. Lincoln was able to make this trip down here. Of course, it's a top secret; his political enemies would have his head if they knew he was visiting the President of Mexico in Texas.

AIDE: We pronounce it "Tejas."

SECRETARY: We are slowly winning the war. Sherman marches to the sea, and Lee will soon meet his Waterloo. Señor González, what do you call those funny little long things that taste like parchment?

AIDE: I can't imagine what you mean, Señorita.

SECRETARY: I bit into one the other day and I swear it tasted just like a . . . corn husk.

AIDE: Tamales! But you eat only what's inside the husk.

SECRETARY: Oh my goodness! (Pause.) Is the situation getting better in Mexico?

AIDE: No, but we are still fighting. We need another Cinco de Mayo.

SECRETARY: Another kind of food?

AIDE: No, it was a battle in Puebla where on the fifth of May, 1862, we defeated the French. A raggle-taggle Mexican army under Zaragoza defeated the vanguard of the French expeditionary force under Lorencez. It showed we had the capability for victory.

SECRETARY: Oh, I think I will sit down, it is getting very hot.

AIDE: Siéntese aquí, I will finish this.

SECRETARY: Moo-chas grass-ias, Zenor González.

AIDE: You're learning the language? (Aside.)

SECRETARY: Dee-me maz, poor favor!

AIDE: Well, originally, the English and the Spanish were going to be involved in the invasions of Mexico under the pretext of collecting a debt which was in arrears. We let them take Veracruz, hoping to trap them there in the hot season . . . (Cut off by Juarez' arrival.)

JUAREZ: ¿Todo está preparado?

AIDE: Sí, mi Presidente.

SECRETARY: Buey-noz dee-ass, Saynor Prez-i-dente.

JUAREZ: Buenos días, Señorita Kennedy. I see it is president Lincoln who is tardy this time?

AIDE: I'll get him this instant.

JUAREZ: This is of the utmost importance, González—we must convince President Lincoln that it is to the best advantage of both countries that he assist us.

AIDE: If anyone can persuade him, it will be you, mi Presidente.

JUAREZ: Show him in.

LINCOLN: (Entering.) President Juárez, I am so glad to see you again.

JUAREZ: And I am so glad that you kept your promise.

AIDE: Would you like coffee now, sir?

JUAREZ: Yes, Mexican coffee.

LINCOLN: Excellent!

JUAREZ: The coffee I had in Washington came all the way from Colombia. We could sell you our coffee at a much more reasonable price. Tráele una botella de brandy al Señor Lincoln. *(Aide exits.)* We have also been making brandy.

LINCOLN: We would like to open up better trade relations between our countries.

JUAREZ Unfortunately your concern is precious metals, just like the Europeans.

LINCOLN: President Juárez, we do not covet Mexico's riches. But like all men everywhere we want the finer things of life. Some think the young America conceited and arrogant, but has he not reason to entertain a rather extensive opinion of himself? Men and machines everywhere are ministering unto him.

JUAREZ: Yes, but beware that young America, in its accumulation of the material, does not contract the gout.

LINCOLN: Juárez, we are in the summer of our youth. Why, after this war . . .

AIDE: Presidente Juárez, ¡¡¡noticias importantes!!! *(Entering, he drops a bottle off at the table and quickly exits.)*

JUAREZ: Excuse me, Lincoln, it is *I* who must leave this time. I've prepared a little dinner party in your honor tonight. You will be staying?

LINCOLN: I can't refuse.

JUAREZ: Fine, why don't you invite your secretary, Miss Kennedy. I think she and Mr. González have taken a fancy to each other. Excuse me. *(Juárez exits. Lincoln picks up the bottle and pours some in his coffee. The strains of waltz music fill the air.)*

Scene 8. Lincoln's Flashback

VOICE: *(The stage blacks out except for a spot on Lincoln's face.)* Do you see that tall man over there? That's Abe Lincoln, one of the finest state senators in Illinois.

VOICE: Why isn't anyone dancing?

VOICE: I believe Mr. Lincoln is monopolizing all the young men. They say he is a great storyteller.

MARY: *(As the lights come on, crossing over to where Lincoln is seated at the table.)* Gentlemen, why are you not dancing?

LINCOLN: Pardon me. *(Rising from his chair.)*

VOICE: Mary Todd, this is Abraham Lincoln.

LINCOLN: Pleased to meet you, Miss Todd.

MARY: Mr. Lincoln, why aren't you dancing?

LINCOLN: Well, I, we, uh, were . . .

MARY: I hear you are a great teller of stories, Mr. Lincoln, but that you also have two left feet. *(Laughter.)* Well then, tell me a story . . .

LINCOLN: *(The music stops. Mary freezes.)* For the first time in my life, I couldn't say a word. I was frozen, as though to the spot.

MARY: *(Coming to life.)* Mr. Lincoln, you stand so tall, your bearing so proper, were you a military man?

LINCOLN: Why yes, I was a military hero, I fought, I bled. It is quite certain I did not break my sword, for I had none to break, but I bent a musket pretty badly on one occasion. And I had many bloody struggles with the mosquitoes. *(Laughter.)*

MARY: Oh, Mr. Lincoln, you are a card. *(She freezes.)*

LINCOLN: Quickly we became engaged. I love you Mary, marry me.

MARY: *(Unglued.)* Merry I will marry you but am I the only Mary?

LINCOLN: You are the only one! You have smitten me! *(Down on his knees.)*

MARY: Do you realize you are just as tall as I am on your knees?

LINCOLN: But due to a desperate and stupid misunderstanding which neither one of us remembers . . .

MARY: Well, there was the curious habit you had of . . .

LINCOLN: Or cares about, we broke off our engagement.

MARY: Followed by amends and a second betrothal. I do, I do, I do, I do. . . .

LINCOLN: In spite of the advice given to her by her high-born kinsmen . . .

MARY: Not to marry this "gangling giraffe."

LINCOLN: We married.

MARY: Lived in a manner most unaccustomed to my rank and station with this philistine . . .

LINCOLN: She helped me through the lean years.

MARY: Until he debated Douglas and came to national attention through his oratory. At Cooper Union . . .

LINCOLN: Neither let us be slandered from our duty by false accusations against us, nor frightened from it by menaces of destruction to the government. Let us have faith that right makes might, and in that faith let us, to the end, dare to do our duty as we understand it. *(Crowds cheering, etc.)* That the South shall not, under any circumstances, secede from the Union!

MARY: Hail Republicanism!! We have won the day!! Abraham Lincoln for President!! *(The lights dim again, Mary exits.)*

Scene 9. Meeting Continues

VOICE: *(Singing mournfully.)*
>"Two brothers on their way
>one wore blue and one wore gray
>all on a beautiful morning . . ."

LINCOLN: *(As Juárez enters.)* Bad news?

JUAREZ: The French are moving north.

LINCOLN: I hope you don't have to leave.

JUAREZ: There is still time. I am used to last minute escapes. The situation is not dangerous, *yet.* On the way out of Monterrey several months ago I was attacked by a traitor, my carriage riddled with bullets. Mostly I fear for my family, they had to leave Mexico.

LINCOLN: That bad!

JUAREZ: The French have occupied the entire northeast of Mexico, including Matamoros. I barely escaped with a few friends, followed by a wagon with the nation's archives. I don't know where my wife and children are. We hope they made it safely to New York with the Counsel.

LINCOLN: I'll make a note to check on their safety. I understand that small units of American volunteers have gone down to Mexico to fight for the Republic.

JUAREZ: Yes, and they have proven themselves very useful. I issued a decree asking for foreign volunteers who will fight for us. I offered, besides the regular army pay, lands worth a thousand, fifteen hundred, and two thousand pesos, depending on the rank of the volunteer.

LINCOLN: You mentioned in Washington a possible intrigue between the French imperialists and the Confederacy.

JUAREZ: There is a scheme by which a former U.S. Senator from California would colonize Sonora with American Southerners and then turn it over to the French. A Confederate general, Magruder, has promised to join the French once they win the civil war. Maximilian, the "liberal," plans to issue a decree to induce Southern planters to migrate to Mexico with their former slaves. Lincoln, what are your plans for the South once the war is over?

LINCOLN: Simply that a *United* States of America will prevail.

JUAREZ Lincoln, we are brother nations, democracies newly hatched in the Americas, both spreading our wings and learning to fly. But be wary that the American eagle does not cast a dark shadow over the hemisphere.

LINCOLN: I do not understand you, Juárez.

JUAREZ: My friend, let us be frank with one another. First Texas was invaded, then you took New Mexico, California, Arizona, Colorado, Nevada . . .

LINCOLN: In regards to the Mexican War, emotions were running strong. Everyone kept silent. Later we realized that President Polk had provoked the war out of greed for more territory. In January of 1848, I took the Senate floor and declared him to be a "confounded and miserably perplexed man." The papers called me an Illinois Benedict Arnold for my efforts.

JUAREZ: I realize that you spoke out against the war and I respect you for that, but still you raised money for it.

LINCOLN: Didn't you do the same for your side?

JUAREZ: Yes, of course, but we were not the aggressors.

LINCOLN: The border lands were badly managed.

JUAREZ: You speak of "Manifest Destiny," but Lincoln I say to you: someday our people will need that land and we shall cross this so-called border to resettle it!

LINCOLN: If you come in peace, we will welcome you.

JUAREZ: Lincoln, you forget, I spent some time in New Orleans. I saw how the white man looked at me because of my color. Granted, Mexico is not free from racial prejudice, but could an American Indian become President of the United States?

LINCOLN: Someday. All people, Blacks included, are needed to build a nation. The reason for which we fight this Civil War is to abolish slavery.

JUAREZ: This is 1865. We abolished slavery in 1821.

LINCOLN: In *name* only! Now, I'll be frank with you, Juárez, every underdeveloped nation has to pay a certain price for progress.

JUAREZ: But not at the expense of liberty! I know, I fear it: you will interfere to protect your national interests.

LINCOLN: We harbor no more territorial ambitions.

JUAREZ: Watch how you will change your position once your poor neighbors have natural resources you can no longer obtain by any other means.

LINCOLN: Nonsense, we have everything we need.

JUAREZ: I don't know what it will be: tin, gold, coal . . . but it will be something. Don't you see, Lincoln, destiny has cast us in the role of adversaries. And when the incredible happens, the world, Lincoln, *the world* will turn against you.

LINCOLN: I refuse to stay and listen to this any longer! Especially from a President without a country!

JUAREZ: I know I have angered you, but at least it has awakened the truth which you Americans are persistently denying. From Plymouth Rock on you have swept aside the red man and segregated him to reservation camps.

LINCOLN: I suppose the Spanish were guiltless!

JUAREZ: No, but they tried to integrate the Indian into their society. I am proof of that. Secondly, you brought the Black man into the New World as a slave. But the seizure of half of the national territory of Mexico was not the act of a democratic nation. Your principles have gone astray.

LINCOLN: You are questioning everything I believe in!

JUAREZ: Because I do not want us to be hypocrites!

SECRETARY: *(Entering with a message.)* President Lincoln, Sherman has taken Atlanta; we have broken the back of the Confederacy. Victory is near!

LINCOLN: Not so fast, Miss Kennedy, serpents have a way of regenerating themselves.

SECRETARY: Oh, but it is good news nonetheless.

JUAREZ: I am glad for you, Lincoln.

AIDE: *(Entering.)* Pero no hay buenas noticias para nosotros. Los franceses vienen para Chihuahua.

JUAREZ: The French are coming north. We must leave at once. ¡Recoge todo, vámonos!

LINCOLN: *(Speaking in a separate scene.)* Send a congratulatory telegram to Sherman. Tell him . . .

JUAREZ: We must make the French rue every minute of every day they stay in Mexico.
LINCOLN: As for Grant—tell him he must press on harder than ever.

JUAREZ: I will pack. Then we depart. *(Exit Juárez.)*

LINCOLN: No, give me a minute to rephrase this. *(Lincoln moves off right.)*

AIDE: Goodbye, Miss Kennedy.

SECRETARY: Adiós, Señor González. I have been instructed to tell you that a shipment of arms will be waiting for the Republican cause on the northern side of the river. *(Handing him an envelope.)* But no one is to know where you received this material from. Also, tell President Juárez his family is safe and sound in New York City.

AIDE: He will be very pleased. Señorita, I hope someday you can come and visit the Mexico I know and love, a Mexico at peace.

SECRETARY: Señor González, it would be my pleasure. I am sorry that Washington D.C. didn't sit too well with you.

AIDE: It must have been something I ate or drank. Perhaps I shall come again—for a visit.

SECRETARY: Perhaps some day you shall be appointed Ambassador.

AIDE: Perhaps I will, and then I shall come calling on you.

SECRETARY: Oh, Mr. González!

LINCOLN: Mary, come here, I need you to proofread this!

SECRETARY: Right away, Mr. President!

JUAREZ: *(Entering with his bags packed.)* ¡Estás listo, González!

AIDE: ¡Sí, señor!

JUAREZ: Lincoln, a telegram for you.

LINCOLN: Thank you. Lee has surrendered at Appomattox! I don't believe it! It's so anti-climactic! It can't be true. Mary, please check the accuracy of this report. Five years and so many lives . . .

JUAREZ: You have won your war, for me it goes on . . .

LINCOLN: Juárez, you have my heartfelt sympathy, and I am one of those who hope that soon you will be at the capital of the Mexican Republic with neither foreign influence nor foreign bayonets to threaten you . . . including Yankee ones, I might add.

JUAREZ: Thank you, President Lincoln, I know you are sincere.

LINCOLN: We are very much alike Juárez, you and I. We may not agree on everything, but wouldn't you say we agree, in principle?

JUAREZ: Yes, I believe we do my friend. *(They embrace.)*

Scene 10. The Speeches

LINCOLN: *(Giving a section of a famous speech.)* "Fourscore and seven years ago . . ." (etc.).

JUAREZ: *(Giving a section of a famous speech.)* ". . . el respeto al derecho ajeno es la paz . . ." (etc.).

(At the end of Juárez' speech, a shot rings out and Lincoln's face disappears. Juárez reacts.)

Scene 11. The Close

SECRETARY: Lincoln has been assassinated.

AIDE: Los franceses partirán de México. Juárez será elegido Presidente de México. El mundo sigue.

SECRETARY: The world goes on. Freedom and oppression struggle.

AIDE: Hay una lucha entre la libertad y la opresión.

SECRETARY: The Ku Klux Klan . . .

AIDE: Porfirio Díaz . . .

SECRETARY: Taft and Díaz meet.

AIDE: La Revolución Mexicana brota como un volcán . . .

SECRETARY: Pershing sets out on a punitive expedition looking in vain for Villa.

AIDE: Marineros norteamericanos ocupan el puerto de Veracruz.

SECRETARY: World War I breaks out.

AIDE: Presidente Cárdenas nacionaliza la industria petrolera mexicana.

SECRETARY: Johnson meets Díaz Ordaz.

AIDE: Hay una estatua de Abraham Lincoln en Ciudad Juárez, Chihuahua.

SECRETARY: There is a Lincoln-Juárez scholarship fund in Washington.
AIDE: Reagan se reune con López Portillo.
SECRETARY: Stories of their famous meeting . . .
AIDE: . . . se cuentan en las calles de Juárez y El Paso . . .
SECRETARY: More meetings between two neighbors are needed now . . .
AIDE: . . . para que los ideales que ellos defendieron . . .
SECRETARY: Shall not perish from the earth.

CURTAIN

This play was written thanks to a grant from Four Centuries/81 and the city of El Paso, Texas.

V. La Hispana: Portraits and Self-Portraits

Naomi Lockwood Barletta

TIEMPO PRESENTE

Aún pienso en ti
en el vapor de las voces
que entran y salen por los pasillos
y se esconden tras tomos de escritorios
en las mañanas rutinarias
del sueldo que gano,
y ando seriamente
disfrazada de profesora
agarrando esas voces
que huyen por ventanas imperturbables,
que se burlan del aire
enamoradas del calor,
y doy los buenos días,
y doy las buenas tardes,
y doy a cada uno
mi cada cual
apropiadamente cargado
de verbos en tiempo
siempre presente
como tú, aún.

Alma Villanueva

SIREN

Who is this woman with
words dangling from
the ends of her
hair? leaping
out from her
eyes? dripping
from her
breasts? seeping
from her
hands? Her

left foot, a
question mark.
Her right
foot, an
exclamation.
Her body, a
dictionary dying
to define life,
growth, a
yearning. Her

love as constant
as the sea—
tangy as salt—
dangerous (even
   to her
self): her
heart ruptures,
mends with each
new poem, word,
breath—but
she'll never
stop questioning,

begging, answering
herself (the word
  is constant now
  in her
ears). She
is a woman
singing to her
death, the
bone's still
marrow, the
womb's fluttering
flesh, love's
lost beauty
always found
at the edge of silence.
She is a
woman singing
in the snow.

If she melts your
heart, she
lives there,
too. A woman's
wish—a mother's
wish—a lover's
wish. Beauty
has no wish, it
simply survives
us. We are her

echo.

THE CEREMONY OF ORGASM

Each time something broke in
me: I cried out beyond
my lips: how

many wounds we carry till
we release ourselves in

love, in
to the earth: this wounding

of the flesh: this making
into words of

small bloody cries
from birth (some
were tended like a
lovely hot house
   flower, some

defied the weather and grew
   tender

and wild): till love

passes you, an ordinary
stranger, and recognizes
your colors, your scent

from a dream and plucks
you brazenly, as love
does, imagining you grew
just for him, your
inarticulate greenery stretching

toward the sun, your
cries, stern roots in
the rotting earth, your
wounds the petals of
the body: the love

we dare imagine like
the sun on a
cloudy day: the heat

in my body that healed
me, I break open and offer
you on a ceremonial platter,

the human heart.

Marjorie Agosín

MUJERES

Indocumentada
con los alfabetos vacíos
y un abanico de huesos
girando entre los dedos
he olvidado las palabras
que nunca existieron
porque ellos me nombraban
al penetrarme en una
redondez de nubes
y secretos consagrados.

Indocumentada
soy la mujer
sin consonantes ni sonidos
sin mi nombre
para pronunciarme
mis cabellos
son granizos, neblinas
tiemblan
al escribirme
al juntar alimentos
porque todos me
echan de los clubes
de los cines
de la sociedad de escritores
los viejos poetas
hacen suyos
mis decires
mientras me llaman
ángel
pez
luz
y puta
por supuesto.

Humberto J. Peña

LA MUCHACHA DEL VESTIDO NEGRO

Hace tres días que he llegado a Miami y todavía no tengo trabajo. Me he pasado esos tres días visitando redacciones de periódicos y revistas. Había estudiado con cuidado y ensayado varias veces lo que le iba a decir a la persona que me entrevistara, pero lo que nunca me había imaginado era que tuviera que visitar tantas redacciones y que me entrevistaran tantas personas y que todavía no tuviera trabajo.

Hoy por la mañana no me quedó más remedio que ir al Refugio y solicitar la ayuda económica que dan a todos los cubanos. En realidad me sentí avergonzado cuando la cogí: un cheque por sesenta pesos y una tarjetica para coger comida. La comida era leche en polvo, harina y no sé que más; la tarjetica se la daré al amigo con quien vivo, el pobre, tres hijos, la esposa y sin trabajo. También le daré algo de los sesenta pesos que cogí; pero eso sí todo se lo devolveré al Refugio en cuanto pueda. En el Refugio me encontré a un amigo, que ya tiene un "transportation" y gana algo llevando a otros refugiados a buscar la comida; me dijo que en la revista "Borcas" estaban buscando a alguien que les escribiera un cuento y que hasta pagarían por él. Fue por eso que compré papel y un bolígrafo y que hace tres horas que estoy sentado en este Parque de las Palomas tratando de escribir un cuento, pero no me sale nada, sólo atino a pensar que no he almorzado y que ya no almorzaré. Si aquí la gente con dinero no almuerza, por qué yo que no lo tengo he de hacerlo; además esta noche iré a la exposición de las pinturas de Clavijo y allí seguramente que dan galleticas y refrescos. Siempre me ha gustado Clavijo—en mi apartamento en La Habana tenía un cuadro de él comprado con un cheque inesperado que recibí del editor de mi primer libro de cuentos.

Empecé a caminar sin proponérmelo y sólo me di cuenta que estaba a las puertas de la galería por el barullo de la gente. Al entrar tropecé con una muchacha vestida de negro, con un escote demasiado pronunciado; le tumbé la cartera. Me agaché a recogerla y cuando se la entregué, ni un músculo cambió en su rostro; la expresión de éste me hizo recordar una careta, no decía nada. Sin embargo, era una careta bonita, tenía una bonita cara. Ella iba acompañada por un hombre que tenía todas las características de un imbécil y que tampoco me dio las gracias. Me dieron ganas de mandarlos para el carajo, pero determiné que ya bastantes preocupaciones tenía para buscarme más. Me dieron el programa y empecé a mirar los cuadros como siempre hacía; miraba todos, haciendo una selección de los mejores. En la segunda vuelta me limitaba a mirar sólo los seleccionados en la primera; entonces los interpretaba y confrontaba mi interpretación con la del programa. Después veía el resto. Por algún motivo oculto, esta vez cambié el sistema—quizás fuera que el quinto cuadro me llamó mucho la atención. Me senté frente a él. Era un laberinto con distintos niveles y siempre en declive. Estaba seguro que ese cuadro me iba a inspirar el cuento que necesitaba. Me figuré varias personas en el laberinto todas cayéndose y después flotando como si estuvieran en el vacío.

De pronto una voz de mujer me pidió permiso para sentarse al lado mío. Levanté la vista: era la mujer del vestido negro de escote pronunciado. Sin esperar mi contestación se sentó. No miraba al cuadro, me miraba a mí; me dijo: "Lo reconocí a usted cuando lo vi de lejos; cuando tropezó conmigo a la entrada no lo reconocí. Si supiera, he leído todos sus cuentos y tenía en Cuba sus dos libros. No, no me diga nada, porque es tal la satisfacción que me han dado que tengo contraída una gran deuda con usted; pero no he venido adonde usted sólo por eso, es que necesito hoy hablar con una persona comprensiva, que pueda entender situaciones que no haya vivido y que no juzgue ni busque explicaciones a las cosas que ocurren, sino que simplemente las acepte como cosas integrantes de lo que se llama vida. . . ."

Mientras hablaba la miraba por primera vez con detenimiento; tenía grandes ojos negros, un pelo negro largo, nariz fina, labios perfectos para ser besados, pero sobre todo los senos, casi se le veían completos, el escote era tan bajo que . . .

". . .usted como escritor, supongo reúna todas esas características. No creo que usted diga que no las reúne; supongo que esté por arriba de esa masa ignorante que es modesta porque no le queda más remedio. Creo que el prototipo de esa masa a la que me refiero es el señor con quien estaba; lo acabo de dejar, me ahogaba. Claro, sé la pregunta que se estará haciendo, ¿por qué salí con él? Pues muy sencillo, porque no tenía otro con quien salir. Conozco a muy pocas personas. Sí, ya sé lo que piensa, que cómo no siendo fea no voy a conocer a más de una persona para salir con ella. Bueno, pues muy simple, he dedicado nueve años de mis veintisiete a un hombre, del que no sé nada desde el martes. Sé que acaba de sacar la cuenta, sí señor, desde los dieciocho años estoy con él; ¿mi familia?, preguntará Ud. No tengo, sí, no tengo familia. Mamá y papá murieron cuando yo contaba ocho años, era única hija de padres que a su vez fueron únicos hijos. Los albaceas de la herencia y mi tutor determinaron ponerme pupila en un colegio de monjas. Allí estuve hasta los dieciocho años en que terminé el bachillerato y en que me capacitaron legalmente para administrar mis bienes. Me entregaron la casa donde había vivido con mis padres y adonde me fui a vivir. Era una casa muy grande, llena de sirvientes; jardineros, chofer, cuatro criadas. Era mucho para mí, acostumbrada a la vida humilde y sencilla de pupilaje en el convento. Mi ex-tutor, que era el nuevo administrador de mis bienes, me aconsejó que sacrificara parte del jardín que rodeaba mi casa y fabricara en él un edificio de apartamentos, y así lo hice. Conocí al arquitecto, un señor de cuarenta años al cual veía casi todos los días durante los seis meses que duró la fabricación del edificio. El día en que le dieron el habitable al edificio, sorpresivamente, me invitó a comer. Comí con él y estuvimos saliendo por dos años. Durante ese tiempo me hizo saber claramente que era enemigo del matrimonio y que una pareja debía vivir junta hasta que se quisieran y ni un minuto más y que el matrimonio era algo que entorpecía el verdadero amor. Me reía de esas ideas y le contraponía las mías, es decir, las que me habían enseñado en el colegio. Pero, con el transcurso del tiempo, me enamoré de él, hasta el extremo de no poder oponerme más a sus ideas y empezamos a vivir juntos; es decir, juntos pero él en su apartamento y yo en mi casa. Es un hombre encantador, pinta, sabe de música y no hay novela que se publique que no lea. Le estoy muy agradecida, se ocupó de mi educación, me hizo estudiar pintura, guitarra y literatura. Es un encanto. El, por su parte, no me dejó de ver ni un solo día, me celaba, al extremo de molestarme a veces, y siempre me hacía muchos regalos. Tengo muchas joyas, joyas buenas y todas regaladas por él. Después vino el exilio, en el cual me considero una privilegiada, pues parte del dinero de papá estaba invertido en este país. Con respecto a él, con la escasez de arquitectos en este estado en seguida encontró un gran trabajo. Entonces, dirá usted, ¿qué ha pasado?, ¿por qué no lo ve desde el martes? Se dirá, estamos sólo a jueves, a lo mejor está enfermo. ¿Ha llamado a su oficina? Sí, ha estado allí pero no contesta a mis llamadas. Claro que hay una razón, una poderosa razón para su comportamiento, yo la sé, pero me costó tanto aceptarla. Verá usted, el martes por la tarde me dieron el diagnóstico definitivo. Lo que tanto temía y sin embargo esperaba. Primero vinieron los reconocimientos, después la biopsia de una pequeña porción de tejido y por último, el martes, el diagnóstico fatal: Era cáncer y me tenían que extirpar el seno izquierdo; me lo extirparán el viernes. Sí, mañana. Esta noche ingreso, tengo la maleta en el automóvil, de aquí voy al hospital. No trate de disimular, la noticia lo ha afectado. Es por eso que me puse este vestido hoy, será la última oportunidad de ponérmelo y créame, primera vez que me lo pongo. Pues bien, esa noche, la del martes, le dije todo. Me calmó, me reconfortó, me hizo sentirme bien; pero cuando nos acostamos supe que ya no lo vería más. No me besó como acostumbraba, ni los tocó. Yo, aun sabiendo que no lo vería más, quería que me besara el seno enfermo, el que iba a perder, quería sentirlo por última vez. No tuve fuerzas para pedírselo, ya lo sabía ajeno."

En ese momento sentí el barullo de gente pasar por mi lado rumbo a la puerta. Los miré cuando ya me daban la espalda. La última del grupo era la muchacha del vestido negro; iba cogida del brazo del hombre con el que la había visto entrar. Me levanté; iban a cerrar el local. No había visto casi nada de la exposición, pero estaba contento, ya tenía el cuento, sólo me faltaba ponerle un final.

María del Carmen Boza

ETRUSCANS

Susana thought she was taking quite a chance with her vacation. Serafín's house, however rural and apparently peaceful its setting, was too near Three Mile Island for comfort, and one year from nuclear near-catastrophe is not a long time. She had looked at a map only after she had written inviting herself. Serafín had told her he lived in the Pennsylvania countryside amid rolling hills. As he drove her from the train station, she could see he did live in the country and that everything in his visible environment conspired to forget that not too far off the power company was still venting radiation from those tall twin towers. Her skin felt electric with fright. The sensation was not altogether unpleasant. It was something of a thrill, as if stepping down into a cellar full of snakes.

The afternoon was under threat of rain. She had feared bad weather during her journey, but, thus far, the dark clouds had held their water, and Serafín assured her she would soon be at his house under cover.

They passed a low, white stucco house in the middle of a large lot on top of a singularly graceful small hill. The house seemed to have been transplanted from a western desert. A few widely spaced tall conifers stood at its log fence, but between them and the house nothing grew but grass. Yet in that unvegetated stretch all space seemed contained, and despite the lowness of the glowing dark clouds, Susana had a feeling of air, air, infinite air. In that instant of perceiving the house—for an instant is all that these perceptions took—her claustrophobic city oppression left her for the summer. Relief came with oxygen, but that was all; the rest remained, she knew—the deep depression, the reasons why she left her work.

The very next house was Serafín's. She was glad to arrive at it already acclimated to the country. It was a solid, comforting house, very different from the house on the hill. The lawn had thick, carefully groomed ground cover. Ivy crept up the façade. Shrubbery and trees were dense on one side. The house inside was cool and dark like a house lined with greenery on a day preparing for rain. The first thing she noticed was the wall covered with bookshelves. She need not have lugged books from the city.

"There are more upstairs," Serafín assured her. "Oh, it's too dark today. You won't get an accurate impression of the place. The back gets a lot of sun. That's where I have my vegetable patch. And you must, you must come see my greenhouse."

Where he grew orchids. For years he had written her about his orchids without making himself understood. Orchids, computers, medicine, everything was details, but the details were in a foreign language.

In a corner near a window of the dark, soothing living room stood a small mahogany table on which Serafín had placed a clear blue vase which concentrated the light in the room and emphasized the dark. A bottle for messages, thought Susana—but, no, its shape was elegantly uterine. In the vase Serafín had stood a stalk with many creamy-white orchid blooms like so many round, flat faces lined up to nod agreement should a breeze be allowed to reach them. The room was closed against the possibility of rain. The flowers' fragrance filled it.

"Lovely orchids," Susana said. She felt weak; she did not say that.

"Vandas, one of the first genera I ever tried," Serafín said fondly. "They grow outdoors in Florida."

"Can you tell me something about the house next door, uphill?" she asked.

"Tom Burns's house." He seemed to have expected the question. "It has a far view of the lake. Unfortunately, we don't. Burns is a strange guy. I don't think he's ever planted a shrub, a vegetable, a flower. Those trees were there when he bought the place. He's one of our summer folk. Absentee landlord the rest of the year. One can't blame him for taking his vacations seriously, I suppose, but when I think of how much could be grown on his land I have a fit."

Susana could easily see Serafín having a fit.

Two days later, during a stroll, she had a chance to see the summer person who grew space on his land. He was a light-framed, sandy-haired man of medium height. As he walked he seemed as spare as his house. He reached his front door and disappeared completely. The glimpse at the mystery was over.

Many of the householders around them, less remarkable than Tom Burns, were also summer people who sublet their dwellings the rest of the year—to students and artists, people willing to rough a winter for the sake of a rustic house. Of the permanent residents, some, like Serafín, were professionals who had chosen to push beyond the suburbs out to the real countryside, as they believed it to be, in exchange for a commute. Serafín was not as road-crazy as the rest of this group; the college where he taught was a reasonable distance away. Some of the neighbors were shopkeepers in the town. Many families had lived in the area for a century or more. There were farms all around them, and some of these were run by old-fashioned farmers who clung to old-fashioned ways of dress and prayer and by their old-fashioned wives who made old-fashioned quilts: "Trip Around the World" without leaving the land you were born in.

Save for the radiation, this seemed a good place for Serafín. He had much of the farmer about him.

Two blocks away from the Miami apartment in which Susana grew up stood a bright pink house owned by Chinese who, like her who was not Chinese, had come from Cuba. The other remarkable feature of this house was that every available inch of ground had been turned into a vegetable garden, a fairly common thing in other parts, but not in Miami. There the soil is sandy and rocky. Coconut palms, dracaenas, croton, bromeliads, and snake plants—plant life that had a pact with the climate—grew in other neighbors' yards, here and there, but roses were difficult and food plants damn near incredible. The residents of the pink house, with magic or stubbornness, coaxed from the sandy ground strange vegetation in farming rows, obviously food crops of a Chinese sort. Apparently, the chief persuader of plenty was an old Chinese man as silent and strange as the greenery. He bent like an old stick permanently over his garden. When Susana and her family drove to church on Sundays they always saw him and her parents made a comment.

Sometime after she got shuffled into the same sixth grade class with Serafín, she found out from one of the other children, Bertha to be precise, that he was one of the denizens of the pink house. The fact struck her as strange. The news of his habitation of a mysterious place made him seem a bit spooky, but the strangeness went deeper. Serafín did not fit into the house somehow. Her family would say as they drove past the pink house on Sundays, "There's Serafín's relative!" But she had found the kinship harder to accept. How could nervous—really, hysterical—Serafín be related to that calm, dignified man? How was it possible that the thin stick man and Serafín's baby-round body and face could be flesh of the same flesh? The man might be an uncle by marriage at the most.

One day after she and the boy had started going to different schools, her mother saw something of Serafín that Susana would rather have passed blindly by. As they walked in front of the pink house, her mother stood still, pointed, and exclaimed, "Look, all of Serafín's relatives!"

Susana grew panicky. All of them? How many? All standing in a group expecting to be introduced, judging her, scowling, demanding reparation? At first she did not want to look in the direction toward which her mother pointed. She did not want to look at the pink house because it was strange, a mysterious place. She finally looked at the house and, to her dismay, through the window which was at eye level and uncurtained and impossible to avoid looking through. Inside the living room, on the wall opposite the window—in fact, framed by the frame of the window—was a wall covered with photographs of Chinese people. Some photographs were new color snapshots. Others were brownish and old; in these the sitter strove for dignity. Two large, serious portraits were set apart from the rest. A chill went through her. She was looking, she was sure, not only at Serafín's far-flung cousins but at his near dead. Serafín had mentioned a grandmother, an aunt, some sisters (number unspecified). He never talked of a mother or father. She had never asked about them. They might be dead; they might be in Cuba. At twelve she had not wanted to know. She had not asked him what his relation was to the man in the garden and she could not do so for years, until she saw him again.

Her mother was amused by Serafín's big family commemorated on the wall, for to her it was just a matter of many relatives. Susana grew annoyed with her. To her mother the thing was simple because she did not know Serafín well. The green growingness of the garden, the flaunting of human generation following generation, such prolificness, were at odds with Serafín, the 12-year-old boy who, with a high-pitched voice, screamed about everything and fluttered his hands in unjustified excitement that reached a level of hysteria with the least provocation.

So little did her mother know him that she postponed a shopping trip to act as chaperone on the day Serafín came to finish with Susana their school project, a fictional magazine. She had written impassioned editorials against Communist takeovers of invented lands. He had reviewed movies he had never seen because they had never been shot. That Saturday afternoon they did the layout on Susana's dining table. They worked well together, much more calmly than when other children were around. Her mother was unobtrusive, but the back of Susana's neck followed her every movement. Her mother was ridiculous. In her twelfth year of healthy life Susana was much taller and more mature, physically and emotionally, than most boys her age, but especially Serafín. There was no sign on him of puberty's approach. And as to his character, he screamed whenever a sixth-grader made an insinuating remark, however mild. From Serafín's hot blood and manly importuning her mother was going to protect her. Serafín accepted her mother's presence as inevitable, for Susana was, after all, a well-brought-up Cuban girl. Susana chafed. She was twice Serafín's size. She could have knocked him flat with one blow.

That was sixth grade. Now that she was Serafín's summer guest, she still had a well-brought-up image to maintain for far-away Miami. Innocent as the circumstances were, she told her parents that Serafín's grandmother, heaven forbid, was living with them. She told the lie easily and did not chafe at having to tell it. She was their 28-year-old, unmarried, hot-blooded daughter. Mendacity was their modus vivendi.

She still felt surprised to be where she was. Now she worked at Serafín's garden in a northerly climate in a house he had filled by himself, apparently to his satisfaction, until she had invited herself upon him for emergency reasons. To get here they had had to meet again after sixth grade, which they did their final year of different high schools. On that occasion, he looked physically the same as in sixth grade except for height; in addition he had acquired the unimpeachable air of being remarkably upstanding, neat, clean-cut, dependable. Susana also looked physically the same, including height, but she had gotten grungier.

She remembered that the day he had gone to her apartment to work on their magazine, he had looked and smelled as if he had just come from a bath and his shirt was newly put on. And there he was, a high school senior going to brainy-student meetings in a blazer, and insisting on carrying her tray, and looking after her solicitously. There he was with so much courtesy when she was eighteen and had come to accept ill treatment from males as the norm from rubs with the wrong kind of guy.

The first evening she saw Serafín in his blazer she was not quite eighteen. It was the fall, or would have been up north, and they had gone to meet with a representative from Brown University. They went to the meeting because few colleges bothered with Florida. Serafín looked so happy to see her—even after the reprehensible way she had treated him, for which she would never forgive herself. He was worried about his SAT math score; so was she. He didn't see how she could worry about admission. Who would reject her? She was much too good, brilliant Susana. Susana didn't say so, but she knew he was at least as good as she was. Serafín waited till she talked to the Brown alumnus, sure she would get reassurance. She didn't, but she got in and then didn't go and neither did he. Her mind was set on international affairs and loose dormitory rules. She got a master's and knew a lot about the lawlessness of nations.

That Brown night, Serafín told her, "I want to go to Harvard because they have a greenhouse where I could grow orchids." He said it with a wistfulness that made her wish that wherever college admissions took him there would be a warm, well-lit corner for his exotic growing.

Orchids remained his love. Over them he toiled and fussed in the greenhouse he had added to his house. The vegetable garden was his gesture toward family. In the severe utilitarianism of their garden he had acquired the attitude that what one did with soil, however unpromising the material, was to squeeze plant life out of it, but in the exquisiteness of his mind he rejected as an end in itself the purely useful and edible. Beauty had him in thrall. He had gotten his wish to grow orchids in college and, while there, had immersed himself in beauty of various sorts. Some of that had paled, now that the requirements of his profession put pressure on him to produce intelligent but uninspired papers and the teaching life had become a cyclical sterility of English writers expounded to unreceptive ears, Milton revealed with a slight accent that his audience would not recognize. They would see Chinese but would not hear the Spanish lilt so familiar to her, not in this part of the world. He had no security, of course. For someone his age, there was no tenure track. He wrote as fast as he could in order not to have to move anywhere before he was ready.

He seemed sometimes to want to be devoured by his orchids. As he approached them his mood and concentration changed. He grew as profoundly silent as his grandfather amid his plantings. He seemed to withdraw into the flowers themselves, as if his soul were sucked in by them, refreshed, and returned to him whole and clean. Susana, watching him, imagined a homunculus Serafín in fetal position in the secret scent place of the flower looking apprehensively at the translucency of the veined walls that surrounded him.

He lost himself in his cultivated wilderness, and she liked to hover about in it quietly as a visitor who would not know every leaf but would see the jungle, tropics, something lost to them before they had it, tropics: gone forever. She had asked him if he had been to Soroa, the waterfall where they grew orchids. He hadn't. She had. She knew what she had lost, with or without a Pennsylvania greenhouse to tell her. He wanted to move to California for the climate. Bullshit, climate. Climates are cruel everywhere one goes.

Yet she could put memory to sleep and she could be at peace in his beautiful glassed-in world that smelled green or heady or rotting depending on what was open. Some of the species were stemmy, odd. They repelled her. She did not know what they were about. She preferred the balance to be tipped in favor of large inflorescences in almost obscenely sexual shapes in colors to stun. She enjoyed the incongruity of his life with his avocation.

For the business of orchid-growing is obsessive coupling. In an excitement that threatened to approach the soprano heights of which he was capable at twelve, Serafín showed her his studbooks. He spoke of the criteria for cross-breeding, one Greek name with a Latin, three Greeks together and a cottagey English surname on the side. He wanted her to like his love. She liked his flowers but hated their anxious history, their ponderous lineage, nature made solemn. It was unseemly somehow that the man who still squeaked nervously at human sexuality should have such a need to propagate and talk about it.

He was neglecting work for pleasure. He suffered the proper amount of guilt for a Christian.

"A colleague of mine is organizing a Shakespeare conference," he said to her, wincing. "I've promised him a paper on Hazlitt's criticism. A criticism of a critic, just the sort of thing I'd get saddled with. I don't want to do it and I can't make myself do it. I'm getting a lot worse with age. Time was I was given a job and I got it over with right away."

"Unlike Susana the Great Procrastinator. Bertha and I never did write the puppet show Mrs. Timothy wanted us to put on for the smaller kids. We just didn't want to."

"There are things I'd rather be doing," Serafín continued obsessively. "The problem is my career is threatening to take time away from my hobby. There are some crossings I'd like to try. I've been planning them for a long time. I think I could get a Brassolaelio-cattleya of prize-winning color. And the Coelogyne are so gorgeous right now, don't you think?"

"Oh, yes. I spent quite a long time staring at them recently."

"Do you know which ones they are?" he asked with suspicion.

"Spot of rust in the middle. Listen, don't forget whom you're talking to. I'm not one of your freshmen staring at the clock, thinking of nothing but lunch. As to the Brassothingies, I think the ones you have already come in good colors. What's the point of fiddling with them any more? Are you trying for a flower that moos in Greek?"

Serafín sighed with an impatience that pretended to be patience. "You're teasing. The very basis of agriculture and horticulture cannot be beyond your comprehension. If vegetable gardeners, for example, had not constantly attempted to improve the quality of their crops through hybrids, our diet and its quantity would not be as good today as they are. Our ancestors ate a far inferior kind of pea, less nutritious and less tasty."

"Yet they survived to the point of producing our other ancestors and that's all nature cares about. And while we're on the subject, I, at least, am the product of weak-kneed human carelessness. That is the attention we give to producing high-quality progeny. When we try to explain we refer to vague markers such as chemistry and a look in the eyes—'Ooh! he's so cute!' As my high school biology teacher pointed out. Too bad you never knew her. Your studbooks so carefully kept, your orchids so perfect—what will be the use of it all when some lunatic produced by random mating blows us all sky high? It doesn't even take a maniac, just an incompetent."

Serafín was sitting with his arms crossed, his head resting on the back of his wooden chair, his eyes closed. His lips were tightly pursed; he always pursed his lips when he was annoyed. "You're in a very nasty mood today, very perverse. Like Bertha almost—don't scream. I can tell when something is bothering you. You take an extreme view on a subject and beat it to death."

"I'm not in a nasty mood."

"Yes, you are, but I'd be happy to drop the subject. If something's bothering you, you have ten minutes to tell me before I have to go check on the duck."

"Thanks," she said, of course not meaning thanks. "All right. I'll tell you. I don't see—" She stopped. She did not even know what she meant to say. She had been going to be peevish.

She collected her thoughts and began again, this time in a kinder tone, "Listen, Serafín, I don't think you should feel bad about the Hazlitt paper you haven't done. Shakespeare is overrated anyway. The conference isn't important. Believe me, it isn't. Have fun with your orchids and leave the guilt of work not done to someone on whose work lives depend."

"So that's it. Poor Susana. I thought you were recovering. All the people you help . . ."

"Sometimes I think I suffer from hubris. Maybe no one's life depends on me. I overrate myself."

"Now and then I read the publications that you send me. Not the details of tortures; that's what has you this way. I read the victory stories. Governments relent. People get released. Not just because of you, of course. Because of everybody working hard at what you do—you're one of the bodies. What you do is wonderful and necessary and they are—we are—lucky to have someone as capable as you doing it. But not many people could stand the sort of psychological punishment you take for long. Just look at you."

Susana felt she would weep, but she checked her impulse. Her voice came out tremulous. "You embarrass me," she said. "I'm sorry I criticized your orchids. You're very nice. You're the nicest person I've ever known."

"Oh, no, no. You're nice in a bigger way."

"That's not true."

"Yes, it is. I'm so glad you like the Brassolaeliocattleyas as they are, even if they don't moo. I'm glad to see you've retained your sense of humor, appalling though it is. But you'll like my crosses, you'll see. They'll be stupendous."

"I also like the Coelogyne and those that have their arms outstretched." Like a person who'd had too much suffering. Like a person worn down by flesh, streaked with blood, calling for help or death—either one, it wouldn't matter. Like the thousands calling out to her.

"Paphiopedilum. You like them all, don't you?" he asked her with beatific eagerness.

"The spindly ones puzzle me a bit, but, yes, I like them all."

"I'm so glad." He looked it.

She wished him happiness in the future that she thought she could read as if it were his past. He would write the paper on Hazlitt. It would be insightful and well documented. He would type it neatly and place it between black pebbled covers for protection, as he had done in sixth grade with his report on presidents. One day he would chuck it all, tell the scholar machinery, politely, to stuff itself. (He might use the word "taxidermy.") He would move to California, leaving Milton for Miltonias, the exposition of immortals for beauty of a more ephemeral, biological kind. At least, she hoped he would. He was such a pudgy thing, in need of a grandmother, happiness, and something to get excited about.

It would have astounded the child Susana to hear that one day she would help a scion of the pink house tend his own garden. Yet that is what she now did habitually, after a fashion.

She had started out with no knowledge of how to behave in a garden, how to move, where to step. She walked stiffly, afraid to crush something important underground with aspirations to see the sun. Serafín had refused to believe that she could be so ignorant on any subject, but the evidence of his eyes had convinced him of the truth. Patiently he explained to her everything, answering her hundreds of questions about the most elementary things.

"I've never had a garden," she said over and over.

Despite her awkwardness, Serafín expressed confidence that she would soon manage just fine.

One thing she was afraid to do was to cut.

"I have peasant relatives," she said. "A cousin of my father once told me that if you don't cut sugar cane in the right place, it won't come back the following year. Cane-cutting is an art, he said, and to truck city people out to cane fields is to court disaster."

MARIA DEL CARMEN BOZA

She looked woefully at the knife in her hand.

"Well, it's different with green peppers," Serafín reassured her. "They don't much care. Anyway, I have to replant most of the things in the garden next year, so don't be afraid. Cut away. As a matter of fact," he said, thinking things over, "you'd be doing me a favor if you kept the squash from coming back. I don't ever want to see another squash plant."

Neither did she. Serafín had planted zucchini and crooknecked squash because they grew so well, too well for the two of them. He had regional cousins he could usually unload the garden surplus on, but they were visiting in Taiwan. He gave some to Tom Burns. She wondered if Tom Burns ever ate as healthy a thing as a vegetable; his skin was greyish. But he accepted what they could not eat.

He would come over to the fence and talk politely to Serafín while looking down sullenly at her, and if she approached him he would ask her, in several versions and never directly, what ever gave her the right to be a do-gooder student of torture and didn't she know that people had their entrails pulled out on the floor of the Stock Exchange? She explained to him, in different ways, that she had never thought her profession required permission and, yes, she knew all about financial eviscerations but that nobody got dragged to them who didn't want to go. She told him once, when Serafín was out of earshot, that the market was like a pervert's penis: always going up and down for the wrong reasons.

Damn impudent he was. Bleeding all over the fence about the perils of investment, to her who had to mooch holiday shelter from friends.

When Tom Burns's dark cloud was not hovering near, Serafín attempted to lower the level of her anxiety by getting her to sing with him while they did mechanical chores about the garden. He always intoned "Oh, Susanna," the song he had pursued and teased her with almost the entire nine months of the sixth grade. "Oh, Susanna, don't you cry for me."

Susana would sing to him,

> San Serafín del monte,
> San Serafín cortés,
> Y yo como buen cristiano
> me arrodillaré.

She liked to sing it when she was already on her knees pulling up weeds and could make it seem that she was kneeling before him, as the song said, because she was a good Christian, which she wasn't, and because he was courteous, which he was supremely. And Serafín would pshaw and wave the song away and look as flattered underneath his dismissal as she felt when he sang her "Oh, Susanna" and she said, "All right, I won't cry for you. Don't worry," ever since she was twelve. He had never heard the Spanish song before she sang it to him as an adult, but, then, she had had a mother to learn it from. One played a game to it, but he never had done it. She wondered what games he had played in the country where they were born. She wondered how different his Cuba had been from hers. But she never asked.

Eventually, she gained enough poise in the garden not to worry about her feet or the secret requirements of centimeters of stem.

One afternoon as she looked up triumphantly from severing the vine of a melon, she saw Serafín standing absolutely still a few feet away from her in the same bare strip, staring with terror at the ground between them. He seemed unwilling even to allow his body the subtle movements of breathing. Susana looked in the direction of his stare. A snake had flared its hood, puffed itself up, and was striking at the air in front of Serafín. What Susana had absentmindedly imagined to be the noise of some tire-inflating activity while she concentrated on the melon she now instantly connected with the horrific reptile before her. A tremor ran through her the moment she perceived it. A snake, fangs, fangs in the ankles normally, but she was crouching—fangs in the wrists—death. Suffering, then death. Death through blood or nerves. Almost unbearable suffering before death. And all the time the knowledge that something must be done. They could not go on standing or crouching still forever.

Ten seconds had passed since she first saw the threatening, stabbing, hissing, puffed-up reptile. She studied the hood whose back was visible to her and not to Serafín. She noticed the shape of its head when it tilted it back before a strike.

She stood up from her crouch, swiftly approached the snake from behind, and, fighting back a primitive caution, touched it. Immediately, it twitched pitifully, then rolled over on its back, immobile. Serafín gave out a piercing scream.

"You killed it!" he screamed. "The cobra! You're wonderful!"

"It's not dead," she said. She turned the snake over on its stomach. It rolled itself onto its back again. Serafín painfully drew in his breath. She picked up the snake and displayed it between her upturned hands like a gift bolt of cloth. She moved forward toward Serafín.

"Don't come near me," he said hysterically, but softly so as not to anger the snake. "You've gone crazy. It's a snake. Take it away."

"It's a *hognosed* snake," Susana specified, but Serafín was not at all reassured. "It's not a cobra. I thought it might be an escaped cobra at first," she continued breezily, "oh, for a few seconds anyway. No, this is a hognosed snake. It's harmless. We're probably scaring it half to death."

"*We're* probably scaring it!" Now Serafín was angry as well as frightened. She was having a wonderful time, even if her knees had not quite stopped feeling weak.

"It has dry, wonderful skin. Come feel it," she urged.

He made a sound of deep revulsion. "You're making me sick," he said, and for the first time seemed to realize that, the reptile captive, he could just turn on his heel and walk away. As he marched to the house he ordered, "Get it out of here! Get it out of here!"

Susana, petting the snake, carried it over to Tom Burns's fence, where she put it down. It quickly slithered away through the grass in Tom Burns's lot.

When she walked into Serafín's house, knowing she would face recriminations, she adopted the attitude of someone who wished very much to do him a favor.

"Really, Serafín, a gardener should be familiar with common snakes. The hognose, for example, likes cultivated fields. You might confuse one with a poisonous snake and kill it, heaven forbid."

"Oh, I might, might I?"

"After they've been in captivity awhile they stop doing their puff-and-death scene. They can be very tame."

"You didn't bring it in here, did you?" he asked with alarm.

"No, of course not. One has to feed them live toads. I like toads. I just couldn't do that to a toad. I set the poor snake loose in Tom Burns's yard."

Serafín produced a strange choking noise but did not otherwise comment on this use of a neighbor's land. "How come a city person who's afraid to step on soil knows so much about snakes?" he asked suspiciously.

"I stayed with a herpetologist for a couple of months. That was in the summer too. I learn something from everyone I stay with in the summer. He had cages and cages of snakes, but the hognose were among my favorites, except at feeding time, of course."

That had been a different sort of summer sojourn, not one of rest, that is to say a love affair of sorts and commuting to work. He had not turned out to be very nice, but the descent into his cool, damp basement where she knew she would find cages of snakes lining the walls, where she might put her foot down next to an escaped snake that was not benign, had kept her interested for two months. As she descended the steps into the dark, animal-filled cellar amid furtive slitherings and tremors in metal she felt a wave of sexual excitement pass through her. The herpetologist had noticed, and invariably he followed her when he saw her go down to visit his cages. No, it was impossible to explain any of it to Serafín, and the man had not even been nice. Serafín would never understand her abiding for one minute behavior less thoughtful and courteous than his.

"You were coming at me with the snake," he remonstrated.

"It was harmless, like a Cuban snake. There were no poisonous snakes in Cuba. I don't know where you got your phobia."

It had not been an escaped cobra. Although she shook through it all a little, she had thoroughly enjoyed herself.

Serafín went to church twice on Sundays. In sixth grade his Protestantism had seemed a quirk, an extreme assimilation. It seemed more fitting to her that as a Cuban Chinese he should be either Catholic or Buddhist. If assimilation it was, it took. Now she imagined him driving off to church in a horse-drawn cart, as people of the land around them still did even though their country was overrun by outsiders whose connection with the territory was frivolous and aestival. Serafín would blend in with these German-descended farmers, their wives, their quilts and hills, until he could not be discerned, a part of the geometric pattern of agriculture. In reality, Serafín drove a gas-economy car with shiny bumpers and went to an unremarkable church for which he dressed up in a blazer, looking like the respectable college instructor that he was. He sang in the choir on Sunday evenings, which were depressingly quiet for Susana.

Her compensation was that she had the run of the house. Unobtrusive as Serafín was, there was a special feeling for her in playing mistress of the rooms through which she wandered without the possibility of anyone reminding her otherwise. Her real empire was a New York studio apartment facing a New York apartment.

As the dusk set slowly in, she made herself lemonade, opened the French doors to the back porch, and sat on the swing, determined to enjoy the shifting of time from light to dark, but an uncharacteristic noise from Tom Burns's backyard impeded her pleasure. Tom Burns, who seemed so unconnected to everything and everyone, had guests. Not only were there adults who chattered politely and now and then laughed, there were children as well. She found it difficult to believe that he could in any way be tied to children. Their whoops cut through the horizontal-log fence and Serafín's planting and forced her to retreat indoors.

She took a volume of Herrick from Serafín's wall-wide bookcase, ran up the stairs to her room, and shut herself in to read. The lamp on the desk in her room shed a yellow light; she hated that. She could not concentrate on Herrick. The sun had shone all day on her room and it was hot. She had to open the window.

The voices of Tom Burns's humans carried through the few trees in small waves to her and she could almost grasp intimacies. The crickets were filling the air with insistence and it all seemed much too much, no space to breathe, a surfeit of song. No escape into the self was possible in that outdoor, open-windowed season. She lay on her quilted bed-spread and resigned herself to listen to Tom Burns's party as she would to distant music, a Mozart quartet perhaps, as the smell of the dusk-opening flowers and the gradually greying green grass seemed to recommend. She thought dispassionately, for it was an old thought, that children's cries reminded her of the youth for which she had had no talent. The sound of the adults' conviviality made her think, passionately, of the crisp sheets under the quilt and of her desire to wrestle with a naked body under them, soon, if possible, and she would not mind if it were done to the sound of other people's over-heard merriment, major or minor. Her mind had not turned to sex much lately—from depression, she supposed—but her long chastity of the summer was unusual for her and her mind turned to sex now in a rush of longing.

The stretch of pine trees around the lake was called by locals The Forest. It was sim-ply land where trees had not been sacrificed to housing. Susana would not bet a nickel on their longevity. Because the day was muggy, she proceeded slowly. The ground was needly and pebbly. She took off her thong sandals and attempted to walk barefoot for a while. She only managed that a short distance before the pain in her sitter's soles became too sharp. She knelt down on the ground to test it. She soon got up and picked off the needles that made deep, red marks. The way to comfort was through the thickness of her shorts, but she did not want to sit.

She got to the lake and began to walk around it, intending to do its whole circum-ference. At one point, where the path came to the very edge of the lake, she saw a dead white fish floating in the shallow water that lapped the ground. Next to it were an empty beer can and two cigarette butts. She got a chilly feeling, which she liked, the day being so hot.

"*El pez muere por la boca*," she remembered. A fish dies by its mouth. Because it was clever, this warning was given to Cuban children in a joking way. It was ostensibly about food. Later on she knew her parents had spoken of desire, and, among desires, of one kind in particular. They may not even have been conscious of alluding to it, but it was the kind most feared by a Cuban parent in an unmarried daughter, and fear abides in the brain like a master gland, impinging on all speech, future actions, and sleep at night.

El pez muere por la boca. A statement to be infinitely re-created. Why delimit what is perfect? She had known all desire to be dangerous. I desire freedom. I desire permission to walk in the sunshine today. I desire your love and your compassion. All, dangerous statements if one meant them wholeheartedly. (*El pez muere por la boca.* Many have died for mouthing their desires.) She had learned to desire without desiring too much. It took keen eyesight, but one could, in time, learn to recognize a worm that came with a hook. She laughed at herself. She had just talked herself into believing she was a Taoist sage. Susana the Undesiring, the same Susana who wanted to make the world perfect. Susana Who Desires with All Her Heart Not to Desire. Ah, if it could be! Ah!

She heard words and splashing. She did not welcome the sounds, for she was not feeling jovial and the splashers were gigglers and laughers. To her relief, the ground where she walked sloped quite a distance from the lake which was edged with large rocks. She peered down from the cover of the trees at the swimmers. She was stunned to see that they were several adolescents diving in from the rocks and clambering back up on them again, and that it was still the early afternoon and they were all totally naked, boys and girls together. She noticed in particular one girl who was now up to her shoulders in the water. She was speaking loudly to the boys currently on the flat rock. She was aggressive, certain of her dominion over whatever audience she chose to bestow her time upon. She could hardly have seen Susana, yet she seemed sure she was a person who was watched. The others went about their fun less self-consciously. Susana was certain they would all end badly. They would all, even the girl up to her shoulders in water, go on to lead perfectly ordinary middle class lives, probably in suburbs, ignoring all important questions, and, perhaps some of them, even voting Republican for reasons described as economic.

Their bodies were young and whole, and yet they seemed unaware of the enormous blessing they had. They wasted its exhibition on trivial aquatics and lame jokes about present and absent contemporaries. Since she had taken her job, Susana's pleasure in museums had diminished. Much of modern art had grown repulsive to her when its subject was the human figure. She did not like to see it distorted or, worse, reviled. She preferred to see bodies whole and sensual and, if not line-perfect, then as in a Matisse, at a feast.

"Looking at the scenery?" said a loud male voice from behind her. She jumped. The young swimmers scattered, the boys laughing, the girls shrieking—Susana made a mental note of this culturally imposed sexual difference. Immediately she turned around and faced Tom Burns and his leer.

Having caught her breath she said to him, "Well, now you've gone and scared away the pretty ducks who'd left off their feathers."

Tom Burns's leer became more hideously pronounced. He seemed to be enjoying himself.

"Tsk, tsk," he said, "if Serafín were to find out. Tsk, tsk. He thinks you're the apex of western civilization."

"Does he really?"

"Now I've discovered you. You're a voyeur. A peeping Thomasina. A twisted person." Tom Burns was actually laughing.

"I'm not going to argue with the evidence," Susana said. "Are you walking in my direction?"

"Which is that?"

"Home. Serafín's home, to be exact." Where she could hide the embarrassment Tom Burns was exacerbating with every cackle.

"You have given me a great deal of pleasure," he said as they walked. "You jumped two feet in the air."

"Oh, I'm so glad to have given you pleasure. You see, a person who derives pleasure from another's embarrassment, discomfort, or confusion has a few screws loose, if you know what I mean, and might be thought twisted himself. Especially since I haven't done anything bad to you."

"But you have! You have given me looks."

"What sorts of looks?"

"There-goes-the-selfish-capitalist-who-does-nothing-for-humanity sort of looks."

"Capitalist!" she exclaimed in wonder. "You're a stockbroker! Small fry! No, if I've given you looks it's because of your house. It reminds me of a photograph I used to look at a lot, of Sacre Coeur on its hilltop. And it has a view of the lake."

"Which you like to look at for reasons you would rather have kept to yourself." His leer was back. He was getting fish-eyed.

"Why do dead bodies float and live ones sink?" she asked abruptly.

"Huh?"

"Dead bodies, of humans and fish, float to the surface. Why?"

"I don't know. Wait a minute. Something to do with the water in the lungs."

"That's what drowns them," she said. "It's probably the gases given off as the flesh corrupts that buoy up the corpse. Carbon dioxide, maybe methane."

"If you knew the answer, why did you ask?"

"I wasn't sure. I think it's the bacteria eating the rotting flesh that make it phosphorescent. What's the matter? Not interested? Kept your nose to economics, did you? None of this nonsense of a general education for you."

"Death and decay don't hold much fascination for me. I can't think why. I prefer livelier subjects. Psychology, for instance. I took quite a few courses in that. In my youth I thought they might prove useful in my future work."

"And you've found the human being is not predictable," she guessed.

"Only the individual. As a group human beings will always do the wrong things: they'll sell when it's low and buy when it's high. I don't have to tell you that, judging from the forceful way you put it to me the other day. Groups are as predictable as May follows April. But I knew that before forcing white mice through mazes."

"You sound . . . disappointed?"

"I ought not to be. The stupidity of the herd makes me rich."

"But contempt naturally creeps in."

"Not by itself. That's why I'm disappointed. I get annoyed at the intellectual depths to which people can sink. Look, you're human, aren't you?" He waited until Susana verified this with a nod. "Doesn't some of your pride suffer when you see large numbers of humans elbowing one another to do something that has no logical defense?"

"Or all rallying around the centerpost and filing quietly into the pens, as in a national election?" she contributed.

"Annoyance is not a sensible attitude. It's not good for the body," he said, frowning.

"But it's something we have in common. There's a lot to be said in favor of nonsense and passionate risk-taking—righteous annoyance, I'm talking about. I was disappointed when you had May following April exactly right without giving it much thought. It shows a too-careful attention to detail. Bad for the body, no doubt. Now, me, I've never cared about trivia like physical fitness." Neither did Tom Burns by the look of his soft, under-developed muscles. "What do voyeurs do when they go home?"

Tom Burns came up with a version of a smile, rather self-satisifed and Mephistophelian—alarming. "I don't think I can discuss that with a woman," he said, "even one I have caught in a depraved act that would have best been done in private. That would have proved difficult, I grant you. Should I tell Serafín?"

"You don't know Serafín, or you wouldn't ask. He doesn't like to discuss such subjects."

"You're trying to protect yourself. You don't want to be dethroned from your reign as Paragon of Goodness."

"I'm not especially good. I say that to you and I'll say it to him, without going into details. To be good you have to be competent at it. Intentions are nothing."

"Then you insist on putting yourself down and depriving me of the pleasure of doing it for you."

"When you said I was twisted, it was the pot calling the kettle black. See you later, fellow pervert. Don't eat any worms I wouldn't eat."

And what the hell had he been doing, anyway, watching her watching naked youth cavort?

In the quiet of the kitchen, as he poured the jasmine tea, Susana sensed in Serafín a loud internal rattling of something to be said. Susana looked at him expectantly. She was afraid he was going to ask her to leave, for some good reason; there must be plenty. Because she cut the green peppers with too little stem? Because years ago she had wronged him?

He picked up his hands, looked at their backs, and laid them down again.

During the years of their separation she had lain awake some nights, wondering where he was, wishing to apologize. Then she had found him, had discussed the trivia of their past, and had not apologized.

Finally he said, "It's silly of me not to have told you before. I sometimes meant to, but I always forgot. I got a letter today—that reminded me; I am getting married."

She had not expected that.

"My goodness," she said. "Congratulations! Who and when? Oh, my god, am I causing trouble by being here? Do you want me to go?"

"Oh, no, no. You can stay, you can stay," and he motioned to her as if the question of her departure involved her chair. "She's in Taiwan. That's why I can't introduce you to her. I met her there last year when I visited. My family knows her family. I want to please my grandmother. She wants great-grandchildren. I'm an eldest son."

Susana looked at him with fondness and annoyance, as she would have in the sixth grade, only now she did not kick him. Heaven forbid. Adulthood had taught her patience a little. And, after all, this was the only way Serafín was likely to enter a marriage. His statement that he was marrying had seemed to her not only awkward but absurd, she now

121

realized. Serafín was a solitary spirit, needing no one, incapable of the loneliness that leads to marriage. He was at peace in a garden with glass walls or not. A republic of one.

He brought her a small photograph of the fiancée. She should have known there would be a photograph. From it beamed a young woman with a zeal for forward movement. No Byronic brooding from that head, no doubts and discouragements. On with the job! Be a light bulb! To please Serafín, she might even study Keats. Her name was Pei-ling: "wearing cleverness." Perfect. She wore cleverness like a shiny translucent enamel coat on every cell of skin.

"She's very nice," he said. "And intelligent. Oh, not like you. But really very smart and hard-working. And cheerful. Oh, not like you. She's studying electrical engineering, and she's determined to learn English well enough to adapt to the United States quickly. She already knows quite a bit."

Smart Serafín: highly employable bride. Oh, what fantasies of orchid-growing she must inspire. Could he even now as they sat in his blue kitchen see himself collecting his belongings from the English department, closing the door to his office, and quietly, but permanently, claiming his life forever? Grandmother's great-grandchildren would be delayed till a sensible time, of course. Smart Serafín. He would move to California, leaving Milton for Miltonias.

"I approve," she said to him cheerfully. "Far be it from me to cross Grandmother."

When she had kicked him on the shins with her saddle shoes in sixth grade she had created a gouge that had sent his aunt into hysterics and his grandmother into a wrath. He had told Susana of his female relations' reaction as if this should suffice to make her stop. Previously she had done it several times without drawing blood. Whether it was his grandmother's anger or not, something made her stop kicking him, no matter how high he shrieked at the slightest occasion for excitement.

He was going to get married. She knew she could not take credit for it, but at twelve her pride had been large enough to hold the concept. He shrieked, he waved his hands frantically, he was afraid of insects, even dragonflies. He acted like a girl, and she was determined to make a man out of him. She kicked him when he shrieked, and he shrieked again. He showed her the scabs for weeks, kept her abreast of the process of what she had done. She kicked him no more. At the time of her persecution of him there had been something inexplicably funny in the kicks, in their very repetition. She laughed; other children laughed. Teachers did not intervene.

As the years passed a sense of shame choked her, so that when their paths crossed again and Serafín seemed glad to see her, she was confused. He liked her so much, he had such a high opinion of her, that he made her more ashamed. And despite the kicks he had liked her then. Her spirits sank. She was in his warm kitchen with her hands around her teacup, which was his, and she was ashamed and sorry and did not know what to say.

"It's not your idea of marriage, is it?" Serafín asked her, misinterpreting.

"It's your life. No, that's a stupid thing to say. Congratulations. She's lucky to get such a kind, thoughtful husband."

"Thank you very much, but I'm worried. This marriage thing. One can fail miserably."

"You make an excellent friend, and that's an important part of being a spouse."

He started to deny his excellence, but Susana interrupted him. "Etruscans," she said.
"What?"

"Etruscans."

"The early inhabitants of Italy?"

"So you do remember."

"What?"

"No, you don't remember. Not the important part."

"What is it?" he asked, his excitement rising.

"I'll give you time to ponder," she said, though she doubted pondering would bring back the memory if the word had not. It must come to him in a flash. They would make a game of it the summer, a game in which she would be tease and, ultimately, villain. It might be better for her that he not remember. She had not played a good part, yet the memory to her was sweet nonetheless. He was keen on the challenge. Already she could see him spinning possibilities. He still liked guessing games, then, and he still latched on to what he perceived as an intellectual dare like a bulldog to a pants' leg.

After his marriage, he would drift away from her. It was inevitable.

He had abandoned her before. Or maybe it had been the other way around. He had stayed in public school after sixth grade, but she and Bertha had been put in Catholic school for their protection, the same school. The day she saw Bertha registering was one of the worst of her life. Bertha pursued her, and she no longer had Serafín to cushion the shocks between them. With Bertha for comparison, perhaps it wasn't so odd, after all, that Serafín had liked her, in spite of everything. Of the intellectual triumvirate in Mrs. Timothy's sixth grade, only Bertha had the killer instinct of the competitor. If you did better than she, she'd want to know why, and if she did better you'd know all the details. Bertha went for Susana's neck like a fighting cock and didn't ease up until their last year of high school when they were both exhausted.

"You should have seen the guy Bertha married. He always looked as if he were about to nod off. He believed in taking life leisurely," Susana said. "Well, she converted. Started not giving a damn about grades after she met him."

"Lucky you," Serafín said.

"It happened too late for me to enjoy the benefits."

"Sometimes I thought you were friends."

"People can get all sorts of peculiar ideas. Didn't you ever wonder how the *h* got in her name, seeing that she's Cuban?"

"Don't your parents want you to marry?" Serafín asked abruptly.

"For having lost but once my prime . . . ?"

"No, not that. They're Cuban, that's all."

"I have a career. They don't have to be showered with other details."

"Are there other details?" Serafín asked with apparent eagerness. He had wanted to include a gossip column in their magazine. Mrs. Timothy had not permitted it.

"I can't imagine marrying any more than joining a political party in a serious way," Susana told him. "Oh, I'm registered with a party but only for the sake of voting in the primaries. Hit and run."

Serafín giggled.

Susana woke up from the dream at 3:30 A.M. Her heart was pounding inside her breast. She had escaped the army man. She had escaped, but he had caught Serafín and had beaten him, and it had all been her fault because she was the one who had insulted the army man—and she had run and left Serafín to be beaten. The army man, all shiny with buttons of metal, was holding Serafín by the scruff of the neck, was beating Serafín, was telling Serafín he could never leave until he died. It had been a dream. It had been a dream. But she felt nervous about Serafín. Perhaps the nightmare had been a message from him. Perhaps he was lying in his room beaten by a prowler or ill. She wanted to check on him, but it had been a dream, and if he were all right and saw her, she would alarm him needlessly. And how would she explain?

She went up to his closed door and stood there quietly listening. At last she heard the sound of someone turning in bed. The sound was normal; nothing about it denoted distress.

She went to the bathroom, which was across the narrow hall from his room. She opened and shut the door noisily, hoping to awaken him and force him to go to the bathroom too.

She sat at the top of the stairs near his room to watch. Surely, if he did not get up now he must sometime. He seemed to her to be the sort of person whose bladder would fill. She sat and waited but he did not get up until 6:30, his usual wake-up time.

"Etruscans," she called out to him as he walked from his bedroom to the bathroom. She was happy to see him and enormously relieved, though she knew, and had known all along, that it was silly to feel anxious because of a dream.

He turned around and looked at her very concerned.

"Are you up so early thinking about Etruscans?" he asked. She assumed he was still confused from his sleep. "Is it that important?" He sat down next to her on the top step. "I looked up Etruscans in the encyclopedia. I don't think I found anything significant."

He was all right, sleepy but himself.

"Did the encyclopedia have pictures of their jewelry? It was very nice." She paused and gave him a teasing look. "You won't find the answer in books."

He pressed on nonetheless. "They had a special concern with death," he said. "I read that their tombs are the most lasting things they built and that they depicted their dead in monuments as if at happy, tranquil banquets. You've been very unhappy with your job. I myself don't know how you can stand it, but you've always been able to cope. You aren't thinking of death, are you?"

"No, but something like it has come over you."

"Something like death? Ah!" He screwed the bridge of his glasses into his face with his right index finger. "Speak, Memory," he said.

"Ah hah," agreed Susana, nodding encouragement.

From a birchy hill Susana spied Tom Burns wending his way home from the lake along the narrow, convex road they had taken together before. He wore only his wet, light blue swimming trunks and held by the ends a tightly rolled up yellow towel he carried around his neck. His expression was one of total abstraction. His body seemed to have no contact with the air it displaced. Lake drops clung to his back. They and his body's blond down glistened in the sun, transmuting the grey stockbroker's flesh beneath into their golden substance, drawing Susana's attention to its texture, which at that moment she realized would reward touch.

Susana spied the bather wending his way home and conceived lust for him.

Susana climbed over the fence of horizontal logs and went up the smooth hill to Tom Burns's house. She knocked at the kitchen door. He smiled sarcastically when he opened it.

"What I should have parried with yesterday," she said, "was that you have a view of the lake and we don't, so you don't have to take as much trouble or run the risk of exposure."

"Is that why you've come? To look out my windows? I'm afraid I don't have a telescope."

"Maybe there are naked bodies to be seen inside."

"Mine perhaps?"

"It will do, but don't leave me standing here at your doorstep."

She went inside banging the door. Tom Burns walked straight upstairs to his bedroom without turning around to see if she was following.

She liked his flesh, as she had expected. She sank her teeth and nails into it, and it proved deep despite the bones, and she was glad she had crossed the fence even though he pulled her hair, which displeased her. They were not friends, but at the moment she relished their enmity more than love. There would be at the end of their silent intercourse no lingering needs, no Janus questions.

When they were done, Tom Burns said, "You're good, much as I hate to admit it."

"We are vain about our goodness and then our past rears up at us," she said.

He laughed, ironic but confused. "This is very strange."

"I'm a strange person. That has already been established. I skulk about."

"You're a scholar and a saint. At least, that's what Serafín says."

As Tom Burns slowly sat up in bed, propping himself with both pillows, she was already up, putting on her clothes, unceremoniously stuffing tissues into her underpants to catch the flood of semen and spermicide. She had come prepared. The act had been premeditated, obviously so. She could not even pretend to Tom Burns that lust had hit her between the fence and the door.

"I wouldn't take Serafín's assessment of half the matter too seriously if I were you. Protestants have a very hazy notion of sainthood. They're out of their territory." Serafín, whom she shouldn't have kicked.

"To do him justice, it was not his actual word."

Tom Burns did not know about sainthood then.

"Ah, well. Bye," she said, and she sped down the stairs.

Tom Burns had actually gotten out of bed and was calling after her, naked, from the landing, "Let's continue this spiritual conversation soon. Don't forget your diaphragm."

From what she could see in her hurry, Tom Burns's summer house was what it ought to be: wooden and sparely filled and white-walled, with room to breathe.

This is what Tom Burns did not know about sainthood:

Many who think they are saints are not. And many who are held by public opinion to be saints are not and, unless a mental cataclysm befalls them, are not ever likely to be. Conventional saints (non-saints) are people with slightly different neural mechanisms. They concern themselves with ills we, the general run of humanity, would rather forget about—lepers, for instance—but they, like the rest of the species, rush to screen out other suffering—the wrongs against healthy women, for instance. The magnitude of the world's suffering is too great a burden for the single human brain to support. The false public saint simplifies problems, selects concerns, and condemns or ignores victims of ills that clash with the adaptations of her special neurology.

The generous, haloless person, member of the general run of humanity, admits that life is complicated and graciously, but with regret, specializes.

Sainthood is not a state to be aspired to but a catastrophic accident. A saint is a naked, screenless pain-sensing mechanism with perfect memory. She cannot choose. The fluid of her neural pathways will not block out some cries and let in others, will not pick music from din. Everything that has to do with pain enters her brain, is recorded there, is not repressed but is permitted to remain ever present in her consciousness, there, to make her responsible—her—responsible and guilty that the world is a round pain and she can offer it no healing. A saint is a cockroach dosed with strychnine. A saint is a human who, if she cannot twitch herself into schizophrenia, will surely outwit painful conscience by destroying it, leaving the mourners at the bare funeral grasping for earthly reasons.

That winter and spring Susana had been in danger of becoming a saint. When she realized her fatal direction, she sought escape and hoped to find in summer salvation.

She liked leaving Tom Burns confused. Confusion was the state where humanity's primeval innocence dwelt. It suited naked men. And it was fun for her.

Serafín had known her when signs of her future tendencies began to appear. She did small things at first—small, she thought, for the great task before her. Her father's brother had been put in prison for ingratitude to the Maximum Leader of the Revolution, a former friend. She and her parents had expected him to be shot, but he got prison and they were thankful to their God. They left for Miami, and at first she was content to utter her uncle's name every time she knelt in prayer, which was often. As the years dragged on with his suffering, she gave up things for him as sacrificial offerings to ineffably exigent God. No parties, no dessert, no meat all of Lent although she was a minor. She treated his picture, in which he stood radiant and robust with his arm around her father, with reverence, as if it were the Sacred Heart. He was not just her father's brother who was suffering, but a symbol of all who suffered preternaturally.

He was holy somehow, like the old Jews on South Beach with tattoos on their arms. Her mother had read *The Rise and Fall of the Third Reich* and had been unable to restrain herself, her lonely mother, from telling her of sinister lampshades and soap and of Jews dying in gas chambers, drowning in their own feces. Susana was nine or ten.

Her father, who worked twelve hours a day, sometimes remembered they lived within driving distance of beaches and took her swimming: He always picked South Beach. To him it seemed the cleanest stretch. There old Jews stood waist-high in the water holding onto ropes and singing songs in a foreign language. As she immersed herself to share their water, her skin became galvanized with the fear of possible contagion of tragedy or desecration of grief, and she looked for marks of a past so terrible that the old person bobbing in the water while the waves billowed up the ill-fitting swimsuit became a totem, an object of distant worship not to be approached, and the ocean they shared, a sea of blood, feces, flesh, terror, unspeakable things, unutterable names.

Because simple prayer was so inefficacious, Susana arrived at the conclusion that a particular absolute amount of suffering was required at all times by the Lord of the Universe. If she was to lessen her uncle's suffering, she must take some of it on herself. The algorithm was simple. At thirteen, she stole twenty-one split peas from the kitchen, wrapped them carefully in a paper bag folded many times over, and hid them in her odds-and-ends drawer. Each night she took them out and arranged them on the floor in two sets of ten, shifting the extra one from night to night. She knelt on them to say her prayers, which often consisted of a whole rosary. When she had finished, she hid them back in her drawer, counting carefully. She had tried rice at first. The pain caused by the digging of the slivers into the flesh was satisfactory, but the grains were too difficult to gather up in the dark. She would never have been sure of having picked up all of them.

The height of her religious fervor coincided with that of hemlines. Concealment of her exacerbated conscience grew more difficult as skirts shrank. At first she took refuge in her mother's conservatism, her ready-made excuse, but when finally in high school she faced ostracism she chose to bare her savaged knees, blaming their state on clumsiness, which her peers and alarmed parents readily believed, or on athleticism, an explanation swallowed only by strangers, such as ladies in bakeries whose curiosity was idle and probably ill-intentioned.

One Sunday, with some relief, she stopped her leguminous mortification. A priest condemned from the pulpit the practice of punishing the flesh to extract favors from God rather than to atone for offenses against him. He did not say so directly, but Susana figured he had had enough of the woman who went up the steps of the church on her knees. He did not say so but Susana guessed that he feared that kind of thing would make Catholics look cracked to a Protestant country. The woman did not stop going up the church steps on her knees. A promise is a promise. She could have been doing it in exchange for a favor already granted, but Susana did not think so. The woman had a pleading face. It looked so frozen in that attitude that Susana was certain the woman would never get what she wanted. Or not until the years had passed and the prisoner had served out his sentence or an amnesty was declared or the government changed and her legs had been crippled by arthritis into a permanent bend.

In two months Susana's knees looked ugly in miniskirts merely because of their natural shape. Years passed and the deity was still not forthcoming with his mercy. One day she stopped praying. And so did her mother. And so did everyone else. The earth stayed on its axis. Things got neither better nor worse. Letters from her uncle seldom reached them. Sometimes they dropped from the hands of the newly arrived who brought news of his condition with varying reliability. One Saturday afternoon, someone called to say that he was dead. After the vomiting stopped, the family sank into a depression, until a recently returned visitor to Cuba came to see them: her uncle lived, but he was in solitary confinement—but he lived. So to speak.

She grew up owning her political prisoner, aware that many around her had theirs too and angry with those of her compatriots who, having one, behaved as if they had none. When time came to choose a career, she chose the one to which she was, aside from jailer or executioner, temperamentally least suited. Armed with a brilliant academic record and no natural defenses, she sought a job gathering data on prisoners of conscience. With luck—good or bad depending on the angle of vision—she got it.

She had nothing to do with her uncle's release. He served his full term and was deported. Her colleagues thought they had had something to do with his not being resentenced. Perhaps they had; she had been kept away from his case. When he finished his twentieth year in prison, she was overcome with a feeling of failure. Not by kneeling on split peas nor by adult dedication had she shortened his incarceration.

When he reached Miami she went to see him. The robust young body that had hugged her father had shriveled within its time-eaten, parasite-chewed wrinkles. He was blind from too little light and lame from too many beatings. The insects, the rats had scurried over him at night. When she went up to him, he smiled with a pure child's joy, and her heart broke within her because when he had last smiled at her she had been a child and that waste of a life, of twenty years of suffering away from her and his wife and his children, seemed to her the saddest thing she had known. Someone had forcibly taken his time away from him and with it his youth and health.

She wondered suddenly why he had lived through the years. His own death should have been easy enough to arrange with the smallest provocation. What point had he been trying to make? Her poor little shrunken uncle who sat beside her, fragile, sick in the kidneys from being bayoneted, and talked incessantly with a frantic need to communicate the only things he had known for twenty years, prison and an apparently constant need to analyze why a fate so monstrous had befallen him, going over the friend's accusations of betrayal (the godlike wrath), the trial, the senseless charges against him—this poor little shrunken uncle had tried to make of himself a monument to the human will. She was angry with him for that. She was angry with herself, too. She wondered if her prayers had worked after all, and if the deity to whom she had directed her supplications in his evil had laughingly prolonged the pain of a good man because a girl kneeling on split peas had no conception of the magnitude of pain. She could imagine it now. She was familiar with the many and varied forms of torture, ancient and new, a highly developed technology. And with the method: the manipulation of time and hope and self. So she asked herself if she should not perhaps have prayed that he get a bullet through the head. Yet he had wanted to live. Each morning when he awoke, his soul said a prayer of thanks like a crow beating against the solid metal cell door, "I live! I live!" He smiled at her now and patted her hand and said she was a good girl because she cared so much about political prisoners and did she remember how she danced flamenco for everybody, clacking brown castanets in the air? She could not give him back his twenty years.

When she returned to New York and wore her only grey tweeds to work, she found herself at a meeting in which, whatever was said, she heard only fruitless effort and pain

128

unassuaged. She ran out quickly enough to vomit into the women's toilet. To the gentle voice and helping hand that appeared she returned only trivialities.

The next morning she could not get out of bed. Her body was too heavy for her to lift, in fact, too heavy to move at all. She lay on her back for hours unable to fall asleep or to answer the telephone that rang three times.

Throughout her physical paralysis her thoughts formicated as in a fever. At first she thought only of her uncle and of despair and her uncle. She seethed with anger against him. The human will, she thought, the human will, of all things to sacrifice oneself over. Was not the will of the torturer also a human will? As the hours wore on the thought passed through her mind that perhaps she was forcing her construction on the thing. Her uncle had maybe merely wanted to live, a desire, she supposed, that would be plain to most people. It was not enough for her. She lay immobile on her back, a prisoner of teleology.

About the time when the hour felt like two o'clock and the small light sneaking into her dark room confirmed this intuition, she caught a glimpse of a thought that flashed while the others merely glimmered or ran their course dully. Her uncle, the thought said, had been an affirmer of the human central nervous system, specifically, of our faculty to formulate concepts about which we can say, "They are true, even if you would have me deny them and make the sky a child's marble."

Serafín. The memory came right after. Serafín. The thought of him filled her eyes with tears for the shame she felt about him. Serafín. And she was ashamed she had wished her uncle had died. Who was she to decide such things? She was able to blink her eyes. She blinked away the tears that were making pools of her eyes in her supine position. Snot was accumulating at the back of her nose and she had to open her mouth so she could breathe. She knew she must set right what she could. She also knew she must stop crying. She was very uncomfortable, but she was so tired she could understand nothing more, and quickly she was overcome with sleep. When she awoke she found herself lying on her side and in her drowsy state realized she was able to move. Her clock read six, the time she usually left work.

The next day she asked for and obtained a medical leave of absence. She wrote a letter to Serafín full of falsely cheerful urgency.

Serafín announced that if the day was sunny, they would clean out the greenhouse. From early morning it was obvious that not a cloud was in the sky. Susana screwed up her eyes in a vain search for cumulonimbus.

Serafín found her yelling up, "We're having a picnic!"

"We're going to clean the greenhouse," Serafín corrected her. "No time for a picnic."

"I know, I know. I was just telling the weather." She sang, "¡Que llueva, que llueva, la Virgen de la Cueva!"

"You volunteered to help, you know. I didn't ask you to."

"How much guilt do you think one body can carry?" she asked.

Susana had been carrying out pots two at a time when he showed up with a small platform on castors.

"That's cheating!" she said to him, hands on hips, trying to keep from wringing her own neck.

"You should be more patient. Give me a lever and I will move the world," he said.

She noticed Tom Burns skulking about his backyard and went over to the fence to say hello.

He said, "Bend a bit over this way, and I'll bring out a folding chair and watch."

"Like to watch me sweat?"

"Well now, as to that, it doesn't take much, does it?"

She watched Serafín go into the greenhouse with the dolly. She quickly kissed Tom Burns on the mouth and walked away.

"You're always running away!" Tom Burns cried out mournfully.

Susana had gone to bed with him because he did not seem to need her. She did not fuck needy cases. That was taboo. Men in dire straits were for hard work and years of declining hope. A taboo also hung over her relationship with Serafín. That was the incest taboo. Weren't they all?

She and Serafín had shared important moments in childhood—at the wane of childhood for her—and so they wore invisible sacred robes for each other. Whatever scorn the adult world might heap upon them, they had seen each other clear and glorious before becoming. They existed as witnesses for each other from a time when they had not yet tumbled to earth or walked the world, grey among its grey multitudes.

Serafín as a witness had an imperfect memory, a blessing in most regards. After she said to him "That's cheating!" she hoped she had dislodged a memory to a more accessible part of the brain, but he had not said, "Aha!"

"That's cheating!" had set off a wave of recollections in her, the principal one being that she used to be much younger. For a long time she had thought that cheating, the childish copying and whispering of test answers, was a mortal sin legislated by the Catholic Sixth Commandment, a then vague commandment whose transgressing was given an aura of unequaled evil and cloacality by priests in distant pulpits and teachers in stuffy, over-crowded First Communion preparation classes. Her error was a direct result of the coyness of the Spanish language. Where English texts on the subject boldly listed "Thou shalt not commit adultery" under number six, the Spanish version for children vaguely declared, "Do not commit dishonest acts."

For most of her pious life, years ago, religion was conducted in Spanish. Even as the odd girl was rumored to be pregnant, the dishonest acts she had most occasion to observe were copying and sending back and forth little pieces of paper with the answer written on them, answers she usually did not need subterfuge for. By cultural osmosis she also picked up that the enunciation of certain words called *bad* was criminal under the same statute. She resolved never to cheat and never to use bad language. Eventually, thanks to English, she got her commandments straightened out. Yet she broke the latter part of her resolution only when she stopped fearing heaven. The first one she kept forever, because she had principles, because she never stopped fearing teachers, because she knew most things anyway, and because she felt she must out of faithfulness to Serafín, who had just brought out the white and blue bottle of Clorox.

The thought of cleaning algae off the panes of glass with bleach had made her tired for a week in anticipation. Now that Zero Hour had come, she sneezed uncontrollably. She hoped Tom Burns was getting a good look at her, sweating, muddy, red-faced, sneezing, cleaning her nose on her sleeve.

She had thought Tom Burns would not need her, but he had surprised her. She had walked into his life uninvited, but, once there, room had been made for her, and he felt a certain emptiness when she was not occupying it. She usually scampered back to Serafín's house after making love, and Tom Burns hated that. He wanted her to stay longer. If he found her walking about the neighborhood, he embraced her and kissed her and coaxed her to his house.

"Enough, enough! Please leave the Clorox to me," Serafín said. "Remember that Miami woman who couldn't stop sneezing?"

Clearly. Susana stepped outside and blew her nose thoroughly—with a tissue. She breathed relatively clean air a bit, not forgetting Three Mile Island. When her sinuses settled down, she went back into the greenhouse with a broom to sweep out dead leaves and such.

"*San Serafín del monte, San Serafín cortés*," she began singing in a still somewhat choked voice.

"Oh, what I got in town the other day!" he said and made tracks for the house.

She soon heard a terrible noise, something resembling music. Serafín was back with a tape of children's songs. A crudely arranged "Oh, Susanna" was blaring away.

"That's cheating," Susana said. And still Serafín did not remember.

When Serafín saw Susana come down the stairs, he hurried out of the living room. It was obvious to her that her appearance at that moment had caused his departure. She looked down at herself to make sure she had all her clothes on. Yes, she was decently clothed, virginally so, almost. She was wearing the white India cotton dress she always wore to summer parties. It reached down to midcalf. She walked over to the entrance-hall mirror to check. There was nothing wrong with her. She still only had one head.

She remembered she had left her purse upstairs and was about to go retrieve it, but Serafín returned rather winded with excitement, holding an orchid lovingly in his hands. It was a Paphiopedilum shot through with red and brilliantly striped in green.

"It's for you," he said. "I wanted to see first what colors you were wearing. I'm so glad you're wearing white so there's no problem."

The flower's purplish red center was like blood waiting to course through the earth's green veins, but Serafín's intentions wrapped her in a sweet calm. He recited like a schoolboy glad to remember:

> Yet it creates, transcending these,
> Far other worlds, and other seas;
> Annihilating all that's made
> To a green thought in a green shade.

"Andrew Marvell," he said. "The antecedent of *it* is *the mind*."

Susana felt weak with a desire to hug his round body and with the need, keenly felt, to hold back.

"I thought you might wear it in your hair," he said, holding up the flower shyly to the side of her face.

She finally took the orchid from his expert fingers and walked to the mirror, a lovely pier mirror framed in fine dark mahogany. She held the orchid above her left ear against her black hair. The heart in the green wood, she thought. Looking past the mirror into the living room she noticed for the first time that the sun was as bright as in a late Miami afternoon.

Serafín, beside her, said happily, "I knew it would suit you!"

She cradled the orchid delicately in both hands. "Thank you," she said. "It's a beautiful specimen. I know that it grows singly, so I thank you doubly."

He dismissed her thanks. "It's not a joy forever, at any rate."

At this they both laughed. Because they were relieved to laugh so much at nearly nothing, their laughter grew more intense out of each other's.

Susana said, girlishly buoyant, "If anyone asks what kind of orchid it is, I'll tell them it's Heart in the Green Wood."

"Not a bad name," Serafín said. "I'll consult with you before I name my hybrids."

"Please don't call a flower Brassavola Dimity Dandy-doo, or any of that nonsense."

"Certainly not."

"Before I came here I imagined days filled with nothing but the twitter of birds and thoughts of what I'd left. I never thought I'd be cleaning dead matter out of a greenhouse for the benefit of Paphiopedilums, Coelogynes, Brassolaeliocattleyas, and Vandas, to name but a few," she pronounced with pride in nomenclature.

"You learn something new every summer," Serafín replied, leaving her weighed down with guilt for having teased him with the snake that had so frightened him, when, suddenly looking hectic and heading for the kitchen, he said he'd better make sure the dim sum he'd made for the party was protected well enough to make the trip and that Tom Burns had better arrive soon or they would be late. She knew the good she had done was greater than the evil, but in the evil the molecules were more densely packed, and the angel only used scales.

Feeling rather less lighthearted, Susana looked at her watch to see if Serafín's franticness was justified. Susana didn't think anybody would give a damn if they were late; everybody else would probably be late, making them be on time. But she'd just as soon go already instead of waiting in limbo, all dressed and perfumed and psychologically armored for a party despite the passing burden of guilt and melancholy. She was not sure—who ever is?—what kind of party it would turn out to be besides potluck. The invitation had come through Tom Burns. Other summer people. Ever since she had gotten on intimate terms with Tom Burns his connection with the rest of the world had begun to be apparent. He held himself at a distance but shook hands all around, and from some other world, she supposed, he had plucked enough friendship to fill a summer afternoon. He held himself at a distance but screwed quite well.

With pride she thought that if there were dancing, she would get both Serafín and Tom Burns to dance, although they would be sure to put up strong resistance. She was a great persuader. She could get them to dance even if it was hot, would pull them away from staring at their drinks pretending to be interested in ice cubes. Oh, but Serafín didn't drink. The flower she held lightly in her hand, not wanting to touch much of its surface, afraid of wilting it, was proof of Serafín's forgiveness. Whatever she had done, all her life, he had forgiven her. She had this orchid, and Etruscans. She'd better go upstairs and see if a bobby pin could be found. She was about to go off and scout when Tom Burns walked in the front door without knocking.

"Did you bring your dish from home?" she asked him.

"You mean my bottle from Scotland. J & B, as per your instructions."

"Do you always follow instructions?"

"As long as they're legal or I don't think I'll get caught. What did you make?"

"Serafín made dim sum. I stood around breathing and looking very willing to lend inspiration. When we were in the sixth grade we were all in the habit of repeating that TV commercial—do you remember?—'Mother, *please*, I'd rather do it myself!' We all intoned it but Serafín did it most often and no one could hit that *please* quite the way he could. He drove me up a wall. I don't even remember what brand of pain reliever the ad was for, but Serafín's *please* is engraved in my memory. I thought I'd take him up on it and let him do the work."

"Elaborate excuse."

"Basically, I'm just lazy."

"Not in everything."

"He gave me this orchid. Isn't it gorgeous? I'll go upstairs and put it on."

As she started up the stairs, Tom Burns grabbed her buttocks.

"Don't do that," she whispered angrily and looked nervously around for Serafín. "He knew me when I was a bulwark of purity."

"You've changed."

"He hasn't. I don't want him to know about us. He gave me the flower. Behave yourself."

When she got back downstairs, purse clutched and flower pinned, and Tom Burns went out to open the trunk of his Mercedes for the dim sum, Serafín approached her cautiously.

"Susana," he said with a clear, Spanish pronunciation, and paused. "Tom Burns was complaining to me that you, well, he used the phrase 'use his body' and leave and never spend the night. He thinks I have something to do with it."

"Good grief!" exhaled Susana and sat down on the second step of the stairs.

"He's upset that you don't stay the whole night," Serafín insisted. "I don't want to cause trouble between you."

"Tom Burns is in the rumor business."

"Then it's not true?" asked Serafín with shocked surprise.

"Oh, it is, unfortunately."

Tom Burns came in to see what was holding things up, the bandit.

"Seen any snakes lately?" she asked him.

The other summer people were quite well off. Susana knew right away she should not have come. She knew it in the car as a vague suspicion and the moment she arrived as a cringing in the gut. She did not fit in. Everybody was a city dweller of a certain type she knew: cold-bitten, rich, and hard. Serafín did not fit in, though he would never let anybody know it. Even Tom Burns, among those loud party people, executive types, seemed out of place, a languid creature who sank his back into a living room wall.

A lot of men called Hal and Dick and Irv and Bill tried to call her Sue. She argued vehemently that she was not a Sue but a Susana. She picked a fight with one of them because he had brought with him photographs he was very proud of for technical reasons. The pictures were all of people he had snapped in an underdeveloped country going about their colorful, underdeveloped activities, such as sitting on a road with a heavy burden.

"See how sharp this image came out. I had to use a special lens."

"You're trying to make poverty look glamorous," she said. It was not what she meant. What angered her was the invasion of privacy committed with the assumption that such people had no right to privacy or no desire. Taking their souls away without asking.

"Poverty itself is not bad. What is bad is a bit of development. Then the country goes to pot," said the man, who was an economist with an influential international monetary policy study commission—what did you expect?

"Otherwise known as the barefoot-and-pregnant theory of nations," she told him over her shoulder as she retreated to find Serafín or Tom Burns or anybody who did not work for an influential international monetary policy study commission.

One man who said he was Stan left her stupefied without a comeback.

"I hear you do kinky work."

"What?"

"Yeah, you like to read about torture and stuff," he said, moving an eyebrow up and down.

She backed away from him as from a tarantula.

"Tom Burns told me so," Stan said.

She went immediately in search of Tom Burns, whose slightly greyish skin was blending in with the vertical bands of acanthus leaves in the wallpaper. He pleaded innocent: a straightforward description of her job had been decomposed through the action of alcohol. Alcohol preserves. Stan Creep. She remembered all their names, even if they tried to make her a Sue. She was good at remembering names of drunks (who were easy), orchids, and political prisoners with long foreign names and complicated histories. It was what she did. She slumped next to Tom Burns, who loosely laid an arm across the back of her neck.

"Want some more Scotch?" he whispered.

"No, don't leave," she asked.

Tom Burns had been talking with a jolly man called Bob who changed the conversation to suit her arrival. "So, do you two know each other from New York?"

Tom Burns? New York?

"No, New Yorkers don't know one another, Bob," Tom Burns said.

Susana was thunderstruck. New York, of course, New York. They lived in the same place. But she had never thought about it.

Tom Burns gave her a friendly shake with the arm he had around her. "Why so shocked, honey lamb? Where did you think stockbrokers stockbroked?"

"All over. Philadelphia and Washington are closer to here . . . Baltimore," she argued.

"My family is from Philadelphia. The whole pack has been down here to visit; maybe you've seen them. I was born in Philadelphia, but I live in New York."

Of course, it was ridiculous. She had thought about him vaguely in connection with Wall Street, but not the actual physical Wall Street that connected up through the marvelous grid of the city with the street where she lived in the New York where they both lived.

Tom Burns laughed. "She thought she was going to be rid of me."

He bent over to Susana's neck and kissed it. "Oh, those heartrending summer good-byes of the hit parade of your sun-drenched adolescence," he said.

"My very early adolescence," she quibbled. "I may be younger than you suppose."

The hit parade and her life had never coincided, early or late. She was inclined to suspect the disadvantage was hers. Especially now. The good-byes may have been heart-rending but they had been good-byes that did not leave dangling in one's trembling hands a relationship begun embarrassingly with a stranger because of the exciting effects of water droplets on bare skin. If she had thought "New York" she would never have shown up openly lusting at his door.

A woman was screaming. At first she thought it was her imagination or a reaction of her ears to excess vibrations. Then she saw the woman's open mouth and distressed face. She was glad to learn the scream had not come from her.

The woman's middle-aged face, as red as the woman's red hair, was wailing, "He's leaving me!"

The whole house suddenly fell into a hush at the sound of weeping and the promise of a story.

A woman, Jenny, gasped loudly, then threw her arms around the red-faced woman and before long they were shaking and crying together as Jenny repeated, "No, no, no!" They appeared to be sisters, one of whom dyed her hair.

Another woman, Francine, stepped up to them and Jenny backed off, dabbing at her tears. Francine was cool with the manner of controlled and controlling comforter. She was the same age as the others but not otherwise like the others. She made the weeping woman sit down next to her on the sofa and solemnly and confidently stroked her hand and calmed her as the party returned to its noise.

Susana could no longer hear them through the chatter, but she watched the red-faced woman tell Francine the story of her pain while Francine sat there inspiring trust, with an attitude full of concern but also detachment, involvement just enough, mature profession-alism to soothe others now and rescue herself later. Susana watched Francine's pro-cedure and Francine herself, what she had made of herself, the short blunt way her black-with-grey hair had been cut not to get in the way of a tale of sorrow, the unmitigated pro-fessionalism even in off hours (she had saved a party), reflected in the way she dressed in neat blouse and neat skirt. Susana recognized all her moves. Francine was someone Susana had not yet become, an older counterpart in another sphere, someone Susana would never become because she did not want to cut her long black hair and transform herself into a sleek ambulatory confessional.

But she had to admit that Francine was good and that, given the wrong situation, she would tell that calm face anything. She wanted to toast Francine secretly, but she noticed that she had no drink and that she probably had already had too much. She left Tom Burns's side and answered questions about her orchid. She found Serafín demonstrating the making of dim sum in the kitchen to a rapt audience. He too had answered a lot of questions about orchids. He didn't want to leave. Tom Burns, still pushing up the same spot on the wallpaper, seemed comfortably ensconced.

Susana passed up many opportunities to be crassly insulted or to make pitches for contributions to a worthy cause. She wasn't much of a fund raiser, although the approach was easy, as everyone who did her kind of work quickly figured out. When she was with conservatives she could stress the crimes committed by Communist governments and when with liberals, the torture tactics of right-wing juntas. There was plenty to go around. She simply never felt like bringing it up. That night she told anybody who asked that she was a quality control expert for Estée Lauder.

"Oh, how nice."

So safe. How nice. No sour reminder amidst festivity. She felt that even if they suspected otherwise—and why should they? well, she hardly wore make-up, that was why—they would be grateful to her for her lie.

When Susana and her two party-animal companions were finally walking toward Tom Burns's car for the long-awaited ride home, Susana saw Francine leaning back over the hood of a car, kissing a guy. He opened the door and they both disappeared into the back seat. Wedged into the front seat of the New York-licensed Mercedes between Tom Burns and Serafín so that no one should feel left out, Susana was glad to see Francine do one minor foolish thing in her professional wisewoman's life.

"I shell sea swells by the sea shore," Susana said slowly.

"No, I do," said Tom. "You're a qualitative specialist for Elizabeth Arden."

"I heard, controlling engineer for Estée Lauder," Serafín corrected.

How rumors spread.

She thought of middle-aged Francine in the back of a Buick, and the thought set off warm explosions within her. She would henceforth call Tom Burns Tom, even in her thoughts, Tom, for whom she had found warm feelings partly because he had done all evening long such a good imitation of a wall bracket and had made people come to him, Tom, of whom she was very fond this boozy summer night when they drove past lush trees filled with sweet resin. She would even forgive him for not being the fascinating loner she had thought he was the first time she saw him dart into his house.

When Serafín got out of the car, Tom, newly Tom not yet knowing his promotion, grabbed her hand and asked her, hot and tremulously, "Sleep with me tonight."

That of so passionate a request sleep should play such an important part. She acceded, and did not return to Serafín's house till lunchtime, ready to do her afternoon chores. Serafín seemed as unperturbed by her unchaste life away from him as he was by his orchids' requirements for sun, food, and water, differing from species to species. She had expected him to react like the twelve-year-old boy, both Cuban and Chinese, who took his hand to his mouth and squeaked like a mouse when someone teased him about a girlfriend. She had forgotten sixteen years.

"Etruscans," she said to him as he rummaged through his tool shed.

"Give me time," he said confidently. "Give me time."

"Serafín, what a summer it's been!"

The days were growing shorter and kinder on the skin. Tom Burns had for some time come to the country only on weekends, and then had stopped coming altogether. She loved his white house especially at sunset and dusk, whether he was there or not, but she missed him now that he was not there. She would soon leave for the city herself.

Serafín had been going over the previous fall's lectures, trying to find a gap where he could add something new to stay alive. He said it would soon be time to plant Chinese cabbage.

"What a summer it's been, Serafín!" she said, stretching her arms out to the sides. "I want to thank you. I've never had a better summer. Here's something you didn't know about me. When I was a kid I just stayed in front of the TV during vacation while life passed by behind me. This year I've done things. I'm not twelve any more."

"You're in a silly mood."

"Yes," she happily admitted. "Thank you, Serafín."

"You've already said that."

They leaned against Tom Burns's fence, where Tom Burns was not. The sky was greying over and the earth smelled of mushroom.

"What a summer it's been, Serafín!"

"Are you feeling better?" he asked. "Well enough to go back?"

"Well enough is well enough, but you can't go back. Though I've been with you and the vacation has been long, like a school vacation. I didn't want to stop being lazy when September came, but I was always curious to know what the new year would teach me. I hoped for significant knowledge, universal insight, at last. Every term I was disappointed with the triviality of the lessons, but every summer I hoped. I remember being that way as far back as first grade in Cuba. I was lucky in my disappointment and didn't know it. I've developed backwards, Serafín. I've shrunk and all around me the world has grown in importance."

"You were an early bloomer."

"Did you look up girls' skirts as they climbed the stairs?"

Serafín screamed. "Certainly not," he said laughing.

Susana jumped off Tom Burns's fence and got back on. Then, holding on to it, she did a deep knee-bend that showed the soil caked to the hem of her blue jeans. Good, honest soil from the family of magic.

"No use doing fancy tricks," Serafín said. "Burns is gone."

She did not answer but did more knee-bends. Perhaps she needed to be with Tom Burns now, but she always needed Serafín to be. What cause had he for jealousy? Besides, the Light Bulb was coming.

"What's going to happen with you two?" Serafín asked.

"I suppose we'll see each other once I'm back in New York."

"You don't sound very much in love."

"We've happened to each other. We share one major undesirable trait, but don't have a hell of a lot else in common. Common occurrence, lack of commonality. I got a big contribution out of him, so his occupation has its good uses. Not that I'm a good saleswoman. He could use the tax deduction. That's not fair. The major trait I mentioned: he's consumed with guilt. He did it for me too, I suppose. He's grown attached."

"A man who does not grow anything on so much land needs his moral caliber improved."

"You sold the pink house," she remonstrated. "Your family sold the pink house."

"That old house in Southwest?"

137

"What other?"

"We were all grown up. My grandparents got a good offer for it and moved out near Homestead where the soil is better. I'm surprised you should care so much."

"The house was torn down," Susana said bitterly. "I took a walk there when I went to see my uncle after he got released from prison. Did I tell you my uncle was out? No? I'm sorry. Yes, he's out. Blind and crippled, but out. The neighborhood has become unsafe, did you know? My mother warned me about walking around. There's more crime now. We didn't have to worry when we were children. They've built apartments in place of your family's garden, crummy apartments, like everywhere else in the area. There's hardly a patch of grass in front of it. I loved that house."

"Were you ever in it?" Serafín asked with surprise.

"No. I loved it anyway."

"I had no idea."

"Serafín, I'm sorry. I'm sorry. I've never done a worse thing in my life. Never as bad a thing in all my life."

"What?"

"I'm sorry I kicked you in sixth grade. Please forgive me. I'm profoundly sorry."

She had kicked him for despicable reasons: because he did not fit the mold and her own expectations. She had kicked him for the reasons of persecutors and oppressors.

"I'm sorry," she repeated, and broke down into sobbing.

Serafín, looking utterly perplexed, put an arm hesitantly around her shoulders. He held his arm there shyly, awkwardly, while all along his mind seemed to be struggling with something incomprehensible in the dark.

"My aunt was upset! Those saddle shoes of yours! Those saddle shoes!" he screeched with laughter. "Sometimes I see a young girl wearing a pair like yours and I get nostalgic. Black and white saddle oxfords. Always shiny, the white so white, the black so black."

"My mother polished them."

"She did a good job."

"Look, Serafín, we're straying from the topic. I've carried this burden of guilt for sixteen years. The least you can do is forgive me."

He lay his hands on her head. "You have won forgiveness. And not only forgiveness! Susana, this is your lucky day: you have won a place in the offensive lineup of the football team of your choice for a whole year!"

Evidently he had also spent his childhood summers watching TV game shows.

"Be serious, Serafín, damn you. This is important."

"Important because you've made it important."

"Well?"

"Well, what?"

"Are you going to forgive me?"

"I forgive you," he said smiling at her. "But you must promise never ever to do it again."

"Oh, never, never again." She was intensely earnest. He was joking.

"Oh, Susanna, don't you cry for me," he sang. "It's been such a long time."

"I suspect you have a bad memory. In a way, that's good."

They were sitting on the grass, leaning against Tom Burns's fence. Susana breathed deeply. Soon she would have to give up air that smelled green and brown and turning.

She watched a bird against the evening-blue sky. She could not identify it. All she knew was that it shook up the loneliness and fear of the future she held locked inside of her. But she was done crying.

"I bet you think I'm never going to penetrate the mystery of Etruscans," Serafín said after a while. "I can tell you what I remember. You tell me if I'm hot or cold."

He could not possibly know, not even if he remembered the circumstances. He could not know how much Etruscans had meant to her.

"It was the history final. Mrs. Timothy read out the question: the early inhabitants of Italy. The answer: Etruscans. I remembered from reviewing the night before. There was a loud groan, or some noise of the sort, expressing general ignorance. After a while, I looked at your paper. The space for the answer was blank. I was surprised you did not know it; you knew almost everything. I pointed to my answer and pointed to my answer."

"You risked detection rather recklessly. There would have been a scandal."

"You wouldn't write 'Etruscans' down. I couldn't understand why not. I could hardly believe it. So I pointed and insisted."

"Wounded pride knitted your eyebrows."

"I was angry with you. You wouldn't trust me. The answer was right."

"And when Mrs. Timothy read it out after the test papers had been collected, you said 'See?' rather caustically. But I had believed you all along. The moment I saw the word 'Etruscans' on your paper I knew it was the right answer."

"Then why didn't you write it down?" he screamed.

"I thought it was a mortal sin to copy. You were tempting me to sin. I had made myself a promise I would never cheat. I was a bit of a prig." Yes, and for a while she believed she had won a moral victory. It surprised her even now that she had once been so young.

"Bertha didn't share your scruples," he said.

"She saw your paper, didn't she, while you were trying to show it to me. She whooped like a hunter and seized upon your Etruscans. You two were the only ones in the class who got the answer right."

"I couldn't explain your behavior to myself."

"The year ended, vacation came, and I didn't see you again for years, so I did not have the opportunity to explain to you."

Neither would she now completely. She would not tell him the extent to which his generosity, in the face of sixth grade's fierce competition, had touched her. That act of his, which had been to her conscience and nerves tantalizing trial, after the pressure of the exam had been removed had crystallized in her memory as the sweetest, purest act of friendship anyone had ever extended to her. Thus she cherished it through the years.

"That was nice of you, Etruscans. What made you remember at last?"

"I was thinking up exam questions last night for the Puritans and Cavaliers midterm and considering the propensity of pre-meds to cheat. Suddenly I remembered. Poor Mrs. Timothy."

"Thank you for Etruscans, Serafín."

"I was a pesky kid, too high-strung," he said, staring at the distance. "You were so smart, don't you remember? And you looked like a grown-up woman."

"I never cheated in school, Serafín, even though sometimes the temptation was strong and the circumstances favorable. Since I didn't cheat with you, I wouldn't cheat with anybody."

"Yes, it's been quite a summer," Serafín said.

VI. Obligaciones y compromisos

Justo S. Alarcón

EL POLITICO

Ya era entrada la noche cuando el Senador Alberto Espinoza caminaba por el callejón. Una nubecilla de polvo se desprendía de los tacones de sus zapatos. El hipo intermitente despertaba ladridos de perros, presos en los pequeños jardines de la vecindad. Una luna veraniega le servía de guía contra los botes de basura, propiedad del Ayuntamiento. Este era su camino favorito que lo llevaba a casa siempre que, con antelación, visitaba "El Tecolote's Bar".

Era a fines de primavera y estaban cerrando las sesiones del Senado en donde se trataba de las apropiaciones para los presupuestos de diversas Instituciones subvencionadas por el Estado. Las discusiones, algunas de ellas acaloradas, entre los miembros del cuerpo legislador, dejaban al Senador agotado. Después de estos quehaceres, y bajo la presión del agobio, solía visitar "El Tecolote", en donde podía desahogarse "with my Raza".

Oscar Ramírez, antiguo compañero de escuela y que conocía bien las costumbres y hábitos del Senador, lo estaba esperando al final del callejón que desembocaba en la calle Molina.

—¿Quiúbole, Senador?
—Hi . . . buddy. What . . . are you . . . doing . . . here?

Entre hipos pudo terminar la frase. Oscar Ramírez lo asió por el bícep izquierdo y lo ayudó a entrar en el Chevy station wagon. Al volante se hallaba Antonio Noriega. Se saludaron y comenzó el viaje sin necesidad de altercados. El Senador Espinoza, reclinado en el asiento de atrás, se quedó dormido bajo una pesada respiración.

Pasada la medianoche, llegaron a la casita arruinada y abandonada en donde dejarían el carro. El Senador Espinoza despertó de su abohetado sueño. "¿'Onde 'tamos?" La media luna se había traspuesto hacia el lado del oeste. La pálida lucidez pegaba de lado en los matorrales. En fila, iban caminando los tres. Las preguntas inquisitivas del Senador recibían respuestas veladas. Sospechó algo y esperó la oportunidad apropiada. Se apartó un poco de la vereda para desaguar. Miró de reojo y se lanzó a la fuga. Creyó haber tenido la suficiente distancia, pero su estado de relajamiento muscular no le permitió alejarse mucho. Oscar Ramírez y Antonio Noriega se echaron encima y lo apachurraron. "Don't you ever do that, jijo 'e tu chingada madre", le profirió Oscar Ramírez. Sacudiendo un poco la ropa, se pusieron otra vez en camino.

Habían llegado a la orilla del río. Era el amanecer y comenzaba a distinguirse el serpenteo de las aguas. Seguían la estrecha vereda que zigzagueaba el borde. El Senador

Espinoza, por el rabillo del ojo, veía las aguas en su movimiento ondulante. El silencio de la oscuridad se le filtró hasta la entraña. Movido por una fuerza intensa y misteriosa quería echarse a correr, pero la cercanía de sus dos acompañantes se lo impedía.

El crujir de las hojas y matorros se tradujo en ruido de huesos y de voces opacas. Clavó la pupila en las aguas y vio un velo grisáceo. Las voces brumosas se sumaron en una, clara y femenil. Se detuvo y, en su rigidez estatuesca, le pareció haber oído un "Ay. . . ." Por sus ojos turbios corría el canal que lo llevaba al Circle-K. Su madre le decía: "Mijo, no tardes mucho, porque al caer el sol es la hora de la Llorona." Tenía que cruzar un pasadizo hecho de tablas apolilladas. Siempre que lo hacía le entraba una fuerte palpitación. Al cruzarlo se limpiaba la frente con el dorso de la mano. Una vez se detuvo en la tiendita con dos de sus amigos que vivían al otro lado del canal. Se hizo noche y sus amigos se fueron. Al querer cruzar el puente de madera sintió un calor que le dejaba por las piernas. Se echó a correr y, al llegar a casa, se metió por la puerta de atrás. Se fue a su habitación y se cambió los pantalones. Un fuerte empujón de Oscar Ramírez le impulsó hacia adelante.

Llegaron a la entrada de la cueva. Dibujada contra el fondo oscuro de la boca, distinguió a la distancia una silueta de mujer que los recibía con una flashlight en la mano. Giró y fueron tragados por la garganta del dormido dragón. La silueta agigantada de la dama se mecía cóncavamente en las paredes. Un olor pestilente invadió las fosas nasales del Senador Espinoza. "Estos taquitos jieden, 'amá." "No te quejes, mijo. Tenemos que agradecérselo a Diosito, que nos da pa' comer." "Pero jieden, 'amá." "Cuando tu 'apá nos envíe más dinero no vamos tener necesidá del welfer, mijo."

Lo sentaron en el cepo de piedra. Sus ojos escudriñaban en la oscuridad del vientre de la cueva. Al fondo, y a distancias razonables, notó algunas figuras. Se acordó de las noticias en primera plana del periódico, *The Frontiersman*. No había duda. "Estos cabrones le hicieron kidnap." Se vio fotografiado en los periódicos del siguiente día, acompañado del titular "Senator Al Espinoza disappeared. The kidnappers struck again." Una temblorina se apoderó de él. "My wife estará enojada 'orita. Poor girl, pensará que andaré pedo. Pero when she knows the truth empezará a llorar. . . ."

—Senator Alberto Espinoza, ¿puedo llamarte Al, como cuando éramos compañeros en la escuela?

—Yes, man. ¿Acaso no éramos camaradas?

Con la invitación al tuteo, al Senador Espinoza se la amortiguó un poco la temblorina. Se acordó de sus años juveniles y de cuando Ms. Fairchild los castigó poniéndolos repetidas veces en la esquina de atrás del cuarto de clase. El pequeño Alberto le había escrito una nota a Betty Walker en donde le decía: "I lof you, Betty." Oscar Ramírez enseñó los dientes.

—¿Sabes quiénes somos nosotros?

—No.

—Somos Los Siete Hijos de La Llorona.

—So you are . . .

—Sí, somos los del periódico . . .

—Oh, my God!

Por los pasillos de su mente desfilaron sus planes truncados. La votación en el Senado sobre la construcción de la cárcel en medio de los barrios, la carretera periférica, el proyecto de ley sobre los campesinos, el programa bilingüe y otros programas que afectaban a la Raza. "You guys can't do this to me, especially 'orita." Ahora que el Gobernador iba a presentarlo ante el Presidente para candidato a la Embajada en México. No podía ser. Pensó arrodillarse ante el grupo y pedirles misericordia. "After all, ellos comprenderán . . .," pensó para sí. Hizo ademán para hincarse de rodillas.

—¡No seas coyón!
—But, ¡Yo tengo planes, man!
—Y nosotros también.
—But . . .
—Estás ante el tribunal de "Los Siete", Alberto Espinoza.
—But . . .
—Tienes que responder a una serie de crímenes.
—But . . . yo no soy criminal, I'm telling you!
—Veremos.

"Crímenes . . ." Su amigo, el Senador Teddy Homestead, lo había guiado por el tortuoso camino de la Política. "Politics is like a game, Al boy." Aunque nunca pudo aprender, el campeón de ajedrez trató de decirle muchas veces: "You have to hide, protected behind your army, your people, the pawns. You are the Knight, el caballero, you know. You move one step forwards and then one step sideways. You kill sideways and then you have to back up, hide again behind the pawns. Very simple." Nunca aprendió a jugar al ajedrez. No tenía necesidad, porque le era fácil ponerlo en práctica.

—Tú fuiste elegido Senador del Distrito #4, ¿que no?
—Sí.
—¿Quién te eligió?
—My constituency.
—Nosotros, los chicanos.
—Right.
—Y, ¿qué le pasó a tus promesas, después de que trabajamos tanto por ti, en la campaña?
—I've tried to keep them. But . . . , it is very difficult.
—Eres un mentiroso, baboso. Tú te vendiste.

Notó Alberto Espinoza que un grupo de cabezas torció hacia donde estaba él sentado. Catorce pupilas destellaban con el resplandor del fuego. Oscar Ramírez se había sentado junto a sus compañeros. Estiraron las manos hacia el fuego formando un abanico. Levantaron las cabezas y fijaron la vista en la oscura concavidad de la cueva. Oscar Ramírez musitó una plegaria: "Madre nuestra Llorona, aquí te hemos traído a este hijo extraviado. Es doloroso que una persona ajena y extraña sea la causa de los males de tus hijos, pero más doloroso es que un hijo tuyo traicione a tantos de sus propios hermanos. Ayúdanos a hacerle reconocer sus crímenes, Madre Llorona." Una voz etérea surgió de las llamas e invadió la matriz de la cueva. "Solamente los hijos degenerados y bastardos son capaces de herir las entrañas de una madre, traicionando y vendiendo miserablemente a sus hermanos. Un hijo Senador que, pudiendo ayudar a sus hermanos perseguidos por la justicia, explotados por el capital y castrados mentalmente por las escuelas, estando en el poder político no lo hace, no es un hijo. Es un hijastro bastardo. No lo reconozco como hijo mío." Simultánea y religiosamente bajaron los brazos extendidos e inclinaron las siete cabezas. Permanecieron unos instantes silenciosamente encorvados. Rompieron el círculo y, de frente al Senador Alberto Espinoza, formaron una media luna.

Oscar Ramírez se dirigió al reo: "Has oído las palabras de nuestra Madre, Alberto Espinoza. Bajo su autoridad, única y absoluta, te juzgaremos nosotros, tus hermanos, y nadie más. Tus crímenes y tus movidas chuecas, que tienes escondidas en esa cabeza podrida y llena de bichos asquerosos, te las arrancaremos con uñas afiladas como espinas de sahuaros en carne viva, Alberto Espinoza. Somos la Corte, el Juez y el Jurado que ahora tiene nuestra familia y pueblo: La Raza. No hay ninguna otra corte, Alberto Espinoza. Uniéndote al Sistema podriste tu ser. Estás contaminado de una enfermedad cancerosa y, jugando el mismo juego, querías contaminar a todos tus hermanos, Alberto Espinoza. Tus hermanos te elegimos para que nos sacaras de la opresión padecida por centenares de años y, asquerosamente, te uniste a los opresores para que el peso fuera más insoportable. Eres un puerco, Alberto Espinoza. Eres un mentiroso, un vendido, un degenerado, Alberto Espinoza. Estás contaminado, estás podrido, estás muerto, Alberto Espinoza. Eres una mierda." El Senador Alberto Espinoza tenía las ventanas de su cráneo abiertas a la inmensidad del espacio. Querían encontrar algo sólido, algo claro, algo tangible, pero se encontraban ante el abismo hueco de la oscuridad de la nada. Nadaba vertiginosamente como un bólido sin origen, sin dirección, sin destino. Como un chango, se echó instintivamente ambas manos al coco, se jaló de los pelos y arrancó de la entraña un grito profano: "Tú eres un hijo 'e tu chingada y puta madre." Oscar Ramírez extendió el brazo derecho hacia atrás y, con la mano extendida, le descargó sus doscientas libras en la mejilla izquierda. El Senador Alberto Espinoza rodó por el suelo bajo el impacto. Después de breves instantes, y a instancia de Oscar Ramírez, se sentó en el cepo de piedra. Chorreaba sangre por la boca y por las fosas nasales. El interrogador sacó un pañuelo del bolsillo y se lo entregó.

—Ahora, Senador Alberto Espinoza, continuemos con el juicio. Tú fuiste Presidente de MECHA, ¿que no?
—Yes.
—Tú nos incitaste a la demostración y a la protesta contra la Universidad, ¿que no?
—Yes. Porque era President.
—Tú dijiste y gritabas diciendo que la Administración era una "racist pig", ¿que no?
—Yes.
—La verdad, Alberto Espinoza, era que tú querías servirte de la Presidencia de MECHA para ser aceptado en CLEO y en el Colegio de Leyes, ¿que no?
—Not necessarily.
—Contesta bien, Alberto Espinoza. Sí o no.
—Pos . . . , sí.
—Desde entonces ya tenías planes para hacer una carrera política, ¿que no?
—Pos, sí. ¿Y qué?
—Pues desde entonces usaste a La Raza. Eras un vendido y fuiste un hipócrita.
—I wasn't.

Antonio Noriega le alargó otro pañuelo. El Senador Alberto Espinoza se ahogaba en su propia sangre. La sangre que corría por las venas de sus dos hijos. "Mis hijos no sufrirán lo que yo sufrí de niño. No serán como yo. Irán a la mejor escuela del Estado. Los mandaré a la Salomon School. Les enseñarán algo, por lo menos a manejar el dinero, que me faltó a mí y a mi madre. Eso, mis hijos serán diferentes, serán banqueros. Irán a la Salomon School." Veía que su sangre escurría por sus dedos y se coagulaba en el suelo, en gotas pegajosas y putrefactas.

—Alberto Espinoza, al terminar tus estudios de leyes agarraste un puesto con el Procurador del Estado, ¿que no?
—Yes.
—Y después pasaste a las oficinas del Gobernador, ¿que no?
—Yes.
—¿Cómo subiste tan pronto?
—Porque I was smart, inteligente.
—Porque te vendiste y te usaron ante La Raza, Alberto Espinoza.
—Not true.
—Después, como querías más dinero, comenzaste una firma, el despacho Espinoza & Zarzosa.
—*De la Raza para la Raza*, don't forget.
—Sí, ya lo vi en el anuncio que pagaste para la TV. Y, ¿qué decías en la TV?
—"Aquí le ayudamos en casos de divorcio, de contratos de casas y carros, y arreglo de pasaportes." Y . . . otras cosas.
—"Y . . . otras cosas." ¿Qué cosas? ¿El caso de Carlos Corona?
—Yes, but . . .

Carlos Corona tenía una casa remolque en donde vivía con su esposa y cuatro hijos. Se había comprado un Toyota usado y solamente le faltaba por pagar la última mensualidad. El carro tenía un defecto que nunca se lo pudieron corregir en la agencia. Carlos Corona se negó a hacer el último pago. El banco envió a dos guardias para notificarle que, si no pagaba, al día siguiente le embargarían la casa remolque y se la llevarían. Carlos Corona les dijo que él estaría allí para recibirlos. Al día siguiente no fue a trabajar. Llegaron los guardias y Carlos Corona, por una ventana abierta, les enseñó el caño de un rifle. Los guardias sacaron la pistola y Carlos Corona descargó dos tiros, matando a uno e hiriendo a otro. Antes de doblarse, el herido había descargado su pistola en la frente de Carlos Corona.

—. . . But . . . tú no quisiste ayudar a nuestro hermano Carlos Corona porque no tenía $500.00, ¿que no?
—Yes, pero . . . es que esos casos cuestan mucho dinero.
—El debía nomás, only $200.00 y tú le cobrabas, "para comenzar", $500.00. ¿No ves qué matemáticas más chistosas?
—Yes, pero . . .
—Pero . . . tú sabías que le iban a quitar la casa, y que la familia se iba a quedar en la calle, y que Carlos Corona no iba a permitir eso, y, sin embargo, tú permitiste mejor que Carlos Corona, tu hermano, muriera a manos del interés bancario, de tu amigo Steinfellow.

—I didn't . . .
—Por pedirle $500.00 que no tenía.
—But . . . , listen . . .
—"De la Raza para la Raza."
—But . . . no comprendes que . . .
—. . . que eres un cochino, Alberto Espinoza.

Miró para el suelo y vio la tierra de color rojizo. Del color de la alfombra de la casa del banquero Daniel Steinfellow. Su mente se paseó por los corredores de la gran mansión en Sunrise Hills. Le habían invitado a un banquete-fiesta a raíz de una de las sesiones del Senado, cuando iban a tratar del porcentaje del interés sobre los préstamos bancarios. La mansión hormigueaba de banqueros, senadores y diputados. El Senador Alberto Espinoza quedó maravillado de la alfombra, de los muebles y de las pinturas. Pero un cuadro del Bosch, colgado de una de las paredes del comedor, le robó la atención. El banquero Steinfellow se percató de ello y le sopló al oído: "Senator, this one is my favorite." El Senador Alberto Espinoza vio a una legión de pordioseros y harapientos tragados por una enorme boca de un monstruo muy raro. Al fondo se fijó en lo que parecía ser una ciudad. La ciudad fronteriza que él tantas veces había visitado para comprar souvenirs. Pordioseros, mutilados, famélicos en las esquinas de las calles. "Como en el welfare. Como cuando yo era niño y mi madre me. . ." Se fijó en la cabeza del raro monstruo y en su hocico aguileño. Parecía un cochino, con nariz retorcida y puntiaguda. Se dio la vuelta y el banquero Steinfellow se le acercaba con una copa de champaña. Lo miró a la cara, a la boca, a la nariz y le pareció haberla reconocido. Dio unos pasos para adelante y después torció para la derecha, hacia la cocina. Sorbió de la copa y, mientras bajaba la cabeza, se fijó en el piso cuadrilátero tapizado de plaqueta. "Don't forget, one step forwards and one step sideways. You kill sideways, never forwards. Then back up, and hide behind the pawns. If you remain in the open you will get killed. Very simple."

—Senador Alberto Espinoza, tú estás metido en lo de la marihuana, ¿que no?
—Well . . . , cuando I was a chamaco, I used to smoke algún leño, you know . . . Como los de mi tiempo.
—¿Y después?
—Después . . . almost nunca.
—Porque lo vendías. Eras un pusher.
—Not in the strict sense of the word.
—¿Cuándo dejaste de ser pusher? ¿Cuando te hicimos Senador?
—Right. Ya no fui pusher.
—Pero, te hiciste dealer, traficante.
—. . . You are a mentiroso. I never . . .
—Tú eres el mentiroso, Alberto Espinoza. Tú y el Senador Homestead tienen un negocio de millones de dólares, ¿que no?
—. . . ¿Cómo lo sabes?
—Tú le dijiste al Senador Homestead que tú te ocuparías del territorio de los barrios de tu Distrito. De La Raza, pues.
—That is . . . not true.

—Tú te compraste tu Lincoln y tu mansión con el dinero que les sacaste a los pobres de tus barrios, Alberto Espinoza.

—. . . Not true.

—Tú te compraste una mansión en la Sunrise Hills pudriendo la sangre de tu Raza con hard drugs, Senador Alberto Espinoza.

—But . . . ¿cómo iba yo a comprarme una mansión and live in Sunrise Hills if I am a Senador de mi District? ¿Can't you see?

—Porque ahora quieres dejar de ser Senador para ser Embajador, Alberto Espinoza. You want to be bigger, quieres importar drogas de México "legally", quieres traer ilegales "legally" para los ranchos del Senador Homestead, quieres . . .

—That's a lie . . .

—. . . chingar "legally" a México y a tu Raza.

—Not true.

—No supiste ser Raza. Eres un vendido, Alberto Espinoza.

"Ay . . . de mis hijos, ahogados en ríos de sangre. Por las calles de mis barrios se pasean las jeringas, las agujas y la savia mortífera que corre por los ríos de sus venas. Cruzan el río para buscar comida, para vivir, para sobrevivir, y se encuentran con las jeringas, para morir. ¡Ay . . . de mis hijos!" El tribunal de Los Siete inclinó sus cabezas adoloridas. El Senador Alberto Espinoza se apretaba la cabeza con las palmas de las manos. Sentía que un pincho de puerco espín le taladraba la sien de parte a parte. Un agudo chillido de niño impotente lo llevaría clavado por años sin fin. No hacía mucho que su prima Dolores Espinoza había sido iniciada inocentemente al gusto y placer del arrullo y vaivén del humo de la marihuana. "Just one, uno nomás, baby." Aquella noche, en el Parque San Lázaro, se dejaron arrullar. Tendidos en el suelo alborearon con la ropa revuelta y las piernas al aire. "¡Oh, Diosito, qué hemos hecho!" Un peso inmenso abrumó las cabezas. Duró varios meses. Una criatura mostrenca gateaba por la casa, escurriendo baba, moco y caca. Emitía sonidos perrunos. Nunca pudo estirarse en dos patas. Dolores Espinoza nunca sonreía, se quedaba azonzada. Imitaba al hijo y andaba a cuatro patas. "¡Ay . . . de mi hijo . . . !" con frecuencia clamaba. Y el tornillo seguía apretando en la cabeza cana. El Senador Alberto Espinoza soltó las palmas de las manos y dejó de apretar la sien. Un grillerío de voces infantiles y perrunas le asaltó los tímpanos. "Shut up, you sons-of-bitches!" Y se calmaron los ruidos. Levantó la cabeza y sintió catorce pupilas que le claveteaban la sien.

—Senador Alberto Espinoza, tú te divorciaste de tu esposa Lupe Arteaga, para casarte con Esther Steinfellow, la hija del banquero.

—That's personal business. Negocio mío.

—Negocio de acciones bancarias y de acciones en la City Water Dam Company.

—Porque tengo dinero.

—Tú votaste por la legislación del aborto, ¿que no?

—Yes, porque . . . there are too many niños pobres.

—Y porque le llevaste la corriente al Senador Homestead, a tu suegro el banquero Steinfellow y al Dr. Greenhouse, que quieren exterminar a La Raza.

—No es verdad. That isn't true.

—La verdad es que tú quieres esterilizar a todas las chicanas, abortar a todas las

147

carnalas, para no ver a tanto buqui, a tanto chamaquito deforme e imbécil, como a . . .

—Shut up! I said, shut up!

—La verdad es que, con tu negocio de traficante de drogas, has sido la causa de una camada, de una generación de chamaquitos retardados y retrasados mentales, Alberto Espinoza.

—Shut up!!

—La verdad es que tú eres un degenerado, un vendido y un hijo de perra, Alberto Espinoza.

—¡Cá . . . lla . . . te!

El Senador Alberto Espinoza se echó las manos a la cabeza y le entró la temblorina. Un sudor frío le salía de la sien y le resbalaba por las mejillas. En el delta de la barbilla se juntaba con las lágrimas que caían por la comisura de la boca. Al rato se fue calmando. Oscar Ramírez se adelantó y lo asió por un brazo y el resto del tribunal se puso de pie. Le dieron una vuelta al fuego y, después, lo llevaron de nicho en nicho. Lo presentaron a cada uno de los rehenes.

—¿Conoces a Su Excelencia el Arzobispo McNamara?

—No.

—¿Conoces al Dr. Adolph Greenhouse?

—No!

—¿Conoces a la Directora del Programa Bilingüe y maestra de primaria, Ms. Fairchild?

—No!!

—¿Conoces al Juez Douglas Wright?

—No!!!

—Eres un asqueroso político, Alberto Espinoza.

—No!!!!

De nuevo giraron alrededor del fuego. En procesión desfilaron por las catacumbas de la cueva. Al llegar a la salida, se pararon todos. Oscar Ramírez levantó el brazo y apuntó con el índice. El Senador Alberto Espinoza fue vomitado por la boca de la cueva. Crujían las hojas secas bajo las suelas de sus zapatos acharolados. Eran las siete de la tarde de un verano estival. Los crujidos de las hojas le subían por las venas calientes, inmensos ríos de sangre y de droga. Los chillidos aumentaban, alaridos y ladridos de retrasados perrunos. Y el río a la distancia de un palmo. Estallidos de bombas, de cohetes y de fuegos fatuos. Metió un pie, luego otro, y la gran vena del río apagó los últimos aullidos y alaridos.

Rosaura Sánchez

SE ARREMANGO LAS MANGAS

Se ajustó la corbata. El nudo se veía derecho. La camisa almidonada le lucía bien. Julio Jarrín se acomodó la solapa, se estiró un poco el saco y se dio el último cepillazo del bigote. Salió en seguida. Era temprano. La reunión empezaba a las 4:00 pero con el tráfico máximo tendría para rato.

Subió al auto y en tres minutos ya tomaba la rampa de la autopista hacia el norte. Era tanto el tráfico que tuvo que disminuir la velocidad a 40 m.p.h. Sería un caso difícil y la votación tal vez fuera totalmente negativa, pero había otra posibilidad. Si no aprobaban lo de la permanencia—y seguro que no lo aprobarían—pues podrían ofrecerle un puesto de instrucción en el departamento. De repente el tráfico se paró por completo. Aprovechó para sacarse el saco.

Ahora siempre andaba de traje y corbata. Sin el uniforme de rigor podrían haberlo tomado por indocumentado. Así se decía cada mañana al mirarse al espejo. Alto, prieto y bigotudo pero trajeado para que nadie lo confundiera. Recordaba que cuando recién había llegado a Los Angeles a trabajar en la universidad lo habían invitado a una recepción en casa de un colega donde daban la bienvenida a los profesores nuevos. Allá por el verano de 1970 tuvo su primer contacto con esas insoportables oleadas de calor que después supo llamaban la condición "Santa Ana". El cambio de temperatura atontaba a las comunidades costeras no acostumbradas a un clima tropical. Ese día había ido a la reunión en camisa sport de manga corta, como los otros colegas.

Le habían presentado a varios profesores y después de un rato de charla se había dirigido a la mesa de refrescos para prepararse de nuevo un wine cooler. Al retirarse de la mesa oyó la voz de una señora mayor, esposa de uno de los profesores, que lo llamaba: "Hey, boy", le había dicho, "you can bring me another margarita."

Disimulando, haciéndose el que no había oído, se había ido a refugiar a la cocina donde conversaba la mujer latina de un profesor anglo-saión. Le dirigió unas palabras en español pero ella le contestó en inglés. Cuando quedaron solos por un momento, trató de dirigir la conversación hacia los problemas de los grupos minoritarios en el ambiente académico, pero no logró interesarla.

"Oh no, there's no discrimination in California. I've never experienced any discrimination whatsoever in the 15 years that we've lived here. My husband and I just love this area, particularly the beach area. We have a place right on the beach, you know, and it's so lovely. My sons just love it; they're really into surfing, you know . . ."

No había vuelto a mencionar la situación a nadie. Su ambición profesional lo llevó a distanciarse de todo lo que pudiera asociarlo a esas minorías de clase obrera. Lo primero

149

fue cambiar su apariencia. Nunca más volvió a salir fuera de su casa sin traje y corbata, ni aun cuando se había tenido que arrancar al hospital el día que se cortó la mano al trabajar en el jardín de su casa. Primero se había bañado, cambiado de ropa y ya de traje había salido al cuarto de emergencia del hospital más cercano a recibir atención médica. No era mexicano. Era americano, con los mismos derechos que tenían los anglo-sajones.

Era la época de las protestas estudiantiles, del culturalismo nacional, pero él estaba muy por encima de todo eso. Cuando los estudiantes chicanos de su universidad habían acudido a él para pedirle apoyo para establecer un programa de Estudios Chicanos, les había dicho que haría lo que pudiera desde su capacidad oficial, como profesor, pero que no esperaran que los apoyara en manifestaciones ni en protestas. El no era chicano. Más de una vez, desde el atril donde dictaba sus conferencias, se había dirigido a sus estudiantes minoritarios para quejarse de la dejadez del pueblo mexicano, recomendándoles que estudiaran para que dejaran de ser mediocres. Se avergonzaba de ellos.

Su contacto con los profesores y estudiantes chicanos, por lo tanto, había sido mínimo. Lo despreciaban. Y él a ellos los consideraba tontos e inferiores por no seguir el camino que él les señalaba. Había otras maneras de lograr cambios. El talento y el esfuerzo individual, eso era lo que valía. Pero desde esos tiempos habían pasado tantas cosas, tantas cosas que prefería olvidar.

No le alegraba para nada la reunión departamental que le esperaba. Sería un caso difícil. Se trataba de un profesor negro, el profesor Jones, buen profesor, con pocas publicaciones. Un caso típico. Se había dedicado más a la enseñanza que a la investigación y eso no contaba para la administración universitaria, ni para sus colegas departamentales que lo evaluarían ese día. Claro que tenía el apoyo de los estudiantes minoritarios, pero eso poco contaba en estos tiempos. Ni los profesores minoritarios del departamento lo apoyarían. Nadie quería arriesgar el pellejo. Nadie quería tener criterio inferior para juzgar al colega. Algunos no lo apoyarían porque querían quedar bien con la administración o con el jefe del departamento. Tampoco él podría apoyarlo. Lo había conversado con su mujer esa mañana.

—Ese profesor negro aún puede colocarse en otra universidad sin mucha dificultad. Su trabajo no es sobresaliente, ni mucho menos, y me temo que le den el hachazo hoy mismo.

—Pero, ¿no dices que tiene un libro publicado?

—Sí, así es, pero nada de calidad.

—Pero, ¿no le dieron el tenure al profesor Smith por poca cosa?

—Mira, bien sabes que para los que tienen palanca, no hay estorbos, y el cabrón Smith había trabajado para el State Department y tenía su apoyo en la administración.

—Y, ¿qué de la protesta de ayer? Salió en todos los periódicos que los estudiantes armaron una manifestación muy grande pidiendo la permanencia para el profesor negro.

—Creen que todavía estamos en los 60. Si esa época ya pasó. Ya viste lo que hizo el Presidente. Se mandó llamar a la policía y los arrestaron a todos parejos.

—Sí, el periódico dice que estaba dispuesto a romper cascos con tal de sacarlos de su oficina donde se fueron a sentar en plan de protesta.

—Sí, sí, es un tipo peligroso. Le entró un pánico y perdió el control. Pudo hacerse un gran desmadre allí. Es un líder débil y dispuesto a cualquier cosa para sentirse en control de la situación.

—Y por eso mismo, ¿no crees que habría que apoyar al joven negro? Bien sabes cuánto ha costado traer a los pocos profesores minoritarios que hay.

—Sí, a los tres que hubo en mi departamento, los traje yo, pero sin protestas ni manifestaciones, usando mi propia palanca.

—Sí, sí, Julio, pero ¿cuántos de esos quedan aún? A todos los han botado y éste es el último, el último de los profesores minoritarios que tú ayudaste a traer. Ninguno ha sobrevivido. Ninguno.

Era tan difícil sobrevivir, pero allí estaba él. ¿Acaso no había sobrevivido? Hasta había alcanzado el nivel más alto de profesor en su departamento. Y eso porque había sabido trabajar duro y abrirse camino, no como profesor minoritario sino como profesor capacitado, excelente en su campo, con una lista de publicaciones en su expediente.

Llegó a la salida de la autopista, tomó rumbo hacia la universidad y subió un corto trecho más hasta el edificio de ciencias sociales. Bajó, se volvió a poner el saco, entró al edificio y se dirigió a su oficina. Allí sobre la mesa estaban los últimos exámenes de sus alumnos. Había uno en particular, el de Alejandro Ramírez, que era sobresaliente. Un joven estudiante de clase obrera, pero inteligentísimo. Podría haber sido su hijo. Al lado de las pruebas estaba el periódico universitario, con fotos de la manifestación estudiantil. Había una del Presidente universitario, con la cara airada ante un policía. "Demolish the place if you have to. Just get them out." Así decía el título al pie de la foto. Se puso a mirar por la ventana. El campo universitario se veía verde, con sus árboles y sus aceras muy bien cuidadas. Un verdadero country club. Y él era miembro de este club campestre, miembro vitalicio.

Llegó al salón después de unos minutos para la reunión departamental. El comité de profesores presentó la evaluación y siguió la discusión. Era buen profesor, atraía a cantidades de alumnos, pero porque era fácil, porque no exigía mucho. Tenía un libro publicado, pero era parecido a su tesis doctoral, y después de todo, el tema—el trabajo laboral de un líder negro durante los años 30—no era realmente académico, le faltaba legitimidad, el trabajo en sí era mediocre, y aunque tenía buenas reseñas y aunque la casa editorial había conseguido muy buenas evaluaciones, le faltaba metodología; no era lo que se esperaba de un profesor universitario en ese departamento, en esa universidad. La discusión siguió y siguió, sin que nadie aportara nada a favor del profesor Jones. Por fin habló el otro profesor negro del departamento para darles toda la razón. Pidió que le concedieran a Jones, aunque fuera un cargo menor, algo que le garantizara empleo. Pero tampoco esto les pareció bien.

Fue entonces que Julio abrió la boca. Les recordó que él había traído al profesor negro. Les recordó que antes no se habían dado clases de historia minoritaria en ese departamento. Les recordó que la universidad tenía una obligación, un compromiso con las comunidades minoritarias que aumentaban cada año y que algún día serían la población mayoritaria del estado. Les recordó que tenían un record atroz en cuanto al reclutamiento de estudiantes minoritarios. Les recordó que no había ni un solo estudiante graduado negro en el departamento. Les habló de la investigación que estaba por hacerse en los campos minoritarios. Les hizo recordar su propia producción a esa edad. Les mencionó precedentes de otros profesores, algunos allí presentes, que habían recibido su cargo vitalicio con poca producción cuando esto sólo indicaba posibilidades de crecimiento y mayor brillantez en el futuro. Les habló por 30 minutos. Al ir hablando se dio cuenta de que no se atrevía a alabar al profesor Jones profesionalmente, tratando siempre de encontrar razones contextuales para fortalecer su propuesta de que le permitieran permanecer como miembro permanente del departamento. Calló un segundo y dijo: "Creo que el Profesor Jones merece el tenure porque su trabajo promete mucho, porque es un pionero en un campo poco explorado que ha suscitado poca investigación. Es un buen profesor, un miembro productivo de este departamento, interesado en períodos y contextos históricos totalmente ignorados por este departamento que prefiere tener quince profesores de historia europea. Repito, el Profesor Jones merece recibir el tenure."

Hubo un largo silencio. Se llamó a la votación y brevemente se anunció el resultado: 20 en contra del protesor Jones y uno a favor.

Se levantaron sus colegas y salieron rápido del salón. Era de esperarse, le dijo el jefe del departamento.

Sintió de repente su alienación. No era una sensación nueva. Lo nuevo era reconocerlo. Se había refugiado en la apariencia de ser parte del grupo académico mayoritario. Y ahora el profesor Julio Jarrín ni formaba parte del círculo académico departamental ni formaba parte de la comunidad minoritaria. Su alienación era completa.

Salió al sol, al pasto verde. Ninguno había sobrevivido. El salvavidas lo había arrojado demasiado tarde para salvar al profesor Jones. Pero no era tarde para volver a empezar, no era tarde para aprender a luchar. Se quitó el saco y se aflojó el nudo de la corbata. Poco después se arremangó las mangas.

Nash Candelaria

MANO A MANO

Emiliano Zapata Rosca was a quiet outsider, but confronting the forces of the Establishment on their own ground turned his usual quiet self to stone silence.

Across the sunken living room he could see his wife, Lola, chatting with the other faculty wives. Mrs. Wedemeyer, wife of the department chairman, was holding forth, bobbing her head of lacquered silver hair animatedly while the wives of junior faculty members hung on every word.

Emiliano balanced a plate of hors d'oeuvres in one hand and a glass of missionary punch (whatever that was) in the other. He would have preferred a taquito and a bottle of Dos Equis. But as long as both hands were full, he did not have to worry about eating the precious little goodies that seemed to sniff their noses at him from the plate.

"Ah." The tall, skinny man raised his eyebrows as if he recognized an old friend in a strange and unexpected place. "Rosca," he said. "Chicano literature. Your first semester at Southwest U, and your first presemester English Department soirée." He popped a cracker covered with a brownish-pink spread into his mouth. "Paté," he said. "Tastes like dog food."

Emiliano was too nervous to smile. He didn't recognize the man. Should he? The man took two quick chews, swallowed, then smiled at Rosca. "Levine," he said. "Sounds like grape vine. Freshman dumbbell English."

"Emiliano Rosca." But what more could he say? Certainly not Chic Lit. Levine had already recognized that. Nor that he was new here. Levine and everyone else knew that too.

"I was in the lines at Delano," Levine said. "While I was doing graduate work at Berkeley."

Be friendly, Lola would have said to him. The man is trying to be nice. But Emiliano was not sure what to say. That he too had struggled in the fields for justice? Not true. And he didn't particularly relish the idea either. No more than his father who had been a chef in a hotel in Tucson. "Field work is for animals," Papá always said. "Not for human beings."

From the other side of the room another strange face lit up at him. Nodding solemnly, the new stranger wove his way through the crowd holding high a half-full glass of what, from the glazed look in his eye, must have been something more interesting than missionary punch.

"Oh, Christ," Levine mumbled. "Van Horn." Then pointedly to Emiliano. "Watch out. We're being assaulted by the forces of reaction. And cul---ture."

"Well," Van Horn said. "So this is Señor Rosca. Dr. Emery Van Horn." A little smile played at the edges of his mouth and once again Emiliano had the uneasy feeling that somehow the name should mean something to him. It didn't.

Van Horn leaned toward them conspiratorially. "I have something in a little flask that makes the punch drinkable." He grinned affably at them. "I understand old Weedy learned the recipe from a native Hawaiian on a visit to that ocean paradise. It seems that they threw a few pineapples into a pot with a white missionary and boiled the brew three days before cooling and drinking it. A little vodka saves it from being completely nauseous."

Levine covered his glass with his free hand "Only the juice of the grape for me," he said. "Union picked of course." He smiled slyly at Emiliano.

Rosca, however, thrust his glass toward Van Horn in the hope that not only the punch but the entire party would become more tolerable. Van Horn slipped from his jacket pocket a small silver flask embellished with a filigree design and poured a quick shot into the glass.

"Rosca," Van Horn said, savoring the name and seemingly reaching into his memory. "We once had a gardener by the name of Rosca. Pedro Rosca. He couldn't be any relation, could he?"

"No. No Pedros in my family." But inside, the question irritated him. No, he should have answered. No gardeners in the Rosca family either. Only M.D.'s and Ph.D.'s. Millionaires and movie stars. Did you know that Ricardo Montalbán's real name was Rosca? As for Van Horn, the only one I ever met was an assistant flusher in the sewer works. Was it your father or your brother?

"Tell me, Rosca." Van Horn sidled up to him and glanced around furtively as if about to disclose a state secret meant only for his ears. "About this Chicano literature stuff. Just what is it? Is it any good? I mean . . . literature. Now Shakespeare, that's literature. Or Milton. Keats. Blake. Seriously. Isn't this just another form of welfare program the government's forcing on the colleges? Literature? Most of those people can't even read or write."

With some, anger came instantly like the stifling blast of heat when the door of a roaring furnace is opened. With others it was a bolt of lightning followed by a torrential cloudburst from above. But with Emiliano Rosca it started from the fires of hell itself, seeping up slowly through the soles of his feet to the roots of the hair on his scalp. His eyes lit with maniacal anger, and he almost spit a swallow of punch into Van Horn's face.

"These right-wing classicists," Levine said. "Never known for their tact."

But Emiliano barely heard Levine's attempt to defuse the tension. In amazement he swallowed the juice of some undesirable portion of a missionary's anatomy and blinked at Van Horn. "What did you say?"

He stared straight at this . . . this unspeakable whatever, but he saw nothing. His eyes looked out on blackness as if he had awakened from a bad dream at three in the morning. He heard, sharply etched because he did not see, the simpering, insinuating tone of voice that communicated, even more than the words themselves, contempt and arrogance.

"Have you been reading some of Shockley's stuff?" the voice asked.

"Oh, Christ!" Levine said.

"Now wait a minute," Van Horn said. "It may be about a different group, but the man has a point. He's a renowned scientist. A Nobel winner—"

"In physics," Levine said. "Not people."

"—whose credentials are very high. Science has the right to ask ultimate questions. Even when it offends the sensibilities of some. I think Shockley's point is well taken. There might well be genetic differences in intelligence among various groups. Not just Blacks. Say Chicanos for instance. By the way—" Now the voice shifted as if it had suddenly remembered something, although all Emiliano could see was a dark gray background with this shadowy form looming out of it toward him. "Rosca. Do you know the difference between a Hispanic and a Chicano?"

Emiliano set his glass on the windowsill in preparation. His hands stiffened into claw-like clutches, ready to harden into fists. It was all he could do to shake his head at the voice.

"Well—" Now Emiliano could feel the vodka breath close to his face. "A Hispanic is a man with a chip on one shoulder. While a Chicano is a man—" Already Van Horn's voice was chuckling. "—with chips on both shoulders."

The reflex was automatic. A right cross aimed at the offending mouth. A pair of hands grabbed Emiliano's forearm and the blow never landed. "For Christ's sake," Levine said. "Do you jackasses want to get fired?"

"I resent—" Emiliano began, but he was breathing so heavily that he could speak no more.

"God damn it, Van Horn," Levine said. "What's the matter with you?"

"I just wanted to make a scientific point." His voice was screeching nervously and he had jumped back out of arm's reach.

"I challenge you," Emiliano said. "I challenge your rotten insinuations to a test. Your students against mine. And if mine lose, I'll resign."

"Keep your voices down," Levine said. "People are looking."

"I accept your challenge. Levine can be the intermediary to negotiate ground rules. And Levine, I'd like someone closer to my point of view to assist. Say—Phyllis Worth."

"Anybody," Emiliano said. "I don't care who."

"Worth is fine," Levine said. Then Van Horn turned on his heel and ambled across the room to another group. "You fool," Levine said. "You know he teaches the Honors English program. Some of them are the brightest students in the college."

But Emiliano did not hear. Now that the gray cloud had faded, he saw his wife, ashen-faced, standing within hearing distance of them trying hard to exchange small talk with other ladies.

"I'll be in touch," Levine said, "after you've had time to cool off and think it over."

As Levine walked away, shaking his head, Lola peeled herself from her companions and came up to Emiliano. "Well, Pata. Now you've done it. This was going to be the place to win tenure. To really dig in and do a job."

"Shut up, woman." But his response was half-hearted. He felt overwhelmed by the forces of reaction, from right-wing academics to liberated Chicano women. It made him want to smash something. Even if it was only a whiskey bottle that he had emptied.

The next morning, as far as Emiliano was concerned, arrived two days too late. All night he had either been staring wide-eyed at the ceiling or thrashing restlessly through a recurring dream.

In his dream he saw himself in tattered denim work clothes, hoe in hand, going endlessly from one verdant field to another. They were not the fields worked by the usual migrant laborers. The main farmhouse was a brick and marble monument with mottoes engraved above the portico in a language he could not read.

On the steps of the entrance stood an official in white-face, like a mime. Behind him stood jeering white faces of others in denim work clothes. The official thrust out an arm with a forefinger pointing off into the distance. Emiliano picked up his hoe and moved on, hearing the catcalls and jeers behind him.

He trudged past the fields where the fruit of the vineyards grew: young people pushing up through the soil with smiling white faces, waiting impatiently to be full grown and picked from the vines. Here a head protruded. There one grew out to the waist. Farther on the older plants had grown out to the ankles as they successfully raised themselves up from their roots. Everywhere the smiling white-faced plants shook their heads and pointed arms imitating the gesture of the official.

"Pata, what's the matter?" He woke in a cold sweat, feeling Lola's hand on his shoulder. "Are you all right? You've been groaning something awful."

"I feel like I have a hangover."

"But you didn't drink last night."

"No, damn it!"

"It was the reception, wasn't it?"

"Please."

"Pata. Sometimes I don't believe that you're a college graduate. A man of education and intelligence . . ."

"Please, Lola."

"He made you angry. You still haven't learned to control your temper with gabachos like that. There will always be those people, Pata. You can't escape them."

"What do you know?"

"I may not have a college degree, but I know plenty. How can I help you, Pata? What can I do?"

But what came back to him was the dream. For at the end of the dirt road beyond the verdant fields was Tortilla Flats, where a brown-faced crowd in tatters watched him approach. As he came near enough to recognize them—his father, mother, brothers, sisters, aunts, uncles, cousins, neighbors—they turned their backs on him in a group.

Emiliano sat up in bed and covered his face with his hands, his voice choked with emotion. "After all they've done to help me," he said, "I'll go back to them in shame. I'll have to resign because of that stupid chingado."

He felt Lola's arm around his shoulder. "Only if you lose, Pata."

Emiliano tightened his lips in a grim smile because her comment reminded him of a variation on the punchline of an old joke. "Does it hurt?" "Only when you lose."

"I'll go see Drs. Levine and Worth and offer to be a laborer in the vineyards." He looked at her suspiciously, wondering if she had been reading his mind. "I'm a good typist," she said. "And a whiz with a Xerox machine. All you have to do is agree on the conditions, one of which is for me to help."

He remembered Lola's offer later that day when he sat in Levine's office. "Worth and I want to suggest that each of you state three conditions for this trial by intellect and that both of you review the other's conditions and agree to them. OK?"

"What happens if Van Horn loses?"

"He hasn't said. The only offer was yours. A damned rash thing if you ask me."

"If my students win I want him to resign."

"He'll never agree to that." But Levine's tone of voice implied even more to Emiliano. That the whole question was, as they say, only academic, since miracles may have occurred in twelfth-century monasteries, but they did not occur on twentieth-century campuses.

"Then what's at stake besides my job?"

Levine shrugged. "Honor. Reputation."

"Son-of-a-bitch."

Levine ignored the expletive and picked up a sheet of paper from his desk. "Here are Van Horn's conditions. First, the questions are to be literary, not general knowledge."

"No IQ test?"

"That's right. No IQ test, Dr. Shockley notwithstanding. Second condition, the test will consist of ten questions. Each of you will contribute five, multiple choice or answerable in a few words but not true-false or essay. That's to make grading easy, yet reduce the likelihood that someone could guess their way to a good score. The questions do *not* have to be approved by the other teacher. The only thing is that they must be literary."

"Like Chicano literature?"

"Certainly. No less than Van Horn's classics. And finally, contestants must be legally enrolled freshmen or sophomores. Each of you to select three from your classes."

"What does that do to his honors students?"

"Some of them are sophomores."

"Hell, I don't even know my students yet. We don't start classes until Monday."

"Those are his conditions, Rosca. Face it. They could be a lot worse."

Emiliano slumped in his chair and stared at Levine's untidy desk. What could this do for the honor of Chic Lit? Students he didn't know against Van Horn's handpicked honors students. And the bastard had not even declared his stakes yet. It should be the same as his: loser to resign. Jesus!

"Well, Rosca. Have you been thinking of your conditions?"

His mind was a blank. "My wife wants to help. To do the typing and Xeroxing."

The look of disgust on his colleague's face was obvious. "Come now. You can do better than that. This is a crusade. A battle of good against evil. Of reaction against progress."

"Of lambs against lions," Emiliano added.

"Seriously now. Three conditions."

"One. My wife to help as indicated."

"Come now."

His headshake was emphatic. "No. I promised her. That has to be condition number one." Levine scribbled onto a yellow pad. "Number two." Emiliano was thinking hard. "The participants are to be selected at random. That is, no handpicking. The names of all Van Horn's students go into a hat or something and he draws out three names. Same for me. If I'm lucky, he won't get any honors students."

Levine nodded in approval. "That's more like it."

"And number three. The test to be on a Saturday morning four weeks from now. That will give me a little time to coach my team."

Another fast scribble before Levine held the pad out at arm's length and trumpeted a sound of completion. "Now I'll just run these by Worth while you think of some good questions."

But Emiliano had already been thinking, and he rose and left the office in thoughtful absentmindedness. He reviewed the questions he had already been pondering. "Who is considered the grand old man of Chicano literature and what is the work he is most noted for?" Then he answered himself: "Villarreal. *Pocho.*"

"What do these writers have in common and what is a major work of each? Alurista, Judy Lucero, Gary Soto, Bernice Zamora."

"What is the profession of the title character in Rudolfo Anaya's most widely acclaimed novel and the title of that novel?"

As he pondered these and other possibilities, the realization came to him that Van Horn was doing the same with his classics. He stopped in the middle of his walk and looked up, surprised to see the bright sun and clear sky. The campus was alive with small groups of students making their way casually and light-heartedly across the lawn, like clusters of contented insects buzzing over the flowers in the lazy sunshine.

The contrast to his mood, to his intense absorption, shocked him. The world went on whatever he and Van Horn did or didn't do. The students, Chicano or not, went on their young ways enjoying life. What was the matter with him that he should leap at the bait of people like Van Horn? Itch at the opportunity to go mano a mano with him?

"Enough, Pata!" he said to himself. "There are things to do and only four weeks to do them in."

The weeks passed quickly. Too quickly. The lottery had been held and both he and Van Horn had, for better or worse, their three contestants. As Emiliano looked at the names of his team, he was grateful for small favors. He had not drawn the name of the big hulk of a football player who sat half asleep in the back row of his eight o'clock class. This Chicano jock only differed from gabacho football players in his dark complexion and Spanish surname.

Emiliano had drawn what looked like good solid students. A liberated young lady who was going to study medicine and go into the Public Health Service to work in the barrio. A young man majoring in business who hadn't made up his mind whether to go into computers or ethnic foods; there was money in both. (Ah, Emiliano thought, millions in micro-circuit chips or tortilla chips.) And another pale ghost of a young man who reminded him of himself fifteen years ago. A poet who would become a teacher. All three of them starry-eyed, eager. God bless them.

As the Saturday drew nearer, Lola too became busy. He heard her typing in the kitchen on Friday night. Between her activity and his this past week, they seemed only to be together while asleep in bed.

The Saturday of the test Emiliano woke at the first hint of daylight. His stomach tossed and swayed like a ship on a stormy sea. He started to tremble and could not stop himself. Finally he trembled Lola awake and she embraced him and reassured him. "It will be just fine," she said. "You'll see."

He was the first to arrive at Room 107, Langley Hall. A few moments later Van Horn strode in and smiled benevolently, as if in his mind he was already certain of the outcome and was showing what a gracious winner he would be.

Luckily the students came in as a group, chattering as if it were a social gathering and not a contest, before Emiliano found himself forced to speak to his adversary. Then Levine and Worth rushed in breathless, although it was fifteen minutes before the hour.

Van Horn rubbed his hands together and looked toward Dr. Worth. "Where are the papers, Phyllis?"

"They're on their way, Emery."

Her clear, bright voice was in contrast to Levine's fast shuffle over to Emiliano. "Where's your wife?" Levine hissed. "She was going to type and duplicate the material."

Emiliano shrugged. Somehow it had never occurred to him this morning and Lola had not said a word. Not asked for a ride to campus. Not asked him to carry the test forms himself.

The students sat and grew more quiet as the hour approached. Beads of perspiration formed on Emiliano's forehead. Where was that woman? It was bad enough to be drawn into this idiotic contest without his wife subjecting him to public shame by being late.

Van Horn approached from across the room and Emiliano sighed. What now? A complaint no doubt. "Rosca," Van Horn said. "You do realize what's at stake in this contest?"

"My job," Emiliano said. "But you never declared yourself."

There was a frown on Van Horn's face. The man looked pained. "Don't you think that's a bit heavy?" he said.

Emiliano bristled. "I gave my word. It's a point of honor."

"Over a silly quarrel? Look. One of my three students is in the honors program. I certainly wouldn't put my job on the line if I were in your shoes. Then there's the administration's attitude. You know what would happen if someone heard of our silly bet?"

"We'd both get fired."

"The punishment doesn't fit the crime," Van Horn said. "The wager should be something more appropriate. Something—"

"Something chicken."

"Well. If you insist on wagering your job. I'm not such a fool. If I lose—and there's little likelihood—I'll cook you a dinner of your choice. You and your students."

A sneer curled Emiliano's lip. Van Horn walked away. The minute hand on the wall clock ticked itself straight up and the door opened. In walked Lola, smiling as pert as you please, just as if she were the hostess welcoming guests at the door.

"It's about time," Emiliano hissed.

"All right, students," Dr. Worth said. "We're ready to start. Mrs. Rosca, would you pass out the tests? You will have one hour. We'll collect papers exactly at ten o'clock. If you're finished earlier you may turn in your paper and leave. And please, don't lift the cover sheet until I give the word."

Lola placed a neat package on the writing arm of everyone's chair. Then she handed one to each of the teachers, smiling at Emiliano as she passed him and went out the door.

Emiliano stared distractedly at the blank top page. He was watching his students poised for the word from Dr. Worth. "All right," Dr. Worth finally said. "You may begin."

Emiliano turned the page and stared in shock at the top of the sheet. There, as brazen and saucy as Lola herself, was the word "Nombre" with a line beside it for the students to write on.

Quickly he stared down the page at the first question. "¿Quién es el viejo grande de la literatura . . ." He could hardly believe his eyes. There was a restless murmur in the room and when Emiliano looked up he saw a red-faced Emery Van Horn rushing at him with a glint of murder in his eye.

"This is a trick!" Van Horn protested. "A cheap trick—"

Dr. Levine hurried up to them. "Please, gentlemen. The students."

"Did you see this?" Van Horn said, waving the test in Levine's face.

"Outside, gentlemen," Dr. Worth said. "You're disturbing the class."

They tumbled into the empty hall while Dr. Worth remained behind to monitor the test. "This is an outrage, Rosca!" Van Horn's voice had risen to a shout. "This is a direct violation of the rules and conditions we agreed upon!"

By now Emiliano had recovered his aplomb. He looked calmly up and down the hall for Lola, but she was not to be seen.

"Do you hear that, Rosca? A direct violation!"

"Ridiculous," Emiliano said. "My first condition was for my wife to type and duplicate the test. We did not agree that it *had* to be in one language or the other, although we did agree that they had to be literary questions. My wife just happens to type in Spanish."

"A fraud!" Van Horn protested. "Outrageously unfair."

"Rosca is right," Levine said. He was trying hard to restrain a smile. "The matter of language is covered indirectly in his first condition."

Red-faced, Van Horn sputtered and stomped down the hall. Levine started to laugh. "Beautiful," he said. "I have to hand it to you, Rosca. And don't worry about Van Horn. Phyllis and I will calm him down."

Emiliano smiled modestly as he re-entered the classroom. The students were working, some diligently, others with shaking heads and furrowed brows, while Dr. Worth kept watch.

"Very clever, Rosca," she whispered. "You keep this up and you'll find yourself a department chairman." Again the modest smile.

An hour later the students passed their papers to Dr. Worth and left. Emiliano stood by the door and nodded as they went by.

"This must be some kind of bad joke," one of Van Horn's students said.

"Piece o'cake, teach," Emiliano's liberated young lady said.

The poet stopped and smiled shyly. "I could have gotten every one in Spanish *or* English, but those others— Well." He tossed his head in the direction of Van Horn's students.

There was no doubt in Emiliano's mind. The day was his, thanks to Lola. He rushed into the hall and almost bumped into her as she approached the classroom. He grabbed her in a bear hug and kissed her.

"Mi vida," he said. "I owe you my job, my honor, and my undying gratitude."

"It needed a woman's touch," she said. "With you men, things are always mano a mano when they should be mente a mente."

"The one thing that would make it perfect is for Van Horn to resign."

Lola's smile faded. "Isn't it enough that you don't have to?" she said. "What if he did resign, which he won't. There would still be others. Maybe in the Physics Department next. Or even some of the students. You can't fight them all. There has to be a better way."

"You mean make friends with the bastard? Never."

"The least you can do is be thankful that Dr. Van Horn is going to prepare dinner for you."

"And for my students. If it weren't for them—and you—I wouldn't be looking forward to a Van Horn fiesta. To begin with, I'll have taquitos and Dos Equis. And then—"

"Don't forget Van Horn's students," she said. "They need encouragement too."

Drs. Levine and Worth came out of the classroom carrying the test papers and nodded at them. Emiliano took Lola's hand and followed down the hall, smiling to himself as he wondered what Lola would be up to next.

VII. War and Death

Rolando Hinojosa

CONVERSATIONS ON A HILL

I

"Hi, how you doin'? I was told to wait here—with you. You know how long we got to wait?"

"I can't say . . . you okay?"

"What?"

"Are you okay? Are you doing all right?"

"Yeah . . . They just brought me in and sent me here. To you. But I'm okay; I'm one of the ones from Charlie Battery, the Two Nineteenth? Been here long?"

"Yeah, but we just set up this morning. We'll probably be moving on again."

"Yeah? Ah, where are you from?"

"The Two Nineteenth."

"No, I don't mean this shit, I mean where are you *from*? Back home?"

"Oh . . . I'm from Texas."

"No shit? I'm from Louisiana; yeah . . . and I've been to Beaumont, Houston, Galveston, Orange . . . all those places. You know where that is?"

"Yeah, that's up the coast from us; I'm from the Valley."

"Oh, yeah? Where's that?"

"That's way down there, by the border. Next to Mexico."

"Is that anywhere near El Paso?"

"No—we're a long way from there, too; we're near the Gulf, by the Rio Grande."

"Oh, yeah. That's way down there, isn't it? How far is that from Houston?"

"I don't really know; I guess it's about four hundred miles . . ."

"You been there? To Houston?"

"No . . ."

"Oh . . . It's a big town, Houston . . . Were you guys in the Pass? I mean, were you part of the bunch that got caught?"

"Sure, all of us were . . . you too."

"Yeah, but I was talking about the firing and the thermiting . . . Able Battery . . ."

"Yeah, that was us."

"Boy, you guys are fast. Was *he* with you?"

"Who you talking about?"

"The red-faced guy . . . you know, the sergeant who brought us in?"

"Yeah; he, ah . . ."

"Is he a friend of yours?"

"Yeah, he's . . ."

"How do you pronounce your name, anyway?"

"What's that?"

"Your name . . . how do you say it?"

"Oh. Buenrostro. Boo N Ross Troh. Buenrostro."

"Run together like that? . . . Spanish, right? My name's Ben Pardue, but they call me Rusty 'cause I'm from Ruston, Louisiana; you know, Louisiana French. I'm a coonass."

"A what?"

"A Cajun; that's what I am, what we all are down there; a coonie. You know, coon-ass . . . You Catholic?"

"Catholic? No . . . why?"

"I am; all of us are. . . . Here comes that sergeant."

"His name's Hatalski—he's okay."

"Rafe, we've got a few minutes yet."

"This is one of the stragglers, Frank; his name's Pardue."

"Rusty Pardue, Sarge."

"You from the Two Nineteenth?"

"Charlie Battery, Sarge."

"What'd you do there?"

"Oh, I spotted some . . . and loaded; fired, too. You know, a little of this . . ."

"You've met Rafe here? . . . Good; you stay with him. You hungry?"

"No, Sarge; thanks . . ."

"Can you operate a phone?"

"Sure."

"You'll do that for a while, then. See you, Rafe. . . ."

"He's okay, eh, Ralph?"

"Yeah . . ."

"What's his name again?"

"Hatalski. Frank. Hatalski."

"Polish, right?"

"I think so . . ."

"Sure he is; look, all those guys with *ski* are Polish; I knew a whole bunch of them in basic . . . Where'd you do yours? . . . Your basic?"

"Fort Sill . . . Oklahoma."

"Oh, I know where it is . . . I've been there, too. . . . You like it?"

"Sill? Yeah, it was okay. . . . Are you all right?"

"What do you mean?" ·

"I mean, are you okay?"

"I'm all right . . . it's just that . . . well, I don't know anybody here. . . ."

"Yeah . . . how about a cigarette?"

"Hey . . . thanks . . . Can I have two more? . . . What'd you do at home? You work?"

"Well, I went to high school and to college, for a year, but my brothers and I, we got some land."

"Ranching, huh? You got a ranch in Texas? With horses and all that?"

"Some, but we mostly do farmwork."

"Yeah? What?"

"Just about everything: cabbage, tomato, carrots, broccoli . . . And cotton."

"Who picks your cotton?"

"What's that?"

"Your cotton; who picks that?"

"Oh . . . We do, and we hire some, too."

"You hire niggers for that?"

"Niggers? Colored?"

"Yeah, you know, black folks for picking . . . That's who picks at home . . . 'Course we pick it, too, but they hire out a lot . . ."

"There aren't that many Negroes in the Valley."

"So who picks it besides you all . . ."

"We do . . ."

"You're Spanish, right?"

"No; I'm Mexican."

"But you're from Texas?"

"Right."

"Oh . . . When do you all pick? Cotton?"

"Usually from around June to August . . . up to September, just about."

"We don't start till later; we pick in July and then we plow under in late September, early October . . . You notice the dirt around here?"

"Yeah, it looks pretty bad. . . . It's a hilly place, Korea."

"You can say that again; and rocky, too . . . You guys dry farm in that place?"

"No . . . we irrigate; we use the river."

"The Rio Grandee? Hey, I bet you've been over to Mexico a lot."

"Sure, it's right across."

"Across what?"

"The river; the Rio Grande . . ."

"Oh yeah . . . you got relatives there?"

"Yeah, like I said, it's right across the river . . ."

"And . . . and you speak Spanish?"

"Sure . . ."

"No shit?"

(Laughs) "Yeah . . ."

"What's so funny?"

"I speak Spanish all the time when I'm home . . ."

"And we speak French, d'ja know that? Yeah. At home. On the street. In the beer joints . . . anywhere . . . Lemme hear you say something in Spanish . . . Come on, Ralph."

164

"Rafe . . . ¿Qué quieres que te diga?"

"What'd you just say?"

"I said, 'What do you want me to say?' "

"Hey, d'ja really say that? That's pretty good. Say it again. Come on . . ."

"¿Qué quieres que te diga?"

"Tell you what, you teach . . . hey, here comes Hotski . . ."

"Hatalski . . ."

"Yeah . . ."

II

"You got a girl back home, Rafe? I don't mean someone serious, you know; I mean, a girl . . . any girl. You know. Someone to write to. Once in a while?"

"No . . . you?"

"I did; ah, I guess I still do—now and then; she was born there in Elton, and I met her when me and my Dad moved there, but then they moved on out to Eunice; that's a big town. Her father's pretty handy with his hands, and he knows a lot about tools, see? His name's Prosper. . . Her name's Suzy. Suzy Postelle. She's kinda . . . skinny, but she's nice. And quiet . . . and real nice. But you must have had a girl in school, right?"

"I was married once, and . . ."

"Hey, I didn't know that. What happened?"

"It was right after I got out of the Army, and . . ."

"You been in before? I *thought* you had. Why'd you come back for?"

"I went in right after high school; a whole bunch of us did . . . And we got out about the same time; we all went in for a short time, eighteen months."

"Yeh?"

"Yeah . . . and then I got married, and I went to junior college for a year, and I worked on the farm, but we planned for me to go to school . . . to college."

"College? Hey!"

"Yeah . . . but she died, Rusty."

"Died? She *died*? No . . ."

"She drowned . . ."

"Oh, Jesus . . . I'm sorry . . . No; damn! I, I'm sorry, man. Jesus . . ."

"It's okay; I can talk about it . . . Now. The reserve called me up right after that; called the other guys, too. Charlie, Joey, Sonny, you know . . . Called up a cousin of mine, too."

"Who's he? You got a cousin, too?"

"I've got a whole bunch of cousins . . . this one's special; you'd like him, Rusty; he's . . ."

"Yeah? What's he like?"

"He's a pretty good guy . . . he's over here someplace."

"No shit? Your cousin is? In Japan or out here?"

"Last I heard, he was here, in Pusan . . . yeah . . . he's a real good guy."

"Hey, I'm sorry about your wife; I mean . . . you know . . ."

"It's okay . . ."

"Gosh, how old are you, then? Twenty-two!"

"Twenty-one in January . . ."

"Coming up? Oh, man, we got to celebrate; no two ways about it . . . Yeah, no shit, we got to . . . Tell you what, we'll get some guys out . . . You know . . . We'll get drunk, right? Like we did in Japan last Christmas? Remember? Over at . . . at that place . . ."

"The whorehouse?"

"Yeah, *there* . . . that was *good*, wadn't it?"

"Yeah; it was good . . ."

"Hey, man, I'm sorry about . . . you know."

"It's okay, Rusty; I can talk about it . . ."

"My Mom died, too. Yours?"

"Yeah . . ."

"And your Dad?"

"Yeah . . ."

"But you got your two brothers . . . and all those cousins, right?"

"Yeah, sure . . ."

"Boy, that's nice . . . I only got *one* brother, and he lives in Lufkin, that's in East Texas . . . Angelina County? His wife's from up there . . . and that's where he lives . . . My Dad . . . he, ah, doesn't work anymore . . . He's disabled, you know what I mean? That's when we moved from Ruston to Elton. . . But he's a pretty nice old guy . . . I like him. He's a good man, but he doesn't know how to write, see, and I send him my allowance *every* month, and it's okay. . . . So you got a cousin here?"

"Yeah, and you'd like him; trouble is, I don't have his address . . ."

"Maybe you could write home and get it . . . Know what I mean? Say, that's silly, isn't it? I mean, you got to write *there* to get his address *here*? It'd be good, wouldn't it . . . Wouldn't it? And meet him? When you going to write home the next time?"

III

"Time to call in, Rusty. Rusty! Call-in time . . ."

"Oh . . . okay . . . Badger Four. Over. Badger Three calling in."

"What's up?"

"Everything's okay up here . . . Over."

"Understood. Out."

"Well, that's that . . . How long now?"

"One more hour, and that's it."

"Hey . . . how far are we from home?"

"What?"

"Home. How far are we from *home*? You know, miles. How many miles are we from home?"

"I don't know . . . Five. Six thousand?"

"Nah; it's got to be more than that."

"Okay."

"No—come on; how far are we, Rafe?"

(Laugh) "I don't know . . . It's a long way, that's all."

"I bet it's . . . I bet it's nine thousand miles."

"I guess so . . ."

"Don't you think about home? Don't you have anything back there?"

"I think about home all the time . . ."

"I do too. . . . What do you think about?"

"I think about home, that's all. Home. People. Home, I guess; I don't know. I think about home, that's all."

"I do too; I think about it all the time . . . I think about it, well, I think about it, you know. I think about home. You?"

"So do I, Rusty."

"I wonder how far it is?"

(Laugh) "I don't know; it's a long way."

"How far is it from where you live . . . to, ah, the state of Washington? Fifteen hundred?"

"Fifteen hundred, two thousand miles . . . I really don't know, Rusty."

"Okay, say two thousand, and how far is it to Hawaii? No; we didn't go to Hawaii . . . Right? Ok . . . let's see: how far is it then from Washington to Japan? Four, five thousand miles, right? What do you think?"

"Sounds right."

"Well, I'll bet it's no less than five thousand miles and you're two thousand miles, right? And, well, we're not too far from Japan here, but how far would you say we are from where my Dad lives in Elton? How far are you from Elton, Louisiana?"

"I don't know. Five? Six hundred miles?"

"How far are you from Houston again?"

"About four hundred."

"Yeah, six sounds about right . . . 'cause we're pretty close to two hundred miles. From Houston. Sooooo, I figure, ah, I figure from Elton to Washington, ah, it's about twenty-five hundred miles and then another five . . . We're about seven thousand five hundred miles from home."

"Yeah, I guess we are . . ."

"You think about it, ha?"

"Yeah . . . I think about it all the time."

"Me too. I got a lot of friends back home. You?"

"Yeah . . . I've got some (laughs) friends. Everybody's got some friends."

"Yeah? Well, I've got a *lot* of friends. I have . . . I've got a *lot* of friends at home. A *lot*."

IV

"Fog's clearing . . ."

"Yep."

"What time is Rafe supposed to get here?"

"Can't be too long . . . I imagine chow's about over. . . ."

"Yeah . . . I was just . . . oh-oh . . . Rusty? Rusty . . . what's that all about?"

"What are you talking about?"

"Well, I don't know. Looks like . . . Looks like there's about sixty of our guys down there."

"Where?"

"Here: take a look."

"Where?"

"Turn to the right. See Two-Tit Mountain?"

"Yeah."

"Okay: go to the right one. Now, come on down to the belly button. Got it? Now, from the belly button, go to three o'clock. Four. Five . . ."

"Oh, shit."

"You see them?"

"Yeah, there's about seventy of our guys down there . . . chowing down . . . Hold it . . ."

"What's the matter?"

"Shit, that's no seventy guys; that's more like a hundred and fifty or sixty of 'em down there. What the hell are they doing? Isn't that a firing lane?"

"I don't think so . . . What the hell is that, Rusty? Is that a patrol?"

"If it is, that's the biggest goddam patrol I've ever seen. What the hell are they doing down there? Ned, are you sure that's not a firing lane?"

"I'm checking . . . No; it's okay."

"When'd you see them?"

"Just now, when the fog burned off and all . . ."

"Hmph . . . well, I'm going to call Brom and let him know just the same."

"Why don't we just wait until Rafe gets here; it'll be just a few more minutes."

"Holy shit!"

"What?"

"You look through these now. Look!"

"Where?"

"To the left, by where Brom should be."

"Gee-zuz! Those guys are Chinks."

"Damn right. How many, you think?"

"Let's see . . . Oh, sweet Jesus, there must be two, three hundred of 'em."

"At least, yeah."

"Man, look at what the fog brought in . . ."

"Yeah."

"Ta-hell's going on, though?"

"I don't know . . . let's see, looks like they're between us and Brom."

"You sure?"

"Well, shit, they're about a thousand yards away, and Brom's what—twelve, thirteen hundred yards . . . A mile, right?"

"Hey, here comes Rafe . . . get down, Rafe."

"What?"

"Down! Get down!"

"What the hell's going on?"

"Take a peek . . . Here . . . No, no, right down there . . . Well?"

"Goddam! That's a lot of people down there."

"Isn't *that* the truth. Now, look to the left. What do you see?"

"Shit! Those guys are Chinks . . ."

"What do you think, Rafe?"

"I don't know . . . they're all chowing down . . . One thing though: they haven't seen each other."

"Yeah? How do you figure that?"

" 'Cause there's a couple of rises between them . . . Ta-hell's going on?"

"That's what we're wondering."

"Well, shit, give me the phone."

"What are you fixing to do?"

"I'm going to call Bromley up."

"Rafe, you think it's safe?"

"Safe? Goddam, Ned, they went right by him. Let's see if he's alive or holed up or something . . . Hold it a minute . . ."

"Yeah? What's the matter?"

"You. Are you okay, Ned?"

"Yeah; why?"

"You sure you're okay?"

"Yeah, I'm fine."

"Okay . . . I'm calling Brom right now. Rusty, what's Brom's call?"

"I think he's Badger Three."

"Okay. Get Batallion on the line, Rusty; tell 'em to hold on till I get through to Brom. Tell Hat I'm on the other line, and tell him about our guys over by Tit. Okay?"

"Any chance they cut the wire?"

"We'll see . . . There, it's ringing. . . . Badger One? I mean, Badger Three . . . Aw, shit: Brom!"

"Hey, Rafe; you okay, buddy?"

"Yeah . . . You, ah, you see any Chinks out there?"

"What are you talking about?"

"I'm saying: you see any Chinks out there?"

"At this hour of the goddam morning?"

"Behind you, Brom."

"What's wrong with you?"

"Look, Brom, there's some Chink infantry between you and us up here. They're about three hundred yards behind you."

"No shit?"

(Sigh) "Brom . . . what are you doing?"

"Well, I'm looking up front."

"Not up front, goddammit. Turn around and put your glasses on. . . . Now, what do you see?"

"Holy shit! There must be close to a couple-a-hundred guys back there."

"We figure close to three or four . . . Listen, now: we've also got close to two hundred of *our* guys to the right. You got that?"

"Yeah? What the hell's going on?"

"I don't know, Brom, but I'm thinking of bringing some mortars in."

"Mortars? Shit; that won't do it."

"You want us to call in some artillery, then? Right on top of you?"

"Hell, yes . . ."

"How deep can you go?"

"Deep enough . . . really, Rafe . . . Rafe?"

"Now, I don't know what our troops are doing out there, but we got to get them out before we fire on the Chinks 'cause once we start up, then the Chink artillery'll open up."

"Yeah?"

"Well, we get ours out of the way on the double . . ."

"Yeah?"

"And when that's clear, we start on the guys down there . . . Now, Brom, you're going to have to tuck. Deep. Hold it a minute, Brom; hang on. Rust, you got Batallion yet? Good . . . Brom! Brom! Okay: when the shit hits, I figure they'll cut and run down the same way they came up: right at you. They sure as hell can't go to the sides; that's too goddam steep for 'em . . . so, they'll run like hell and right back at you. You're going to have to put up with a lot of shit . . . you know, first ours and then theirs . . .

"Go ahead."

"Give us a few minutes to get Batallion to get those guys moving."

"Check."

"Don't hang up, Brom; leave the line on, I don't want any ringing."

"Gotcha . . ."

"Rust, you still got Hat on the line? . . . Good . . . Hat? Rafe. Hat, we got some Chinks about a thousand yards up front . . . No, they're chowing down . . . Bromley . . . Yeah, but there's a snag: We got some two hundred of our guys over by Two-Tit . . . We don't know, but if you can move them, Rust and Ned'll work out the coordinates for this place . . . Yeah . . . Okay, hang on, I gotta get back to Brom. Hey, Brom! . . . Look, it'll be a few more minutes; you hang on for a little while . . . Ned and Rusty and I are getting the stuff ready for Batallion. Hang on. . . . Okay? Stay on the line now."

"Go ahead."

"How you guys coming?"

"It's all here."

"Okay. Hat? Hat? Rafe . . . that's good. Good! Listen. Rust'll give you the poop, I gotta get back to Brom. See you. . . . Brom!"

"Go ahead."

"Hat says our guys are moving out now. Here goes: we've got every bit of ground sensed, and we're going to shell the shit right out of them. Rusty's passing all the coordinates to Batallion . . . yeah, all of them and in sequence of fire. Got that? Now, we're going to fire past you all the way to Eddie Boy Ridge."

". . . Eddie Boy Ridge; got it."

"After you and I sign off here, you then count for three minutes and after that we'll open up short and then long. We're going to stop two hundred yards short of you and then, two minutes later, we're going to fire two hundred yards further up . . ."

"Two hundred yards . . ."

"We'll wait another two minutes after that. Got it? . . . Okay. And then, we're going to fire all the way to Eddie Boy at hundred yard intervals: Able, Baker, Charlie; Charlie, Able, Baker; and like that. . . ."

"You'll be spotting hundreds all the way to the Ridge. . . ."

"Good boy! Listen: Ned's got his eyes on the Chinks and Rusty's looking to ours; so don't worry about *our* guys. I'm going to start counting, Brom, and it's going to start raining shit down there. You tuck in now. Wad up. I'm signing off; I've still got Hat on the line and you've got three minutes, Brom, three minutes starting: NOW!

"Hat? We're all set . . . We'll be okay . . . Sure . . . Yeah . . . Yeah . . . Okay . . . *Right* . . . *okay*, I'll watch him. Over and out and all that good shit, Hat. What? Right; see you, now."

V

"Rafe, you remember the time ole Ned blew up? You know, when the Chinks? At Eddie Boy Ridge?"

"Sure . . . I remember . . ."

"You know *why* he blew up, Rafe? You know *why* he went crazy?"

"Why?"

" 'Cause he talked a lot. Well, I talk a lot, too, but I mean he talked a lot to himself. And that's not right. He heard voices; he told me so. You can go crazy that way, and that's why he blew up . . . Don't you know about those things?"

"You hungry?"

"What?"

"Are you hungry?"

"No!"

"I wish I had a candy bar; one of those goddam Snickers; you remember them?"

"You went to college, didn't you?"

"Just the one year."

"Well, I didn't finish high school, but I read about that kind of stuff. . . . Talkin' about Ned. We had a good school there in Elton. Elton, Louisiana, yessir . . . I went as far as the tenth grade; well, *up to* the tenth grade . . . that's pretty good, right? I mean, that, that's being a sophomore. Right?"

"Right. Call in, Rusty."

"What?"

"Call in. Batallion."

"Right. Right."

"There. . . . You remember when we caught the Chinks there, at Eddie Boy Ridge?"

"Sure I do."

"I wasn't angry at 'em, you know."

"What do you mean?"

"Well I, I don't *hate* 'em; I used to hate 'em. A lot. But not anymore."

"Why not?"

"I don't know . . . I just *don't*. Now, *last* year, when they caught us in the Pass? And they, ah, they put it to us?"

"Yeah?"

"Well, I really did then, boy; I really hated hated 'em then . . . I really did: they're shootin', and it was cold, and we were caught there. Like rats, you know. Just like rats, and boy . . . I really did. I *hated* their ass. Man, they . . . why, shit, I'd-a-killed one of them if I'd-a-seen 'im . . . I would've, boy, right there. Boom! You know? Bring in the guns, yeah! But . . . I don't now. I don't mean I don't *hate* 'em, you know, but they're not my friends, right? And, and that's why we're here and that's why they're over there on that other hill . . . but . . . but, ah, I don't know, it's funny."

"Yeah . . ."

"Remember that time?"

"Sure . . ."

"Boy, that's a long time ago, right? Eddie Boy Ridge? How many yards is that, Rafe? Years, I mean, how long ago . . . was it?"

"Well—about seven months, I guess. Right."

"Let's see . . . Well, we can work it out . . . Yeah, ole Ned. He was a nice old guy . . . I wonder where he's at?"

"Probably home."

"Yeah—he got out on one of them Section Eights or them Section Nines. Boy, I sure don't want one of them. . . . I want to go *home*, but I want to go home *right*. Know what I mean? Be somebody when I get home. I don't want nobody to go around pointing their *goddam* finger at me . . . How about you, Rafe?"

"Yeah, I want to go home, too . . ."

"You okay, Rafe?"

"Yeah, I'm just tired . . ."

"What are you going to do when you get home, Rafe?"

"I don't know; I'm just going to go home for a while, but I want to get out of here first."

"Well, *I* want to get out of here first too, you know . . . I, I . . . we're not home safe, I know, but . . . but I don't think we're going to get it. Shit, we've been through too much, right? Remember? We were in the Pass . . . 'Course, Charlie died, but . . . Hey, those are nice guys, right? Those are good friends you got. I got friends like that too, but they're not here, they're, they're at home, but you got friends here . . . You know. You got Joey, and, and that crazy guy, what's his name? Sonny . . . He's a case, isn't he? Ain't he a lick, though? And I sure had a good time with you guys in Japan. That was good, boy; I, I really liked that. You guys really know how to have fun. I'd never, *never*, been to a . . . to a whorehouse. Anywhere. You know—no money. But that was *good*; I liked it there, but you know, those, ah, girls . . . they're not really whores, are they?"

"Oh, they're whores all right."

"Yeah, but I always figured that they, ah, that they'd be real *old*. Those are young girls, I mean, they're shit, they're *my* age, *your* age, right?"

"Yeah."

"Yeah . . . Boy, I sure had a lot of fun. Did you?"

"Yeah, I had a lot of fun, too, It was good . . ."

"I did . . . I really did . . . That was nice. That was a lot of fun. Yeah . . ."

Miguel Armenta

LA MISMA LEJANIA

Hacía más de media hora que habían salido del Cañón de Guadalupe y el viejo automóvil avanzaba dificultosamente a través de la yerma superficie. Pronto estarían en la carretera principal y enfilarían rumbo a Mexicali. El calor era agotador pero había valido la pena el paseo, además de la oportunidad de buscar algunas huellas de vetas que podían significar un nuevo giro en la maltrecha economía. Pedro miraba de soslayo a su hijo y se sentía orgulloso de verlo, sano, vivaracho, con todo un mundo por delante. Sí, a base de estudios y de esfuerzo, su muchacho llegaría a ser un buen profesionista, tal vez médico o licenciado, algo, en fin, que le hiciera la vida más fácil de lo que había sido para él. Los sueños de Pedro se mezclaban con los espejismos que, allá adelante y a los lados, a lo lejos, parecían ofrecer venturas sin fin. Era tan interesante esa superficie árida, amplia, sin estorbos, franca, que Pedro no pudo menos que sentirla como una profunda expresión de sí mismo y de su gente.

Arturo, su amigo, guiaba el automóvil y parecía absorto también en la lejanía, como si estuviera ansioso de llegar pronto a aquella carretera que se antojaba tan distante. Luis, el hijo de Pedro, muchacho alegre, sano y de excelente humor, se rebullía en su asiento como con deseos de bajarse del auto y echar a correr para llegar más pronto al crucero. De pronto, el motor dejó de funcionar; con el impulso que llevaba, el auto avanzó todavía unos metros pero pronto se detuvo totalmente. Arturo lanzó una exclamación de impaciencia y se bajó, dirigiéndose al frente. Abrió el cofre y una oleada de vapor lo hizo retroceder. El motor parecía estar ardiendo por dentro y por fuera.

—¡Caray, Pedro, ésta sí que es mala suerte! Precisamente en plena Salada nos tenía que pasar esto.

—No te preocupes —respondió Pedro—, vamos a echarlo a andar.

Los dos estuvieron intentando hacer funcionar nuevamente el auto pero fue inútil. Además, no traían agua para echarle al radiador. Ni siquiera traían para beber. Les había parecido tan fácil el viaje que no tomaron esas precauciones básicas para transitar por la Salada.

—Y ahora, ¿qué hacemos? —dijo Arturo—.

—Mira —dijo Pedro, señalando con el índice a lo lejos—, allá se ve polvo, debe ser un camino; si nos vamos caminando podemos llegar allá con tal de no perder la dirección. De todos modos, andando en línea recta llegaríamos a la carretera de San Felipe.

—No —dijo Arturo con gesto preocupado—, no creo que sea prudente hacer eso. Es demasiado lejos. Creo que lo mejor sería esperar aquí a que pase algún carro y nos ayuden.

—Pero, ¿quién crees que va a pasar por aquí, hombre? —replicó Pedro—. Aquí nos podríamos estar días y sin agua y comida nomás no. Mira, vamos haciendo una cosa. Tú quédate aquí y Luis y yo nos vamos caminando hasta salir a la carretera de San Felipe. Luego venimos por ti. O si pasa alguien, que lo dudo, pides ayuda. Tú, ¿qué piensas, Luis? ¿Te animas?

—Claro que sí, papá. Caminando aprisa fácil llegamos. No es cosa del otro mundo.

—No lo creo prudente de todos modos —advirtió Arturo— pero si están decididos, pues, ¡buena suerte! El que encuentre primero ayuda irá por el otro. Espero que pronto pase alguien por aquí.

—Buena suerte y no te preocupes, Arturo, —añadió Pedro confiadamente—. Nos vemos pronto. Hasta luego.

Pedro y Luis se pusieron ansiosamente en camino. Sentían el sol a plomo sobre ellos y el calor que la arena devolvía como poderoso reflector. Pero ellos eran de Mexicali, ya estaban acostumbrados al calor —¡qué caray!— no había por qué amilanarse. De vez en cuando volvían la cabeza para ver a lo lejos el auto hasta que éste se convirtió en un punto y, finalmente, ya no lo vieron más. Camine y camine siguieron los dos. Al principio habían intercambiado palabras y hasta habían bromeado. Pero ahora, después de mucho caminar, sentían las piernas pesadas y el agotamiento empezaba a manifestarse, mientras una cierta aprensión empezaba a invadir su espíritu.

Pedro se hacía fuerte, pues no quería que se trasluciera su preocupación para no inquietar a su hijo. Este caminaba con denuedo y determinación. Sin embargo, llegó un momento en que Pedro ya no pudo precisar si realmente estaban caminando en la dirección tomada al principio. Al iniciar el camino había parecido fácil, teniendo como punto de referencia el lugar donde se habían detenido y el mismo auto. Pero ahora parecía que tras de caminar y caminar, aquellas siluetas lejanas frente a ellos seguían iguales, imperturbablemente iguales. Pedro había esperado que al avanzar, poco a poco se irían percibiendo con mayor nitidez aquellas crestas, pero no sucedía así. ¡Pesaba tánto ahora el propio cuerpo! Y aquel maldito sol que parecía chuparles la poca agua de su cuerpo. Si tan sólo hubiera alguna pequeña sombra para descansar al menos un momento; siquiera para no sentir aquella hornaza que los envolvía. Pero los pocos cactos no ofrecían sombra alguna aprovechable. La única esperanza era arreciar el paso y tratar de llegar lo más pronto posible a la carretera.

Pero, ¿dónde diablos estaba la carretera? ¡Si al menos supieran con certeza a qué distancia estaba! Eso les daría más ánimo para continuar. Pedro quiso decirle a su hijo su idea de arreciar el paso pero se quedó atónito al ver que no podía articular palabra; sentía la lengua pegada y casi paralizada. Esto lo aterrorizó pero, sacando fuerza de flaqueza, con un ademán le indicó a Luis que había que apretar el paso. Pronto se dio cuenta que era inútil el esfuerzo; allá a lo lejos seguían las siluetas igualmente distantes. Pedro sintió que estaba dando vueltas en una danza infernal sin sentido. Volteó a ver a su hijo y sintió una puñalada en el corazón. Luis tenía una expresión desesperada, con la boca abierta, seca, y con los ojos casi vidriosos. La angustia invadió a Pedro. Era urgente beber agua, pero ¿de dónde? Vio unos cactos y tuvo una idea. Le indicó con la mano a Luis que se detuviera y se aproximara a él, junto a los cactos. Sí, él había visto en una película cómo un hombre perdido en el desierto había abierto una de esas plantas y se había salvado chupando el ansiado líquido. Pero, horrorizado, recordó que no tenía cuchillo como aquel hombre de la película.

Su hijo estaba allí, a su lado, con los ojos desmesuradamente abiertos, como presintiendo la tragedia. Pedro no podía soportar ver a su hijo así; había que hacer algo; sí, con las manos arrancaría la corteza del cacto y beberían su líquido; primero su hijo, su amado hijo, que se moría de sed ante sus ojos. No esperó más; se abalanzó sobre el cacto para arrancarle la corteza, pero sólo sintió las horribles punzadas de las agudas espinas; quiso arrancar la corteza, pero era inútil, ya las fuerzas no le alcanzaban; quizá si lo hubieran hecho antes, cuando todavía no estaban agotados . . . quizá . . . Volvió los ojos hacia su hijo y sintió que una oleada de amargura le llenaba la boca, aunque la siguió teniendo seca. Su hijo ya no podría beber agua aunque la hubiera. Ya no podría masticar el cacto aunque lograra descortezarlo. Se había quedado inmóvil, con los ojos desmesuradamente abiertos, fijos, vidriosos, con la mueca inconfundible de la muerte.

¿Y si todo esto fuera una pesadilla? Debo despertar —pensó Pedro— despertaré y veré a mi hijo a mi lado, en el auto, mientras nos dirigimos hacia la carretera; mi hijo vivaracho, sonriente, lleno de vida . . . mi hijo . . . ya vamos a llegar, sí, a Mexicali, a la casa, vamos a abrazar muy fuerte a mis otros hijos, a mi esposa . . . vamos a tomar agua fresca . . .

Pero allí estaba el sol, como ascua; nunca lo vio así antes. De haber sabido, ¡Cómo se me ocurrió! mi hijo . . .

Terminó de desplomarse sobre un costado, con una mano clavada en el cacto todavía, la otra como queriendo inútilmente alcanzar aquel cuerpo calcinado, seco, de su hijo. Sentía que el calor de la arena le invadía todos los huesos, se sentía ya sin líquido en su cuerpo, con una sequedad mortal. Sentía que el sol bajaba y lo tenía ya encima, con un resplandor inimaginable, como una llama inmensa, implacable . . .

Y luego, sólo quedó arena, arena, cactos, dos cuerpos secos y allá, a lo lejos, las siluetas engañosas, iguales, con la misma lejanía.

Leo Romero

THE BUTTERFLY COLLECTOR

You were chasing butterflies
when you fell
You felt the heavy wings
pounding in your chest
and then they were silent
as if caught in a net

And you did not chase butterflies anymore
for you were caught
The bright red butterfly of your heart
was very still
The jungles of Mexico turned blue
and the world stopped on its axis

NOTHING MORE CAN
HAPPEN TO YOU
WHEN YOU ARE DEAD

I do not understand the skeletons
they try to communicate with me
but their words are garbled
as if they had cotton in their mouths
But their mouths are empty
They do not even have tongues

The skeletons pat me on the back
as if they were old friends
Where is it that we knew each other,
I ask them, there is something

so familiar about you
I wish you had eyes, I tell them,
then I would know who you are
The skeletons raise their bony fingers
to their empty eye sockets
and it seems to me as if they're weeping
But there are no tears

I feel lonely, I tell them
You are all so different from me
I am soft and warm
and you are hard and cold
I cannot imagine embracing you
And I cannot imagine any greater terror
than having you by my side in bed

The skeletons leave me alone
They go off in pairs
At least they are not alone,
I think, and realize
that I am lonelier than they
And it is I who have the harder chore
For they have no worries
they are dead, and there is
nothing worse that can happen to them

Alvaro Cardona-Hine

A DRUNKEN POEM FOR BARBARA

in Baja
at Ernesto's
a flower without an adjective
because of all the booze
the beer and mescal that I have drunk
to find that adjective
and
of course
missing you
missing your shoulder
that road in the night
between cemeteries and three-legged dogs

last night
while the moon tried hard to soften dread
I looked the ocean in the eye
and it wasn't my mother
a cemetery behind us held plastic flowers
choked with sand in its poor throat
I waited against the blank side of my wanting to embrace you
having always known that light is the beginning of curvature
the stamp that seals two wings in flight

oh female in the sting of memory
absent flower
absent offering
absent presence
last night that same wild moon
stuck its feet through the windows of our car
the sky was tight with stars
and you were absent as perfume
absent as comfort
I went and sat by the beach
the fog was half my sleeping bag

it came in truant
late
an unpaid whore

strange place this Ernesto's
a resort in the dust
six miles of dirt road into the wind
(Miguel's knife cuts the little crab in half
don't hesitate I tell him
cut
cut
three legs on either side
try that now for bait)
the afternoon waves its arms of ancient linen
the air
once the wind gets into its soluble posture
smiles and is cold
moving its branches
my mother is what I see with kindness
children gathered into cords of laughter
poverty nibbling at the dirtied flesh of sunlight
a horizon of something dead on its back
overturned cars in the fields
cockroaches on a thin diet of running
a vast unfinished sadness
women and sand dunes each softening the other

at 1:30 a.m. the lights of a car in the distance
speak to me of your leap into the arms of New Mexico
yesterday
before the sun went down
an albatross came and sat on a calloused dream
the last ridge before the liquid foams out of darkness
near it
a goat dead on its own heap of bones
had collapsed into stillness
I recall how correct how splendid they seemed
those few white vertebrae above the chunks of fur

seagulls caress a thigh of wind
coasting sideways as if hunger were lighter than air
ducks fly with necks outstretched
heads almost independent
smaller birds travel the length of each wave
its gathering mountain

and at the last escape from under
the sun wades in blue pastels and greens
golden with foam
the trip settles into this
days of crazed iodine and lives of unindictable madness
oh girl far off in Santa Fe
with your grace told in my heart
our separate journeys end here
a pattern of mist and joy

Martín Espada

WAITING FOR THE COPS

In front
of the public housing project
someone, a big man,
was murdering a junkie.
A scream falsettoed
through Brooklyn's
blind street-vendor night
in two languages.

This junkie tried
to steal a car
under the one street light
that wasn't broken,
and now he was telling
the neighborhood
about the dizzy rush of death,
a crazy sidewalk mystic
predicting his own
assassination.

The buildings were priests
with nothing to say,
a squat and pious brick.
Windows awoke
in dim and yellow fear,
overlooking a one-act play.

Down below,
someone, a brown man,
walked out
and stopped the killing
of the junkie.

His wife called the cops.

Three men
wrestling, stiff-armed,
in the street,
voices broken bottles
slashing at the moment,
nerves protruding like wires
from a blasted fusebox,
waiting for the cops
to arrive
to start the killing
so that the cops could stop it.

Three clowns
playing to an empty
coliseum,
gravediggers
trying to avoid
the subject of death
and waiting for the cops.

Waiting for the cops.
Waiting at the welfare
and the free clinic
and the jail (can't make bail).

Waiting for the gypsy cab,
or the ambulance.

Waiting for the boss
and his punchclock lectures,
waiting for the landlord's
pipe-busted heat,
waiting for the caseworker's
ritual humiliation
and then the check.

Waiting for Jesus.

Waiting for work.
Waiting for the liquor store
to open,
or the pawnshop.

Waiting in fluorescent cubicles,
abandoned hallways,
chain-gang shuffle lines,
haunted bus stations,
weary laundromats,
prison visiting rooms,
all faintly smelling
of frustrated urination.

Waiting
waiting to wait
waiting not to wait
waiting tables
waiting for the sake
of waiting
hating the waiting.

"Call back if somebody
gets hurt, lady."

Waiting for the cops.

Noel Rico

ON HEARING
OF THE AILING
JOHNNY WEISSMULLER

Tarzan's call
to the animals
that

once followed
him
across
the screen in
directed
stampedes

now
puts holes
in the late
night
quiet
of a hospital:

All the
other
patients
are
startled
out
of their dreams;
and
the nurses
arrive
annoyed
at this old man:
But

he does
not see
them.

He waits only
for Death
to come
to his aid.
Somewhere
inside
the clouds of dust
the stampeding
animals
have raised
in his dreams;
somewhere
inside
the roar and
the mighty muscles

Death
approaches,
wearing
the tailored
bushjacket
of
the white
game hunter,
carrying
the one rifle
Tarzan
didn't
get to smash
against
a tree trunk.

EXCERPT FROM THE SOUTH BRONX XX
(The Assassination of John F. Kennedy)

The day the television set
Showed us the outcome of those fatal shots
I was home with my grandparents:
The good Catholic president,
                              As my grandfather's friend
Called him,
              Was now dead.
              At the pull of several cords,
Which my grandmother tugged at slowly, the windows
Closed their eyes and shed dark tears that were shadows.
My grandmother's muffled cries
Reached my ears;
And made my tongue turn into something quiet.

Soon the neighbors arrived:
And one of them said
That somewhere else
Men were laughing
Over a game of cards,
As the vodka was being passed
From hand to hand;
And that there was a fat man
                              Pounding one of his shoes
Against his desk, from the great joy he felt.
My grandfather nodded in agreement.
I knew nothing about politics and presidents:
But I knew that vodka
Was a drink that looked like water,
And suspected
That it must taste just
As bad as the whiskey
My grandfather once gave me.

The Authors

MARJORIE AGOSIN is a Chilean poet born in 1955 who has done her graduate work in the United States and who now lectures at Wellesley College. She is the author of two volumes of poetry: *Chile: gemidos y cantares* (1977) and *Conchalí* (1980).

JUSTO S. ALARCON, Assistant Professor of Chicano literature and Chicano culture at Arizona State University, is the founder of the journal *La Palabra*, which publishes Chicano literature and scholarship written in Spanish. He is presently finishing a novel, *Los siete hijos de la Llorona*.

MIGUEL ARMENTA was born in Mexicali, Baja California. Formerly head of the Department of Philosophy at the Centro de Enseñanza Técnica y Superior, he is presently Asesor Académico of the Universidad Pedagógica Nacional.

MARIA DEL CARMEN BOZA was born in 1952 in Havana, Cuba, where her father was managing editor of a newspaper. At the age of eight she emigrated to Miami with her parents. "Etruscans" is her first publication. She has recently completed a novel, *Death of the Virgin*, which explores attitudes toward history and virginity.

NASH CANDELARIA, author of the widely praised Chicano novel *Memories of the Alhambra* (1977), is a descendant of one of the pioneer families that founded Albuquerque, New Mexico. *Not By The Sword*, the second novel in his projected series about the Rafa family, will be published by the Bilingual Press in mid-1982.

ALVARO CARDONA-HINE has published nine books of poetry and translation, including *Agapito* (1969), an elegy in prose form. He has also translated Vallejo's *Spain, Let This Cup Pass From Me* for Red Hill Press.

RAFAEL CATALA is a Cuban poet and essayist. He is the author of *Caminos/Roads* (1973), *Círculo cuadrado* (1974), and *Ojo sencillo/Triqui-traque* (1975), and coauthor of *Cinco aproximaciones a la narrativa hispanoamericana* (1977).

MARTIN ESPADA was born in the Brownsville section of Brooklyn, New York, the product of Puerto Rican and Jewish parentage. He is presently a paralegal with the Dane County Welfare Rights Alliance in Madison, Wisconsin. Mr. Espada has been published in *Abraxas. Plumbline,* and the *Journal of Contemporary Puerto Rican Thought*.

RAFAEL JESUS GONZALEZ was born and raised in the bilingual-bicultural setting of El Paso, Texas. Currently he teaches literature and creative writing at Laney College in Oakland, California. He has published extensively in the United States, Mexico, and abroad, and his collection of verse *El hacedor de juegos/The Maker of Games* has gone into a second printing.

ROLANDO HINOJOSA is the author of the novel *Klail City y sus alrededores*, which won the Premio Casa de las Américas (Havana) in 1976, the first time a Chicano novel was so honored. His other works include *Estampas del Valle y otras obras* (1973), *Korean Love Songs* (1978), and *Mi querido Rafa* (1981). "Conversations on a Hill" is from *Rites and Witnesses*, the forthcoming sixth part of the Klail City Death Trip series.

189

THE AUTHORS

EL HUITLACOCHE is the author of several stories and poems in *The Bilingual Review/La Revista Bilingüe* and the *Mexico Quarterly Review*. One of his stories, "The Man Who Invented the Automatic Jumping Bean," was selected for the anthology *The Best of the Small Presses* and subsequently praised in the *New York Times* as a "masterpiece." His poems will be published in the forthcoming book *Five Poets of Aztlán*.

ENRIQUE R. LAMADRID, teacher, writer, and cultural worker, born in 1948, Embudo, New Mexico, raised in Albuquerque, is currently teaching at Northern New Mexico Community College at Española. His poems have been anthologized in *Flor y Canto I, The Indian Rio Grande*, and *A Ceremony of Brotherhood* (the Tricentennial Anthology of the New Mexico Pueblo revolt) and in magazines: *Sunstone, El Cuaderno, Goathead, New Mexico Magazine,* and *Plural* (Mexico City).

NAOMI LOCKWOOD BARLETTA, born in Mayagüez, Puerto Rico, and currently pursuing graduate studies at the State University of New York at Binghamton, has had the following books published: the text *Fair Poetry* (1980) and the poetry collections *Sueños y señales* (1979) and *Alrededor de un encuentro* (1981).

PAT MORA, a native of El Paso, Texas, has taught English at the high school, community college, and university levels. She is presently assistant to the Vice President for Academic Affairs at the University of Texas at El Paso. Her poems have been published in *Puerto del Sol, New America's Women Artists and Writers of the Southwest,* and *Kikiriki: Children's Literature Anthology*.

CARLOS MORTON is a distinguished playwright, poet, and fiction writer who is currently in the Drama department of the University of Texas at Austin. His work has appeared in *Revista Chicano-Riqueña, Tejidos, Caracol, Nuestro, De Colores, El Grito,* and numerous other publications.

ELIAS MIGUEL MUÑOZ, born in 1954 in Camagüey province, Cuba, is currently a doctoral candidate at the University of California, Irvine. He has been published in *Chiricú, Maize,* and in the literary review *El Puente* (Madrid). His first novel, *Los viajes de Orlando Cachumbambé*, will be published soon in Mexico City.

GUADALUPE OCHOA THOMPSON, born in 1937 in La Feria, Texas, is currently teaching at the University of Oklahoma. She has published her poetry in *La Voz* and has given readings of her work before the Popular Culture Association. She is an assistant editor of *Minority Voices*.

JUDITH ORTIZ COFER, currently in the English department at Broward Community College, has been published in *Kansas Quarterly, New Mexico Humanities Review, SEZ, South Florida Poetry Review*, and many other publications. She is the author of the chapbook *Latin Women Pray* and is poetry editor of the *Florida Arts Gazette*.

HUMBERTO J. PEÑA, born in Havana and trained as a lawyer at the University of Havana, is currently a professor of Spanish and of literature at West Virginia State College. He has published a collection of short stories, *Ya no habrá más domingos* (1971) and a novel, *El viaje más largo*. He has an anthology of Cuban poetry in press.

NOEL RICO is a writer from the New York area who has recently taken up residence in Hialeah, Florida. His work has appeared in the magazines *Contact II, Y'Bird, Revista Chicano-Riqueña*, and others. In 1978 he was awarded a creative writing fellowship from the National Endowment for the Arts. He has appeared in the films *The Nuyorican Poets* (1976), *New York Español* (which aired on Italian television), and *Isabel la Negra* (starring José Ferrer, Raúl Julia, and Miriam Colón).

ALBERTO RIOS has had fiction and poetry published in *The Salt Cedar, New America, Blue Moon News, North American Review, Prairie Schooner, The Little Magazine, Citybender, Tequila Press Poetry Review*, and many others. In 1977 he won the Academy of American Poets Poetry Contest, Tucson. He received a Fellowship Grant in Creative Writing from the National Endowment for the Arts in 1980. His forthcoming book, *One Night in a Familiar Room*, won the 1981 Walt Whitman Award sponsored by the Academy of American Poets.

DIANA RIVERA, born in Puerto Rico and educated at Teachers College of Columbia University, currently teaches art in Spanish Harlem. She has had paintings exhibited in New York City and Puerto Rico, and her poems have appeared in *Plaza* (Harvard), *Central Park: A Review*, and the anthology *I Call Myself Daughter, And It Is Good*.

J. W. RIVERS, born in Chicago and educated at the Universidad de las Américas (Mexico City), has published poetry in some eighty literary magazines such as *Pikestaff Review, Poet and Critic, Southwest Review, Puerto del Sol, Maize, New Mexico Humanities Review, Southern Humanities Review*, and *Akros Review*. He has also published a chapbook, *From the Chicago Notebook* (1979).

ALFONSO RODRIGUEZ, born in 1943 in Guerrero, Coahuila, Mexico, migrated to the United States in 1954. He currently teaches at the University of Northern Colorado, where he specializes in Mexican-American Studies. His work has appeared in *Cuadernos Americanos, Cuadernos Hispanoamericanos, De Colores, The Bilingual Review/La Revista Bilingüe*, and others.

LEO ROMERO has published poetry in various anthologies including *We Are Chicanos: An Anthology of Mexican American Literature* and *For Neruda, For Chile: An International Anthology*. His work has also appeared in the literary magazines *South Dakota Review, San Marcos Review, The Greenfield Review, Revista Chicano-Riqueña, Berkeley Poetry Review*, and *Pembroke Magazine*. His chapbook *During the Growing Season* appeared in 1978.

JIM SAGEL, born in northern Colorado in 1947, moved to Española, New Mexico, in 1969, where he was reborn. An instructor of bilingual creative writing and Southwest literature at Northern New Mexico Community College and Española Valley High School, he has published extensively in southwestern magazines and anthologies. His published books include *Hablando de brujas (y la gente de antes)* (1981) and *Tunomás Honey* (1981), a collection of short stories which won the prestigious Premio Casa de las Américas (Havana).

THE AUTHORS

ROSAURA SANCHEZ is an Associate Professor in the Department of Literature at the University of California at San Diego. She received her Ph.D. in Romance Linguistics from the University of Texas at Austin. Her work is primarily in sociolinguistics and Spanish linguistics, but she has also written several short stories which have been published in Chicano literary journals.

JOSE SANCHEZ BOUDY was born and educated in Havana, Cuba. Currently he is a professor at the University of North Carolina in Greensboro. He has published numerous books, including *Cuentos grises* (1966), *Poemas de otoño e invierno* (1967), *Ritmo de Solá* (1967), *Soledad de la playa larga* (1975), and *Tiempo congelado* (1979).

ARNOLDO C. VENTO's early childhood was spent in San Juan, Texas, in the Rio Grande Valley, where he recalls as a child witnessing Chicano political rallies, overt discrimination, and hundreds of Mexican inmates serving time in the Edinburg County Jail. Currently he teaches at the Unitersity of Texas at Austin. His publications have appeared in *De Colores, Canto al Pueblo: An Anthology of Experiences* (1978), *Grito del Sol, La Raza, Revista Río Bravo*, and many others.

ALMA VILLANUEVA is the author of *Bloodroot*, a collection of poetry, and a long narrative poem entitled *Mother, May I?* Her work has also appeared in the anthologies *The Next World, Contemporary Women Poets,* and *I Sing the Song to Myself,* in addition to the magazines *ChismeArte* and *El Nauhtzen.* Her poem "La Chingada" will appear in the forthcoming book *Five Poets of Aztlán,* together with a translation by her mother.